C000272895

AIRBUS

The World in 2008

EDITOR: Daniel Franklin
MANAGING EDITOR: Harriet Ziegler
DEPUTY EDITORS: John Andrews, Leo Abruzzese
EDITORIAL ASSISTANT: Olivia Malone
COUNTRIES EDITOR: Alasdair Ross
INDUSTRIES EDITOR: Carla Rapoport
DESIGN AND ART DIRECTION: Bailey and Kenny
ART DIRECTOR: Anita Wright
CHARTS: Phil Kenny, Michael Robinson, Peter Winfield
ILLUSTRATIONS: Steve Carroll, Derek Cousins, James Sillavan
PICTURE EDITOR: Juliet Brightmore
RESEARCH: Ariel Ramchandani, Carol Howard, Sophie Brown, Paul Pedley, Jason Palmer, Janek Schmidt
EDITORIAL ASSISTANCE: Ingrid Esling, Sheila Allen
ADVERTISING DIRECTOR: David Weeks
ADVERTISING MANAGERS: Harry Whitbread (UK), Sarah Jane Lindsay (Europe), Nick Mesquita (MEA), Suzanne Hopkins (North America), Terrie Lam (Asia)
CIRCULATION & MARKETING DIRECTORS: Yvonne Ossman (UK), Anna Rawling (Europe), Matthew Aylmer (Asia)
PRODUCTION: Sharon Simpson, Michael Mann, Andrew Rollings, Amy Brown, Katy Wilson, Robert Banbury, Tom Scott
INTERNATIONAL RIGHTS & SYNDICATION MANAGER: Rebecca Brunt
Agent: Hutton-Williams Agency
PUBLISHER: Des McSweeney

The Economist

25 St James's Street
London SW1A 1HG
Telephone: 020 7576 8133
E-mail: worldineditor @economist.com

For more information, including podcasts, go to: www.theworldin.com

11 **From the editor**

Leaders

13 **China's great game**
The Olympics and China's foreign policy

14 **One more year**
America under George Bush, and beyond

18 **A grand bargain**
Iran and America should strike a deal

21 **The economy: twin track**
The rich world struggles, emerging markets soar

24 **Clean the planet**
Time to get down to the details

26 **The culture wars go global**
God will be everywhere

28 **The rediscovery of discretion**
Oldies extend their social networks online

30 **Diary for 2008**

Britain

33 **The Gordon and David show**
Politics becomes a competitive sport again

34 **The battle for money**
Army, navy and air force fight it out

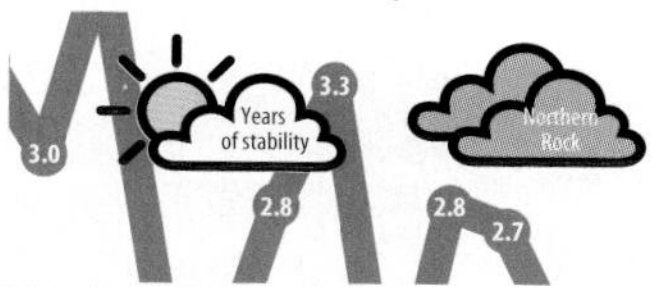

35 **The storm to come**
The economic horizon is fast darkening

38 **An academic exercise**
Who's the smartest of them all?

40 **Health concerns at 60**
Labour's drive to reform the NHS falters

42 **007 in 008**
Back to your books, Mr Bond

Europe

45 **A plateful for Brussels**
Plenty of tricky issues for the EU

46 **Trendy talk**
With an Italian accent

51 **Germany's double act**
Economic traction, political friction

54 **Defining Sarkozism**
Crunch time for France's president

56 **Sour grapes in France**
No longer world champion for wine

56 **Then there were two**
New parties, same old problems for Italy

57 **Not just another business**
Michel Platini on European football

58 **The second transition**
Prepare for some pain in Spain

58 **To coin a phase**
Making mischief with maps

60 **Putin's pyramid**
Russia's politics will be unstable

61 **Beyond Ataturk**
Turkey struggles to redefine itself

62 **Unoriginal sins**
Eastern Europe's "halo effect" will fade

63 **France in a challenging world**
Nicolas Sarkozy on foreign policy

United States

65 **The Democrats' year**
The betting is on a Clinton presidency

66 **The $1 billion campaign**
The costliest ever—but so what?

67 **After the binge**
A hangover for America's economy

68 **Green expectations**
Nancy Pelosi on global warming

69 **The new buffalo**
Good odds at the casino for Indian tribes

69 **Home and away**
American tourists watch the pennies

70 **Cautious conservatives**
The Supreme Court nudges to the right

72 **The city club**
Michael Bloomberg on city power

The Americas

73 **Who'll dance with Chávez?**
A test of the region's new-found resilience

74 **Homeward dollars**
Migrant money falls, but still matters

75 **Canada goes greener**
Farewell Kandahar, hello Kyoto

76 **Mexico's road**
Felipe Calderón on Mexican reforms

China special section

79 **The challenge to Beijingoism**
China prepares for the games—and critics

80 **Dire straits**
Taiwan heads, turbulently, to the polls

81 **Chery-picking**
Global temptations for Chinese companies

82 **No kids, more money**
Watch out for China's empty-nesters

82 **Smelling a rat**
Worries about China's economy

83 **Flashing red**
The world's hottest stockmarket

84 **China's e-commerce**
Internet entrepreneurs bloom

85 **The new champions**
Who's rising up the statistical charts

85 **Win-win Olympics**
Team China strikes gold in Beijing

86 **In 2008, be nicer to your neighbours**
The Dalai Lama on compassion

America votes

One more year of George Bush, *page 14*. Then the Democrats' turn in the White House, *page 65*? A costly campaign, *page 66*, and its impact on Wall Street, *page 149*. **Michael Bloomberg** won't wait to see who does what in Washington, *page 72*.

China's games

The Beijing Olympics are China's chance to show off to the world, but don't expect big changes in the government's behaviour, *pages 13* and *79*. The **Dalai Lama** asks for understanding, *page 86*. China's great leaps forward, *page 85*, and its e-commerce revolution, *page 84*. But there's more to Asia than just China, says **Bill Emmott**, *page 87*.

Euro-vision

Nicolas Sarkozy defines his foreign-policy agenda, *page 63*. Defining Sarkozism, *page 54*. The EU's coming Kosovo crisis, *page 45*. **Joaquín Almunia**'s vision for the euro, *page 154*. European football is not just another business, argues **Michel Platini**, *page 57*. The outlook dims for the City of London, says **Lionel Barber**, *page 156*.

Asia

87 **Much more than China**
The continent's powers need to be friends

88 **Hard-slogging India**
Will the economy's run rate slow?

89 **An unquiet periphery**
India should help its neighbours more

90 **The enduring caretaker**
The LDP regains its balance in Japan

90 **A wish to lead**
Japan and climate change

91 **Falling here, rising there**
Asia's forests

92 **Australia's coal question**
Can Innamincka provide an alternative?

94 **A new miracle for tigers and dragons**
Surin Pitsuwan on tackling poverty

Middle East and Africa

95 **Solving the insoluble**
Israel and Palestine, in the shadow of Iran

96 **A bitter shmita**
Israel's rowing rabbis

97 **On and on in Iraq**
The Americans won't be leaving yet

98 **Arab federalism, anyone?**
An idea whose time is yet to come

99 **Wanted: jobs for Africans**
Between boosterism and desperation

100 **Criteria for a continent**
Mo Ibrahim on governance in Africa

International

101 **The paradoxical politics of energy**
The urge to get off oil—and to find more

102 **Predictably right and wrong**
A look at our own track record

103 **Stopping the plagues**
Better health creates stronger economies

104 **A world in flux**
Plenty of people on the move in 2008

105 **Artistic fireworks**
A preview of the year's cultural highlights

106 **A year for accountability**
Angelina Jolie on war criminals

107 **Hope against dope**
Sport's war on drugs

107 **The year of the spud**
Food for thought

108 **The spirit of principled pragmatism**
Ban Ki-moon on the United Nations

110 **The future of futurology**
Think small, think short—and listen

111 **Six of the best**
Our selection of trendspotters' tips

The world in figures

113 **Forecasts for 80 countries**

123 **Forecasts for 15 industries**

Business

129 **Freeconomics**
Online, you really can get a free lunch

130 **Movers and shakers**
The European business stars of 2008

132 **Lightening up**
Leave the laptop behind

134 **Buying and celling**
Pay with a wave of your mobile phone

135 **Cash on call**
Mobile payments in the developing world

136 **Not enough people in China**
Staff shortages mean employers take risks

139 **Cheap but not so cheerful**
The world's lowest-priced car

140 **OPEC rules again**
The oil cartel is riding high, for now

143 **The responsible company**
Indra Nooyi on performing with purpose

144 **The good jargon guide**
The perfect storm reaches a tipping point

145 **For the love of mankind**
A big year for big giving

146 **Sustainable maths**
Environmental reporting for companies

Finance

149 **History lessons for the markets**
Investors will be watching politics

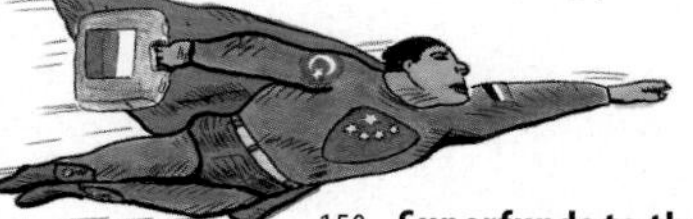

150 **Superfunds to the rescue**
Or are sovereign wealth funds a threat?

152 **Back to basics**
The banking industry must relearn its craft

154 **The euro zone: bigger and better?**
Joaquín Almunia on monetary union

155 **Fearful or cheerful?**
The prospects for world trade

155 **Square dance**
Four powers hold the key to Doha

156 **London loses its cool**
Tougher times ahead for the City

157 **The spread of political risk**
A growing threat to foreign investment

158 **The rise and rise of private equity**
David Rubenstein on a booming industry

Science

161 **The great melt**
The Arctic will be a hotspot for scientists

162 **A whole new dimension**
Rich homes will afford 3D printers

163 **Visiting Neptune's kingdom**
Welcome to inner space

164 **The power of thought**
Restoring movement to the paralysed

165 **The next space race**
Peter Diamandis on private exploration

Obituary

166 **Out with the old, in with the new**
Goodbye to two New York stadiums

Saving the planet

Combating climate change is high on the agenda for America's Congress, says **Nancy Pelosi**, *page 68*. It's a priority for the UN, stresses **Ban Ki-moon**, *page 108*. But will the politicians disappoint, asks **Emma Duncan**, *page 24*? Responsible companies must play their part, argues **Indra Nooyi**, *page 143*. Saving lives in poorer countries is a big opportunity, says **Michel Kazatchkine**, *page 103*. God is everywhere, suggests **John Micklethwait**, *page 26*. And it's judgment day for war criminals, hopes **Angelina Jolie**, *page 106*.

Freeconomics

Prepare for the great online giveaway, predicts **Chris Anderson**, *page 129*; and an almost free car, *page 139*. The rich will be giving money away, *page 145*. But OPEC will keep oil expensive, *page 140*. Rich countries' economies, especially Britain's and America's, face a rough ride, *pages 35* and *67*. Emerging markets, meanwhile, will be hot, *page 21*. Too hot, perhaps, in Shanghai, *page 83*.

Reaching for the stars

Entrepreneurs will lead a new era of space travel, believes **Peter Diamandis**, *page 165*. But futurologists have toned down their cosmic predictions, *page 110*. Exploring the ocean, *page 163*. Reaching for the latest gadgetry, *page 132*.

PHOTOGRAPHIC SOURCES
Alamy Images: Artpartner-images.com, Bora, Danita Delimont, Kevin Foy, Ralph Henning, ImageState, Stockbyte, David Wall. Associated Press/AP Images: Oded Balilty, Charles Krupa, Massimo Pinca, Mark Wilson. Corbis: Bettmann, Marcelo Garcia/Miraflores/epa, Laurent Gillieron/epa, Hulton-Deutsch Collection. European Community, 2007. Getty Images: China Photos, Tal Cohen/AFP, Eric Feferberg/AFP, Larry Goldstein, Henning Kaiser/AFP, Pascal Le Segretain, John Moore, Alexander Nemenov/AFP, Eric Piermont/AFP, Joe Raedle, Reza, Horst Tappe, Teh Eng Koon/AFP, Gali Tibbon/AFP. Anatol Just/inition.co.uk. Panos/Natalie Behring. Michael Pilkington. Reuters: Luis Enrique Ascui, Shaun Best, James Boardman, Claro Cortes, Michael Dalder, Vasily Fedosenko, Santiago Ferrero, Caren Firouz, Albert Gea, Hannibal Hanschke, Lucas Jackson, Issei Kato, Kamal Kishore, Jason Lee, Joshua Lott, Luke MacGregor, Rafael Marchante, Brendan McDermid, Hamid I Mohammed, Yuriko Nakao, Herbert Neubauer, Morteza Nikoubazi, Punit Paranjpe, Hazir Reka, Parth Sanyal, Sheng Li, Aly Song, Jameson Wu. Rex Features. Still Pictures/A Rose. White House Historical Association (White House Collection).

Printed by St Ives PLC, Plymouth, England

Printed on UPM-Kymmene Star 80gsm

Published by The Economist Newspaper Limited.

ISBN 0 86218 207 6
978 0 86218 207 6

The world is growing by more than 70 million people a year.

So is that a problem, or a solution?

With our planet's population continuing to increase, and the quality of life for millions in the developing world improving daily, our demand for energy is also growing. And to meet everyone's needs 25 years from now may take 50% more energy than we use today.
Finding and developing all the fuel and power we need for our homes, businesses and vehicles, while protecting the environment, could be one of the greatest challenges our generation will face.
The key to ensuring success is found in the same place that created this need: humanity itself. When the unique spirit we all possess is allowed to flourish, mankind has proven its ability to take on, and overcome, any issue. It's a spirit of hard work, ingenuity, drive, courage and no small measure of commitment. To success, to each other, to the planet.
The problem...becomes the solution.
This human energy that drives us to succeed has been there every day since the beginning. And it will be with us to shape many tomorrows to come.
So join us in tapping the most powerful source of energy in the world. Ourselves.
And watch what the human race can do.
Chevron
Human Energy™

Two big events will frame the year ahead: America's presidential election and the summer Olympic games in Beijing. The race for the White House will be a marathon, from the front-loaded primary season in January and February to the general election in November. The betting is that the winner will be a Democrat—with a strong chance that a Clinton will again be set to succeed a Bush as leader of the free world. China, meanwhile, will hope to use the Olympics to show the world what a splendid giant it has become. It will win the most gold medals, and bask in national pride and the global limelight. But it will also face awkward questions on its repressive politics.

America and China will be prime players in the matters that will concentrate minds around the world in 2008. One of these is the world economy, which can no longer depend on America, with its housing and credit woes, to drive growth. America should—just—avoid recession, but it will be China (for the first time the biggest contributor to global growth) along with India and other emerging markets that will shine.

Another focus of attention will be climate change. As China replaces America as the world's biggest producer of greenhouse gases, serious efforts on global warming depend on the serious involvement of those two countries. If 2007 was the year when this rose to the top of the global agenda, in 2008 people will expect action. It is striking that green is a theme that links all the contributions from political leaders in this volume, whether at the city level (Michael Bloomberg), the national level (Felipe Calderón, Nancy Pelosi, Nicolas Sarkozy) or the supranational level (the UN's Ban Ki-moon, ASEAN's Surin Pitsuwan). The politicians have talked the issue up; will they now let people down?

America should—just—avoid recession, but it will be China along with India and other emerging markets that will shine

A third preoccupation will be geopolitical risk. The conventional wisdom is that America is heading for a showdown with Iran over its nuclear ambitions, while in its Olympic year China will avoid serious ructions with independent-minded Taiwan. In fact, the opposite is perfectly possible: a "grand bargain" between America and Iran, and a crisis over Taiwan, which faces noisy elections in 2008. For sure, political risk will become a hotter topic in both think-tanks and boardrooms.

Along with the usual matters of markets and profits, businesses will grapple with the question of how to be good. Consultants will urge them to elevate "sustainability" into strategy. And the most successful businessmen and bankers will contemplate the example of Bill Gates, who will step down from his day job at Microsoft to focus on philanthropy.

In general, the world will be on the move. Scientists will swarm over the Arctic. Migrants will cross borders for an ever more complex range of reasons. Chinese empty-nesters will take to tourism. Americans, however, will be tempted to stay at home, shocked and awed by tales of $8 cups of coffee in Europe.

Predicting the future is, of course, a hazardous affair. Indeed, our article on the future of futurology notes that the age of identifying sweeping megatrends may be over. That does not stop a few sweeping predictions from surfacing in this volume: the dawn of a new space age, for example, and the spread of the culture wars beyond America. But nowadays uncertainty looks smart and small is fashionable: there is a growing industry in spotting microtrends.

You will find many of these in *The World in 2008*. Seasoned readers will notice a few additions: a special section on China; expanded country coverage in "The world in figures"; even, somehow, an obituary page. As ever, not all of our forecasts will prove 100% accurate. But two things we know. For Chinese, 2008 will be the Year of the Rat. And the UN has designated it the International Year of the Potato. Happy nibbling.

Daniel Franklin
editor, *The World in 2008*

China's great game

Simon Long argues that those hoping the Olympics might swiftly change China's foreign policy for the better will be disappointed

"China is on the world stage," according to one of its leading diplomats. "But it has its back to the audience." This is an exaggeration, of course: China's leaders are acutely conscious of international opinion. But it contains a germ of a truth worth recalling as China prepares for what it has become a cliché to call its "coming-out party", the Beijing Olympics in August 2008. Its government's priorities are primarily domestic: dealing with the wrenching changes wrought by its spectacular and prolonged economic boom, and coping with the frustrations of those left behind. The Olympics themselves are naturally a chance to show off China's rapid modernisation to the outside world. But far more important is the audience at home, and the opportunity to prove just how much China's Communist rulers have achieved in restoring the country's prestige.

This places some constraints on China's behaviour. It does not want its Olympics to be marred—like Moscow's in 1980 and Los Angeles's four years later—by politically inspired boycotts. This was the argument many used to justify the controversial decision to award the games to Beijing, that it would force China to rein in its abuses of human rights. Otherwise it risks, at worst, international ostracism and, at best, a bad press: the Olympics might be remembered less for the transformation of China's capital or the triumphs of Chinese athletes than for the thuggery of its police and the suffering of its silenced dissidents.

In practice, there may have been some slight easing of repression in China, but it has had next to nothing to do with the Olympics. The impact of the games on human rights is likely to be on balance negative. The world spotlight will invite those with grievances to try to air them. The government will do its utmost to stop them.

So attention has turned to China's behaviour abroad, and the hope that the Olympics will help it become the "responsible stakeholder" in the international system that American officials have advocated as its role. There are some signs that such a China is beginning to emerge. It is no longer so wedded to traditional friendships or commercial ties with rogue or objectionable regimes that it automatically blocks attempts by the West to rein them in.

Again, however, the Olympics may not have had much to do with it. Take North Korea, where China is given credit for having co-operated with the other members of the "six-party talks" (America, Japan, Russia and South Korea) to persuade Kim Jong Il to begin dismantling his nuclear facilities. But this is less a concession to the concerns of its negotiating partners than recognition of China's own self-interest in preventing the collapse of the government in Pyongyang. Whatever else it achieves, the aid that will flow thanks to the nuclear deal will help prop up that brutal dictatorship.

Nor can the Olympics claim exclusive credit for China's distancing itself from the government of Sudan and its decision to take a rather higher profile in the United Nations-led effort to bring peace to the Darfur region; nor for ▶

> The impact of the games on human rights is likely to be on balance negative

Simon Long: Asia editor, *The Economist*

China's failure to veto criticism of the junta ruling Myanmar at the United Nations after its brutal suppression of monk-led protests in September 2007. In both cases, the isolation of the regime was such that China had little to lose from moderating its stance. In both cases, too, China's self-interest lay in a peaceful outcome.

The Olympics will have some impact on China's handling of two issues that it resolutely insists are "internal" affairs, but that much of the world sees as foreign-policy issues. It will continue to engage in desultory talks with representatives of the Dalai Lama, Tibet's exiled spiritual leader. But these seem more designed to give some sort of sop to international opinion than to reach an accommodation with the Tibetans. The Dalai Lama, who, unlike many of his followers, is willing to forgo full independence for Tibet for the sake of genuine autonomy, represents the best hope of such a settlement. But China seems to have decided its interests are best served in waiting for his death. In 2007 it approved rules intended in part to give the Chinese government a claim to a veto on any reincarnation.

An Olympic window, or a post-Olympic crisis

Among Taiwanese, as among some Tibetans, there is talk of the "window" that is open before the Olympics, when China might be expected to refrain from taking extreme measures. In Taiwan 2008 is an election year and, as ever, relations with the mainland will be the most divisive campaign issue. Taiwan's governing party also plans to hold a referendum to endorse its doomed application to join the United Nations in the name of "Taiwan" rather than "Republic of China" (under which name it lost its UN seat to China in 1971). This will enrage China, which will see it—as will many in Taiwan—as a step towards a formal declaration of independence.

China will exert indirect pressure, especially through America, to ensure that Taiwan does not go further. This will probably succeed. America will do all in its considerable power to dissuade Taiwan from provoking the crisis in American relations with China that would follow increased belligerence.

However, it is still reasonable to predict another Taiwan Straits crisis in the coming 18 months. The cause may be less Taiwanese provocation than the Olympics themselves. Like the reversion of Hong Kong to Chinese sovereignty in 1997, this is a great symbolic event celebrating the basis on which the Communist Party now builds its legitimacy: it has made China rich, and has made it a great power again. It will lead to a wave of patriotic pride. The party will then face the difficulty of how to control this surge of nationalist fervour; and how to explain its continued failure to complete the last unfinished task on the nationalist agenda: "reunification" with Taiwan. ■

One more year

Christopher Lockwood expects a frustrating but fascinating final year under George Bush

Love him or hate him—and the polls show that around a third of Americans do at least still approve of him—George Bush will be president for the whole of 2008 and the first 20 days of 2009. But with a Democrat-controlled Congress (not to mention a Republican Party that increasingly wants to distance itself from Mr Bush) and the distraction of the most open presidential race for 80 years, 2008 is likely to be a year of profound stasis.

On the domestic front, where nothing can be done unless White House and Congress agree, the gridlock will be almost total. On the foreign-policy side, where the president has more freedom to act alone, the chances for progress ought to be better. But this particular president is so weakened, and the problems he faces are so intractable, that there will be little room for progress here either.

It could have been very different. History is full of examples of divided government producing powerful results, because only when political risk is shared equally by both parties can the boldest reforms be made. But 2007 was a dismal year for domestic policy: an attempt to reform immigration policy was killed by attacks from right and left; the president's plans to reform health care were pronounced "dead on arrival" in the House of Representatives; the budget was negotiated amid acrimonious talk of vetoes and veto overrides.

> Iraq will be the most emotive subject of the campaign. But the most significant issue could well be health care

It will be better in 2008 only in that, in the absence of serious attempts at policymaking, there will be fewer clashes. One possible area for co-operation (though don't hold your breath) may yet come over global warming. The White House has moved a long way towards accepting the man-made nature of the problem. Although the administration is most unlikely to endorse Democratic plans for capping carbon emissions, there may be ground for agreement on some incremental changes, such as somewhat tighter standards for car emissions. But the other big domestic issues that urgently need reform—immi-

Christopher Lockwood: United States editor, *The Economist*

gration, health and social security—must all wait for the arrival of a new administration.

American foreign policy could potentially be more interesting. Mr Bush and his secretary of state, Condoleezza Rice, have tried hard to rebuild bridges to American allies in Europe and Asia, and Ms Rice's charm offensive is sure to continue in 2008. The task of improving transatlantic relations has been hugely helped by the advent of Nicolas Sarkozy as president of France, just as Angela Merkel has overseen a transformation in relations between Germany and America. European diplomats hope that the gradual coaxing of America back towards full engagement in multilateral bodies like the United Nations will continue. Progress in "denuclearising" North Korea could lead to a more fruitful period in American-Asian relations, too.

But Iraq and Iran will overhang all other areas of foreign policy. In Iraq, the president has made it clear that he is determined to maintain a large number of troops (probably more than 100,000) until the end of his presidency, barring either a catastrophic deterioration or a marked improvement there. The Democrats in Congress, who tried and failed to end the war in the summer of 2007, are unlikely to devote more than token energy towards trying again in 2008. This means that Mr Bush's successor, whoever she or he is, will inherit the business of disengagement from Iraq as their most awkward first-term problem. But it is Iran (see separate leader) that may hold the key to how the last Bush year will unfold. The administration has worked hard on a multilateral diplomatic approach that has borne no fruit. It remains quite plausible that America will attempt unilateral military action in 2008, which would set back its relations with most of its allies significantly.

First personalities, then policies

But few people, in America at least, will be paying much attention to any of the sterile arguments that will rattle up and down Pennsylvania Avenue. The year's political oxygen will be wholly consumed by the 2008 presidential race, and to a lesser extent by the Democrats' bid to secure a proper working majority in the Senate rather than the measly one they have now. And it will be a fascinating ride, falling into two quite different stages. The first few months of the year will be taken up by the primaries, which will be more about personalities than policies. But once the party nominations are settled, a profound argument about policy will begin.

This is because there is a striking degree of agreement within the parties, but very clear differences between them. All the main Democrats, for instance, but none of the Republicans, favour remarkably similar plans to introduce universal health care to an America that badly needs it. All the Democrats, and none of the Republicans, want to rescind Mr Bush's tax cuts. And so on. Voters may be hard-pressed to see much difference between Hillary Clinton's views and those of Barack Obama on anything (though Mrs Clinton is more cautious than Mr Obama when it comes to withdrawing from Iraq and more hawkish about Iran); but there will be profound differences between whichever of them wins and the eventual Republican nominee. The Republican candidates, it is true, are deeply divided over moral matters such as abortion and gay marriage, but these are matters for the states, not the federal government.

Iraq will obviously be the most emotive subject in the campaign. But the most significant issue could well be health care—unless there is a major new terrorist attack on America in 2008 (in which case security will become the dominant issue and the Republican candidate will probably win), or else a serious recession (which would help the Democrat). On health, American voters will get a real choice. They will be asked to say whether they are prepared to see a significant amount of federal money—anything from $100 billion to $200 billion—spent on the almost 50m people who lack health insurance and are not covered by the Medicaid and Medicare government programmes, and who consequently live in fear of serious illness which can ruin them even if they fully recover. And beyond the 50m are tens of millions more who fear that losing their jobs and the health insurance that goes with them will expose them to the same risk.

It may not sound glamorous. But the absence of a universal health-care system is a main driver of the feeling of economic insecurity that will be a big feature of the 2008 campaign. ■

A grand bargain

It's time for America and Iran to explore the art of the possible, argues **Peter David**

What follows is not so much a prediction, more a thought experiment. It is not likely, but nor is it impossible. It is this: in 2008 America and the Islamic Republic of Iran strike a grand bargain. They stop competing for dominance over the Middle East and agree to respect each other's spheres of influence.

What makes such a deal possible is that the alternatives are dire. Without some such rapprochement, an explosive mix of Iranian technology and American politics will make 2008 the most dangerous year yet in three decades of confrontation.

Iran is close to mastering the skills it needs to enrich uranium for an atomic bomb. Though most analysts say it would take Iran until 2010 to build a deliverable weapon, it could perhaps master the art of enrichment, and so cross a technological point of no return, in 2008. George Bush has come to see Iran as the main author of America's woes in Iraq, and is running out of time to order a strike on Iran's nuclear facilities: the coming year is his last chance to end his presidency with a military bang.

A collision between Iran and America can be prevented only if both decide to swerve out of the way. Since both think they have too much at stake to risk showing weakness, neither will swerve on its own.

Iran's leaders probably believe that the very survival of their theocratic regime is in play. Economic failures have weakened domestic support for the mullahs. But President Mahmoud Ahmadinejad's nuclear defiance of America is popular, and he has turned this into a test of national pride. Even the moderates may therefore be unwilling to back down. The Bush administration, meanwhile, feels that America is competing with Iran for domination not just of Iraq and the oil-rich Persian Gulf but also of the Middle East as a whole. In Washington, DC, it is not just Mr Bush who believes that America's status in the region will unravel unless it prevails against Iran.

What if they could strike a deal under which both saved face?

In short, neither side seems willing to budge. But what if they could strike a deal under which both saved face?

At different times in recent years the old enemies have quietly signalled their willingness to talk—and therefore to trade. In 2003 the Iranians promised (via the Swiss) that if America was willing to talk Iran was willing to be flexible, not only on the nuclear question but also on de facto recognition of Israel. In return Iran wanted America to end sanctions, stop threatening "regime change" and recognise Iran's legitimate regional security interests. At that time, the Americans, feeling powerful just after toppling Saddam Hussein, ignored this offer. In 2006, however, America softened. Now it promises not only to help with the political and economic rewards that Europe has offered Iran in return for stopping uranium enrichment, but also, once Iran stops, to talk directly about all the subjects that have bedevilled relations between the two countries.

More in common than you might think

Why have the Iranians rejected this offer? It may be that it is their turn to feel strong. Or Iran's intransigence may reflect the conservative turn in its domestic politics since the election of Mr Ahmadinejad. Either way, the mere fact that the two sides have exchanged feelers suggests that they recognise some strategic interests in common. Here are three: both support a united Iraq under its present Shia-dominated government; neither wants the return of the Taliban in Afghanistan; and both have a vital interest in securing the free flow of Gulf oil to world markets.

If America and Iran did sit down to talk, they would swiftly bump into two much harder issues: Iran's nuclear ambitions and Israel. But even these might be smudged. After all, Iran says all the time that it wants nuclear technology, not a nuclear weapon, so negotiators have wriggle room. As for Israel, even under the mullahs Iran has until recently been content to denounce "the Zionist regime" without taking any action against it—and sometimes even co-operating with it (Iran bought arms from Israel, for example, during its war with Iraq). Who knows what Iran might agree to in the context of some Persian version of Nixon-to-China that leads to a grand bargain with America? In 2008 it might at least be prudent to find out. ■

Peter David: foreign editor, *The Economist*

Twin track

Financial excesses will hold the rich world back, but emerging markets will keep soaring, says **Robin Bew**

It couldn't last. The past few years rivalled the champagne days of the late 1980s. Equity prices surged. Interest rates were low, borrowing was easy. For many, it was a time for splashing out on a second home. The lucky few were buying a second Picasso. But the party mood ended abruptly in mid-2007. Suddenly, the economic future looks a lot less bubbly.

For years America has been the engine of the global economy. Many a job elsewhere is reliant—directly or indirectly—on American consumers' willingness to spend with abandon. But the double whammy of an ailing housing market and tighter credit means the odds of recession have risen. Since a slump in America would spell trouble for the global economy, this is something the whole world needs to worry about.

Yet an American recession is not inevitable. Indeed, the most likely scenario is that America pulls through. If so, 2008 looks set to be a reasonable year for the world economy as a whole. Lay-offs will go up a bit, but most people will keep their jobs. Pay will still rise, if more slowly. Businesses will keep investing, especially in the emerging world.

But the sun will not be shining on everyone. The wine bars of Mayfair and Connecticut—and other haunts of bankers and buy-out merchants—will be a little quieter. Homeowners in many countries face difficult times. Those who borrowed heavily in the belief that house prices would move ever upwards will discover that the laws of gravity, as well as economics, apply to property markets. Home builders, too, can expect a tough year.

Home truths

House prices in America began to slip in some metropolitan areas in mid-2006, and that downwards pressure went nationwide in 2007. As low-income borrowers defaulted on their debts, the subprime crisis rocked the global financial system.

Yin and yang

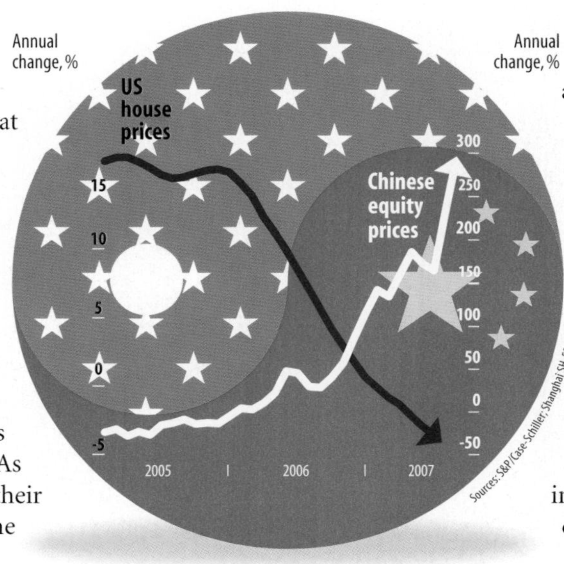

In 2008 these housing-related problems are set to get worse. Many low-income borrowers took out loans in 2005 at "teaser rates" which started to move to a more normal level in 2007. More defaults will follow in 2008, prompting a further round of home sales. The construction industry will take another hit. And consumers, seeing the value of their homes decline, will spend less. Bruised financial institutions will push up lending rates—meaning even good borrowers will pay more, and businesses invest less. But America's Federal Reserve will be anxious to prevent an economic rout, and lower interest rates will mean that, though housing, construction and finance will look sickly, other sectors will keep growing.

> The coming year will sharpen the shift in world growth

Europe and Japan will feel America's woes. The euro and yen will rise as the dollar sinks, hurting exports. Banks will be stingier with credit. But if America avoids an outright recession, both Europe and Japan should be able to keep their economies growing at a decent, if slower, rate.

Meanwhile, emerging markets will be buzzing. If the Fed succeeds in keeping the American economy afloat, the chances of their being hurt by financial turbulence are low. Indeed, many emerging economies are now suppliers of capital to the rest of the world, not borrowers. China is a case in point: far from experiencing a credit crunch, it has more liquidity than it knows what to do with. Exports will slow modestly, as America's appetite for foreign goods wanes. But domestic spending, on investment but also on consumer goods, will continue to soar. India and Russia will also remain hot, thanks respectively to a strong service sector and high oil prices, while most other emerging markets will do well.

The risks are high—higher than for many years. The global economy could take a pummelling. But it seems more likely that the coming year will sharpen the shift in world growth. Developing economies will surge ahead, expanding by about 7.6%, leaving the rich countries' 1.8% growth looking distinctly sluggish. After America's decade, 2008 will be the year of the emerging markets. ■

Robin Bew: editorial director, Economist Intelligence Unit

General Insurance
Life Insurance
Risk Management
What if you can't find the 32 hidde

Clean the planet

Time to move beyond rhetoric and get down to the details, argues **Emma Duncan**

Over the past couple of years, climate change has arrived on the political map. A lot of different people helped to put it there: Al Gore, who came to life inspiring Americans on the topic; Sir Nicholas Stern, who counted the cost in a report to the British government; American businessmen, who started lobbying the administration to take action; American legislators, who have been pushing for measures to combat global warming since 2006; voters, who according to the polls began to take a serious interest in the subject; and journalists, who always jump on a bandwagon when they see one rolling by.

Now that the world has recognised the problem, it wants a solution. That is good, but dangerous, because expectations are mounting and the rhetoric is running high. There is a risk that 2008 may be a let-down, for the two big things needed to combat climate change are unlikely to be put in place next year.

What won't happen

The first thing is serious federal climate-change controls in America. The Democrats, by and large, want federal controls, and they are in charge of the legislature. But some Democrats—especially those associated with organised labour—are hostile to the idea. Some don't want legislation yet because they want to keep the issue alive during the presidential election. The more radical greens want to wait until a Democratic president is ensconced, on the ground that they'll get a tougher scheme if they do. Opposition from such groups, as well as from Republicans, and the sheer complexity of carbon-emissions controls, mean that anything more than minor tinkering will have to wait.

Second, a framework for a new international agreement is needed. The Kyoto protocol can claim some achievements (such as Europe's Emissions-Trading Scheme) but it has failed in its main aim—of getting the world's big polluters to agree on how to cut carbon-dioxide emissions. If America and China are to be included, a new agreement must be reached. That's not going to happen in the coming year, either.

Still, 2008 is crucial for climate change, in two ways. First, America needs a president committed to the issue; as the year unfolds, it will become clearer which candidates would take serious action. Hillary Clinton, Bill Richardson, John Edwards and Mitt Romney probably would; Barack Obama is less committed, and nobody knows where Rudy Giuliani stands.

Second, the world needs to work at enticing China (and other big developing countries) and America into an agreement of some sort. George Bush gestured towards a "new international framework" before the 2007 G8 meeting, calling for big polluters to accept emissions targets. China, whose leaders used never to mention global warming, in 2007 unveiled its first plan to combat climate change. It included a commitment to increase energy efficiency by 20% by 2010 and to double the use of renewables by 2020. But China is still a long way from accepting emissions caps.

> The world needs to work at enticing China and America into an agreement

The rich world has to help China move in that direction. It has to work out how it is going to compensate developing countries for the higher costs of cleaner energy—for instance through a fund that subsidises the adoption of clean technologies and eases the transfer of such technology. And poor countries have to find some way of accepting cuts in their emissions. One way of doing this is through no-loss targets, whereby poor countries would be rewarded if they hit their targets, but not punished if they missed them. An alternative option could be sectoral targets, under which poor countries would accept limits on emissions from, say, their iron and steel industries but not from their economies as a whole.

It will be dull stuff. It will not make the headlines. But if the many officials and politicians involved can beat out some such agreement, 2008 will be a good year for climate change. ■

Emma Duncan: deputy editor, *The Economist*

The culture wars go global

God may feature less in America's election—but more elsewhere, says **John Micklethwait**

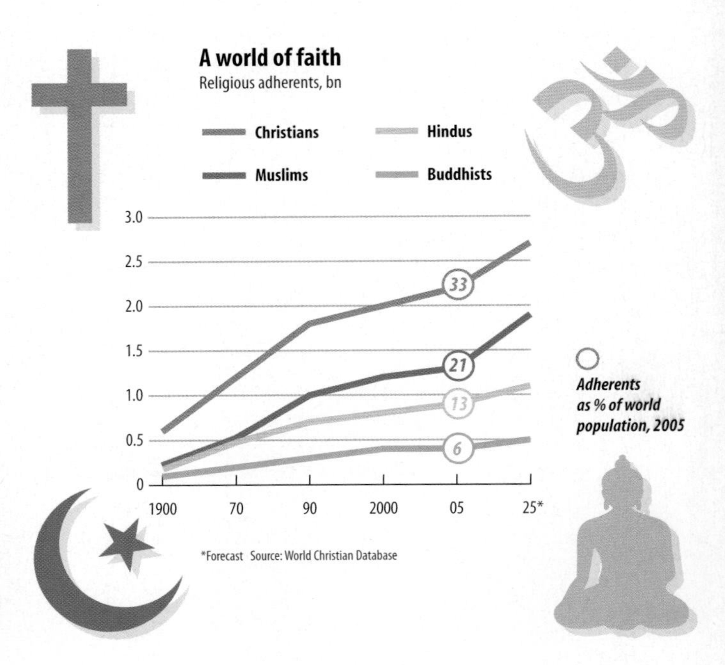

One of the most remarkable changes in American politics in the past half-century has been the rise of the "values voter". Religious conservatives have helped make the culture wars a part of American politics. The easiest way to tell whether a white American is a Democrat or a Republican has not been to ask him how much money he has but how often he goes to church. Over half of George Bush's votes in 2004 came from white evangelicals.

In 2008 the culture wars may well count for much less. Even evangelicals are fed up with the Republicans' incompetence and sleaze. And most of the Republicans on show present problems for the religious right, whether by their attitude (irreverent John McCain), their liberal views (Rudy Giuliani, who supports abortion rights) or their choice of religion (Mitt Romney, who is a Mormon). Meanwhile, the leading Democrats have toned down their side of the culture wars, talking less about "reproductive rights" and more about their own religious credentials.

> Religious belief is growing—especially outside western Europe

The idea of the "values" vote evaporating into this mushy centre will annoy the old warhorses of the religious right. Do not entirely rule out hard-core religious conservatives running a third-party candidate. But that reeks of desperation and would surely help a Democrat into the White House. God will probably not be as omnipresent in the 2008 presidential election as he has been recently.

Expect instead to hear more talk of God in politics outside America. The culture wars that have dominated American politics are gradually going global. That is partly because politics in many countries is following the American model. With most of the big economic debates settled (witness the minimal difference between Conservative and Labour spending plans in Britain) politics is focusing on cultural issues—such as the importance of the family in society. That is giving a fresh role to the West's traditional cultural warrior, the Catholic church, but also to younger evangelical outfits, many of them American imports. Focus on the Family, the heart of America's religious right, already has sister outfits in 54 countries.

Second, religious belief is growing—especially outside western Europe. And most of the faiths doing well are of the hotter sort. Above all, religion is becoming a matter of choice not inheritance—and once you choose to be a born-again Christian, a fundamentalist Muslim or a committed Hindu, you are more likely to make a fuss about religion in public life.

Thus, if India goes to the polls in 2008, its possible nuclear deal with America may be overshadowed by the fury about a bridge that the god Ram and a team of monkeys built to Sri Lanka: the secular Congress party has talked about blowing a hole in the bridge (which it argues is a natural ridge and mainly underwater) to make room for shipping. In Turkey there will be a clash over the constitution: the Islamist AK party wants to get rid of the ban on headscarves at universities. South Korea's Protestant megachurches have formed a New Right Movement partly to demand a tougher approach to North Korea.

Reasons to wage war

Many of the issues in the global culture wars will be familiar ones, such as abortion and gay marriage. Three new ones could emerge on the global scale. The first is the United Nations—long a target for American conservatives because of its ungodly ways (in the "Left Behind" series, the Antichrist returns as the UN secretary-general). The second is cloning—a cause that unites anti-abortion activists with the wider chorus of believers who think science is now playing with the unknown. And the last is the environment—or "creation care", as religious people like to call it. The idea that man is ruining God's dominion could yet become the biggest culture war of all. ■

John Micklethwait: editor-in-chief, *The Economist*

The rediscovery of discretion

Older people, too, will extend their social networks online without feeling awkward, says **Andreas Kluth**

For the first 200 millennia of the species, human social networks remained technologically stable. People sat around campfires, told stories and cultivated connections. Literacy and letters, and later the telephone, helped to extend these across distance. But the trickiest part involved figuring out the right balance between divulging too much or too little to the network, and between coming on too strongly or too coyly in requesting new friendships, copulations and alliances.

Then, during the first decade of the 21st century, the internet briefly promised to solve these conundrums by breeding online social networks—with names such as MySpace and Facebook—that appealed to the fragile psyches of one generation, nicknamed "Y", while mystifying or horrifying the preceding generation, called "X".

What drew the Ys was the sheer scalability of the medium (yielding enormous efficiency gains when prowling for dates), its suitability for self-marketing (with photos of bacchanalia, say, to advertise popularity) and above all the temporary reprieve from the awkwardness that comes with "friending" in real life. The old conundrums around discretion seemed technologically obsolete. What mystified, then horrified, the Xs, who often arrived on these networks as inquisitive parents of the Ys, were those same features. Don't these kids realise that potential employers can see this stuff? And what happens emotionally to my daughter when her boyfriend breaks up by simply toggling his online status to "Single" or "It's complicated"?

The point is that the uses of these networks are for the users to decide

In 2007 things got more complicated for the Xs. Thanks to Facebook, many middle-aged office types were expected to join in. But there was no rule-book for how to reject the "friend" request of a boss, or whether doing so was permissible at all. If not, should he be allowed to see the naked baby photos? While some Ys became more cautious after their excesses in 2006, many Xs began squirming in new forms of awkwardness in 2007.

This will change in 2008, as social-networking technology changes to fit human nature, rather than forcing human nature to fit the technology. The industry leaders in 2007 were really old-fashioned "walled gardens". They came in generic templates, with the crucial sociological aspects—what sort of information to give on a profile, for instance—pre-determined by programmers. Yes, they allowed users to customise their start pages, but so did the walled gardens of the early 1990s, online services such as AOL or CompuServe.

Those closed services crumbled and gave rise, after the Netscape browser and its emulators made it possible, to the open and polyvalent web. The same thing will happen in 2008 in the world of social networks. In place of today's walled gardens of awkwardness, open toolkits will arise to allow anybody, with a few simple clicks, to create his or her own social network, which will be an extension of existing connections in real life.

Anyone for yoga?

One example is Ning, a provider of just such networking tools (co-founded, as it happens, by Marc Andreessen, who once built Netscape). Using Ning's tools a mother, say, can start a social network with other mums to schedule playgroups for the kids—by inviting the other mums, while making the whole thing private for security against stalkers. If she also likes yoga, she can start another network, with photos, videos and reviews of yoga studios. And so on.

The point is that the uses of these networks are for the users to decide. Once reassured of this, people will then not so much "join" new networks as "log on" to their existing human networks around hobbies and other passions. It will be like sitting around campfires again, only now with vastly superior tools for sharing, bonding and planning. As for the old dilemmas between telling all or too little, between making friends wisely or not, 2008 will offer no progress at all. ■

Andreas Kluth: San Francisco correspondent, *The Economist*

Diary for 2008

Our selection of events around the world

JANUARY

Slovenia assumes the presidency of the European Union, and Cyprus and Malta both join the EU's euro zone.

Movers and shakers from politics, business and the media meet at the World Economic Forum in Davos, Switzerland.

Smoking is banned in France's bars and restaurants, adding to the restrictions already in place in offices and public buildings.

America's presidential hopefuls take their chances with the voters in the Iowa caucuses and the New Hampshire primary.

Africa starts its Cup of Nations soccer tournament, depriving European teams of many of their best players.

President George Bush delivers his last state-of-the-union address.

FEBRUARY

Chinese around the world begin the Year of the Rat: supposedly clever, charming and quick-witted.

Brazilians and foreigners alike dance to hedonistic excess at the Rio de Janeiro carnival.

Hollywood, for the 80th time, hands out the Oscars to the film world's finest—one day after the Golden Raspberries for the film world's direst.

On the 5th, a "Super-duper Tuesday", a score of states in America hold primaries that could point to the presidential nominees.

MARCH

Iditarod dog-sled race, in which mushers drive their huskies across more than 1,000 miles of snow-covered Alaska wilderness.

Russians elect a president to succeed term-limited Vladimir Putin.

Zimbabwe holds a presidential election. The last, in 2002, led to charges of fraud and intimidation.

Fifth anniversary of the American-led war in Iraq.

Western Christianity celebrates Easter on the 23rd, the earliest date since 1913.

APRIL

Environmentalists celebrate Earth Day, to encourage energy efficiency and deplore ecological waste.

No more Harry Potter books, but parents will still celebrate International Children's Book Day.

The *QE2*, destined to become a floating hotel in Dubai, ends its final round-the-world cruise.

MAY

Workers around the world celebrate May Day.

Cinema people gather for the Cannes film festival—and TV viewers tune in to the kitsch of the Eurovision song contest, live from Serbia.

Israel throws a party for its 60th anniversary; Palestinians mourn the *nakba* (catastrophe).

London elects its mayor, pitting the Labour Party incumbent, Ken Livingstone, against the Conservatives' Boris Johnson.

JUNE

Roger Federer hopes to win the final of the French Open, the only grand-slam tournament so far to have eluded him.

France delights in the Fête de la Musique, free live music in the open air for the whole nation.

America celebrates Gay and Lesbian Pride Month.

UEFA's Euro 2008 football tournament takes place in Austria and Switzerland.

The hurricane season officially begins in the North Atlantic, threatening the Caribbean region in particular.

With the help of contributions from foresightnews
www.foresightnews.co.uk

JULY

All but the most minimal amounts of trans fats will be banned in New York restaurants.

France takes over the EU presidency from Slovenia.

Japan hosts the G8 summit in Toyako, Hokkaido.

Cycling's Tour de France, three weeks of drama and drug-testing, starts in Brittany.

AUGUST

China plays host to the Beijing Olympics—and the athletes pray for clean air.

After an exhausting primary season, the Democratic Party gathers in Denver to anoint its presidential candidate and lambaste the Republicans.

Scholars, journalists, geeks and other fans of Wikipedia, an open-access internet encyclopedia, meet in Taipei for Wikimania 2008.

SEPTEMBER

The Republican Party holds its pre-election convention in Minneapolis-St Paul to anoint its candidate to succeed President Bush—and to lambaste the Democrats.

Some 4,000 disabled athletes from around the world meet in Beijing for the Paralympic games.

The UN General Assembly meets in New York.

Hong Kong elects a new 60-seat Legislative Council—half by direct popular vote and half indirectly.

OCTOBER

Azerbaijan holds a presidential election; Belarus holds a parliamentary election. International observers will doubtless find electoral imperfections in both countries.

Lithuanian voters choose a new, four-year parliament.

The Rugby League World Cup, featuring ten teams, begins in Australia. It is the first for the tough types of rugby's 13-a-side code since 2000 in Britain.

The International Salon of Taste opens in Turin, organised by Italy's Slow Food Movement, a group founded in 1986 to protest against the opening of a McDonald's restaurant in Rome's Piazza di Spagna.

The French-speaking world, boasting 200m people in some 68 countries (with French an official language in 32 of them), celebrates *la Francophonie* in Quebec.

NOVEMBER

America chooses a new president. Voters also elect all 435 members of the House of Representatives and a third of the 100-seat Senate. Several states elect governors, too.

The world's tobacco industry meets in Macau for World Tobacco Asia 2008—recognition that while the West persecutes smoking, China, already with 350m smokers, remains a growth market.

In a joint venture with Bharti Enterprises, Wal-Mart opens its first store in India.

DECEMBER

Signatories to the 1993 Chemical Weapons Convention (in force since 1997) meet in The Hague: 188 countries have signed the convention, and 182 have ratified it.

Leaded fuel for cars and lorries, already eliminated from developed countries, is due to disappear worldwide, following a programme begun in 2006 to phase out leaded petrol in less developed countries.

End-of-year deadline, after four years, for European Union nations to recover or incinerate 60% by weight of their packaging waste.

Also in this section:
Military money wars 34
The economy: clouds ahead 35
Our own university rankings 38
The NHS turns 60 40
James Bond: back to his books 42

Britain

The Gordon and David show

Andrew Miller

British politics becomes a competitive sport again

There will not be a general election in Britain in 2008. When the prime minister, Gordon Brown, humiliatingly pulled back from the vote he came close to calling in the autumn of 2007, the idea of holding one in the spring of 2008 was abandoned as well. But 2008 may nevertheless be a year in which British politics becomes more compelling than it has been since Tony Blair's landslide victory of 1997. Compelling in both the ways that politics can be: the competition will be closer, and it will feature more genuine policy disagreement than has been the case for most of the past decade.

The volatile beginning of their match-up in 2007 is a poor guide to how Mr Brown and David Cameron, the leader of the Conservatives, will fare against each other in 2008. Mr Brown's clunking style once looked likely to be bested by Mr Cameron's slickness. But the prime minister was quicker to see that the public had tired of Blairite panache, and his sombre gravitas at first went down well, giving him a bounce in the polls. After the bounce, however, came the fall of Mr Brown's panicked election decision. So it is only in 2008 that the two leaders will square up in normal political circumstances: both established in their jobs, with no distorting prospect of an imminent election.

In theory, Mr Brown can afford to drop the tactical manoeuvring that dominated the first few months of his premiership, which he mostly devoted to cosmetic efforts to attract small-c conservative voters. If he is to justify his reputation as a deep-thinking policymaker, he needs to do so in 2008. In particular, Mr Brown will be obliged to clear up what, in domestic-policy terms, may be the most important uncertainty about his leadership: will he pursue the market-based reforms that, albeit belatedly, Mr Blair tried to implement in the public services? Or will he abandon them, as some subtle smoke signals emitted by his ministers have implied?

Brown's gravitas...

That was the bet that the Tories placed on Mr Brown when he took office: that he would retreat to a more centralised philosophy, thus allowing them to inherit Mr Blair's agenda. If Mr Brown does so—and, for example, diminishes the limited freedom that had been granted to some secondary schools, or neglects the contribution that the private sector has begun to make to the provision of government-funded health services—he will need to find another way to deliver the improvements he has promised. Money alone cannot be the solution: economic growth will slow, and with it growth in government expenditure.

In the blue corner

For his part, Mr Cameron will try to achieve what Mr Blair did in the final few years of the last Tory government: persuade the country that his party is a credible government-in-waiting, rather than just a skilful debating outfit with a few eye-catching ideas. He probably will. Most Tories will at last adopt the conviction that Labour adopted under Mr Blair—that opposition parties must actively win elections, rather than relying on governments to lose them. For Mr Cameron, that will mean taming those Tories who, after Mr Brown persists in refusing to hold a referendum on the European Union's new treaty, will want to continue campaigning on that issue more than on domestic ones. Mr Cameron and George Osborne, the shadow chancellor, will discuss Britain's tax burden more freely than their predecessors.

The sparring between Messrs Brown and Cameron will make for an entertaining spectacle. Sniping about Mr Cameron's posh background will intensify. So will ▶

...versus Cameron's charm

An Australian-style, points-based **immigration system** begins in March, designed to restrict entry to those whose skills are in demand.

2008 IN BRIEF

Andrew Miller: political editor, *The Economist*

2008 IN BRIEF

The Isle of Man belatedly follows its British master on March 30th by **banning smoking** in enclosed public places.

efforts to unsettle Mr Brown.

If Mr Cameron gets the upper hand, whispers about Mr Brown's leadership, and jockeying among his many would-be heirs, may begin in the Labour Party. Watch the demeanour of David Miliband, the foreign secretary and the closest thing Labour has to a dauphin. Mr Brown will consider changing Britain's first-past-the-post voting system to a nominally fairer version that would discriminate against the Tories and favour Labour and the Liberal Democrats. For their part the Lib Dems, Britain's third party, will try—under new, more energetic leadership—to transmute their ideas into higher poll ratings. Alex Salmond, Scotland's nationalist first minister, will continue his canny efforts to turn Scotland against Westminster.

The more embattled Mr Brown becomes, the more likely he is to accelerate the phased withdrawal of Britain's troops from Iraq. That will disappoint George Bush even more than Mr Brown's cool rhetoric has already; the prime minister will calculate that Mr Bush's imminent departure from office will mitigate the impact on Britain's "special relationship" with America—and pray he is not called upon either to endorse or to denounce an American strike on Iran. But thousands of British troops will remain in Afghanistan, a conflict that will become more prominent and controversial.

> Although there won't be a general election, there will be another, entertaining vote: for mayor of London

Although there won't be a general election in 2008, there will be another, entertaining vote: for mayor of London. The incumbent, Ken Livingstone, will face Boris Johnson, the Tory challenger. Mr Livingstone (who will probably win) is caricatured by his critics as a cranky socialist; Mr Johnson, as much a liability to his party as an asset, is portrayed by his detractors as "a fogeyish, bigoted and upper-class twit". Those are also, roughly, the labels that the Tories and Labour would like to attach to Mr Brown and Mr Cameron. The coming year will determine whether those labels stick. ■

The battle for money

Anton La Guardia

Army, navy and air force will fight it out

Britain's armed forces are feeling unloved, and their hearts will sink further in 2008. They have fought alongside the Americans in Iraq and Afghanistan, losing more than 250 soldiers, but with nothing like the same support in terms of money or public respect.

Wouldn't it be nice, mused the British army chief, General Sir Richard Dannatt, if British soldiers could be given more American-style homecoming parades? Wouldn't it be nice, reply his colleagues, if we could just have more cash?

The Labour government claims to have overseen the longest period of rising defence spending since the 1980s, but in truth it has fought two wars on a peacetime mindset. The core budget, excluding the cost of the wars, has been fairly flat, rising by about 1% a year in real terms since 2000. As a share of GDP it fell to about 2.3% in 2006, in contrast to a sharp rise in America to 3.8%.

Chunks of money will be taken up with rising manpower costs, better military housing and new submarines for the Trident nuclear deterrent. As a result, important military kit will be cut or delayed in 2008 to close the £1 billion ($2 billion) hole that has opened up in projected annual spending.

This will lead to a nasty fight among the services. Despite the announcement that two new aircraft carriers will be built, the navy could come out worst. Its surface fleet has been hollowed out (some ships go to sea without air or submarine defences) and the likelihood is that it will continue to shrink. Disputes over what planes to put on the carriers (and how many) will fester.

The air force, which is receiving expensive Typhoon fighter jets, has been strengthened by the need to respond to the return of Russia's long-range bombers around British skies. Even so, the state of its transport fleet is a disgrace.

The army, for its part, expects to be involved in counter-insurgency for a generation. It wants more men (the American and Australian armies are growing) and the speedy delivery of the long-delayed new family of armoured fighting vehicles. But Gordon Brown's priorities lie elsewhere.

Britain will tiptoe away from Iraq. Mr Brown plans to reduce troops there to 2,500 in the spring, and may bring them out altogether by the end of 2008. Pride demands that it intensifies its effort in Afghanistan, but after two bitter and indecisive fighting seasons in Helmand the army's performance will be questioned unless it can show real progress in 2008. Expect many medals, but no ticker-tape parades. ■

Anton La Guardia: defence and security correspondent, *The Economist*

Pass the cash, Tommy

The storm to come

Anatole Kaletsky

Britain's economic horizon is fast darkening

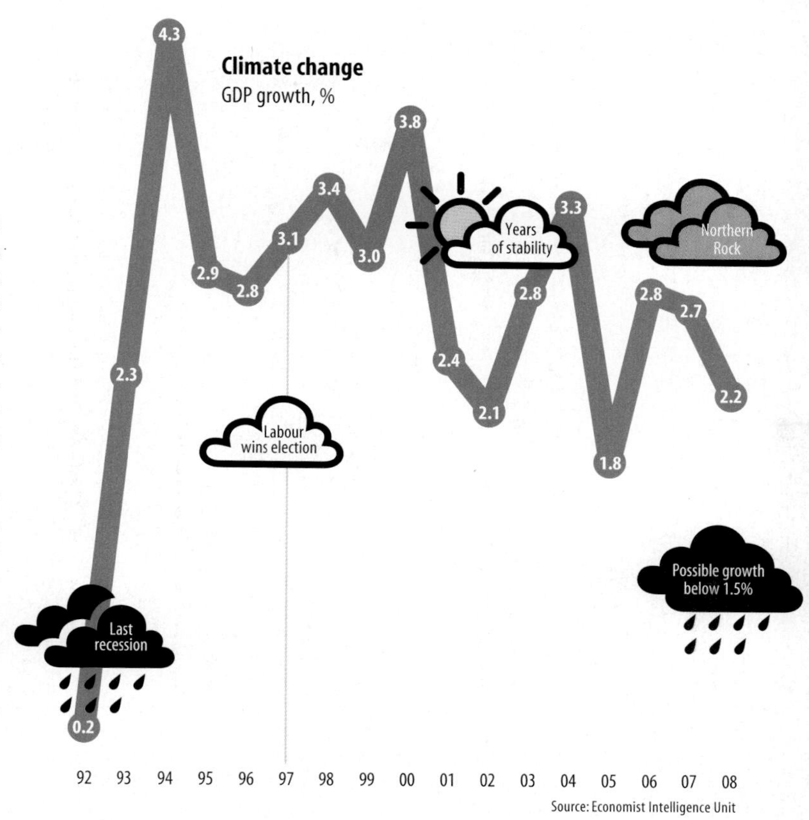

For the first time in 15 years, Britain is facing the prospect of a serious economic slowdown. After the longest period of uninterrupted economic growth in modern British history—and a world-beating decade of price stability, rapidly rising living standards and low unemployment—the era of prosperity is not completely over. But consumers, homeowners, workers and financiers are entering a leaner period than anything they have experienced since the Labour government came to power in 1997.

An outright recession is still unlikely, unless the credit crunch and the weakening in the American and European economies turn out to be much more severe than suggested by the evidence up to the end of 2007. But the nice, gentle slowdown assumed by Gordon Brown's government, and required by the Treasury to prevent a serious deterioration in Britain's public finances, seems almost as unlikely as the other, pessimistic extreme. Alistair Darling, the chancellor, was technically correct to say in his October economics report that his budgetary assumption of growth ranging between 2% and 2.5% was consistent with private-sector "consensus" forecasts, but he neglected several important caveats.

Economists typically get their forecasts wrong at cyclical turning-points or periods of major structural change—and it looks increasingly as if 2008 will be just such a year. To make matters worse, private forecasters have mostly been clustered near the bottom of the Treasury's 2-2.5% range. Moreover, several of the forecasts completed after the summer credit crunch and the Northern Rock crisis were producing results of 1.5% or below. If growth ends up anywhere near this low figure, then 2008 will be by far the worst year for the British economy since the end of the last recession in 1992.

Of course, Britain will not be alone in suffering some economic hardship. But in contrast to every previous slowdown since the early 1990s, Britain could well do worse than America and continental Europe in 2008. Britain's unaccustomed difficulties stem from four separate sources.

Four horsemen of the apocalypse

The first is the 2007 credit crunch, which is likely to have an even greater impact on Britain than on the United States or any other G7 country. This is partly because house-price inflation in Britain has been even faster than in America, while consumer leverage is higher than in most European countries. According to *The Economist*'s index, real house prices rose by 205% in Britain in the ten years since 1997, compared with 103% in the United States, 137% in France and 184% in Spain. Meanwhile, British households' mortgage debt stands at 125% of disposable income, compared with 104% in America, 65% in France and considerably lower figures in other European countries. There are other factors, such as strict restrictions on land use, that partly offset the vulnerability of house prices to an American-style meltdown. But the threat of a significant correction is clear.

What makes Britain even more vulnerable to the specific form which the global credit crunch has taken is the importance of the financial sector to the broader economy. The banking and insurance industries account for 6.5% of gross value-added in Britain, compared with a share of only 4-5% in other European countries. And, significantly, the parts of the business which have grown the fastest—hedge funds, wholesale finance and international securitisation—are the ones due for the biggest setbacks in the year ahead.

According to the Centre for Economics and Business Research (CEBR), wholesale finance and the related high-value business services based in the City of London have accounted for around 16% of the growth in the British economy over the past four years. These activities are not about to collapse, since Britain still enjoys an international comparative advantage in wholesale finance—and will probably continue to do so even after the Treasury's tax raid on foreign workers announced in October 2007. However, the phenomenal gusher of wealth that Britain has enjoyed from the City of London is bound to slow down in the year ahead. According to the CEBR, which makes a speciality of tracking financial employment, London's 350,000 high-end jobs in finance and business services will fall by about 5,000 in 2008. This may not seem much, but it will still represent ▶

> The phenomenal gusher of wealth that Britain has enjoyed from the City is bound to slow down

2008 IN BRIEF

The number of Britons celebrating their **100th birthday** passes 10,000. In 1911 in England and Wales there were only 100 centenarians.

Anatole Kaletsky: partner, GaveKal Research; editor at large, the *Times*

How would it feel to drive a car so considerate, it charges the battery when coasting, and stops the engine when the car is stationary and the clutch is out? Brake Energy Regeneration and Auto Start Stop, part of BMW's EfficientDynamics programme: Lower fuel consumption. Fewer emissions. Group hug. **Seehowitfeels.co.uk**

BMW
www.bmw.co.uk
Tel. 0800 325 600
The Ultimate
Driving Machine

a shock after four years of growth at 10,000 annually. Much worse, the City bonuses which have powered the London housing market and consumer economy are likely to fall by 30% over two years, according to the CEBR—to £6.2 billion ($12.4 billion) in 2008 from £7.4 billion in 2007 and £8.8 billion in 2006. This would represent a much bigger loss than the 12% decline in bonuses experienced between 2000 and 2002.

As the hedge funds and investment banks start firing staff and reducing bonuses, the London economy, which represents roughly 20% of national GDP, will suffer a significant loss of income. The damaging effects will quickly trickle down to the rest of the country through the housing market and retail sales. Moreover, the Brown government's unexpected attack on the generous tax treatment enjoyed by foreign-domiciled workers could do long-term damage to Britain's comparative advantage in this sector and turn what should have been a temporary cyclical slowdown into a permanent structural decline.

The third threat to the British economy is closely related to the problems of the City. For the past 15 years Britain has enjoyed an enormous terms-of-trade benefit from the fact that the exports in which it specialised (largely business services) were going up in price, while its imports (largely commodities and mass-produced manufactures) were getting cheaper. In 2006-07 this terms-of-trade gain, which has lifted Britons' real incomes and consumption without the need for them to work any harder, was reduced by rising commodity prices. But in 2008 the terms of trade could even go sharply into reverse, as financial incomes start falling, while the cost of imports from China and the rest of Asia goes up.

The final problem will be partly the result of weaker incomes and spending: government finances will suffer an even tighter squeeze than the Treasury assumed in its downgraded forecasts—and as a result the boom in public-sector spending which has spread wealth from the City of London to the rest of the country will subside or even reverse. According to the official forecasts, public spending should rise by 2.1% annually in real terms from April 2008 onwards. Presumably there will be some overshooting, as a result of which budget deficits will keep on rising and the government's fiscal rules will have to be torn up. But public-sector workers and managers cannot even dream of a return to the 4%-plus growth rates they enjoyed from 2001 until 2006. With housing, consumption, financial services and government spending all slowing abruptly, one can see why Mr Brown was tempted to call an early election—and why he is very unlikely to do so in 2008. ■

An academic exercise

Helen Joyce

Who's the smartest of them all?

By far the biggest research project undertaken in British universities in 2008 will be one in which academics examine themselves. In the "Research Assessment Exercise 2008" (RAE2008), 67 panels of over 1,000 academics will rank the work done over the past seven years by every university department in Britain, on a scale of "world-leading" down to merely "of national interest" (or, horrors, "unclassified"). Each "research-active" academic must submit his best four pieces of work since the last such stocktaking, in 2001. And each department must submit nine electronic forms detailing everything from the number of its research students to the quality of its facilities.

The stakes are high: not only government money is at stake (the lion's share of research funding goes to the world-leading; worthwhile crumbs to the internationally excellent; nothing to the rest), but so are universities' positions in league tables that are scoured by ambitious students when choosing where to study. So prolific professors have been poached at exorbitant salaries (by academic standards, anyway), their publication records coming with them. And less stellar performers have been humiliatingly redefined as "non-research active", to stop them letting their side down.

Some attempt at ranking universities to determine the share-out of money is probably inevitable. But surely there is a simpler way? Future RAEs are to rely mostly on "metrics": measures of quality that piggyback on the judgments of others—citations by other academics, for example, and a university's success in raising funds from elsewhere.

To help point the way ahead, *The World in 2008* spent one journalist-day compiling its own citation index: the number of times individual British universities have been mentioned in *The Economist* over the past ten years.

The London School of Economics comes top (well, perhaps we have a slight bias in favour of economics departments), followed by Oxford, Cambridge, University College London and Imperial College. It will be interesting to see whether thousands of hours of painstaking academic research yield anything very different. ■

Helen Joyce: education correspondent, *The Economist*

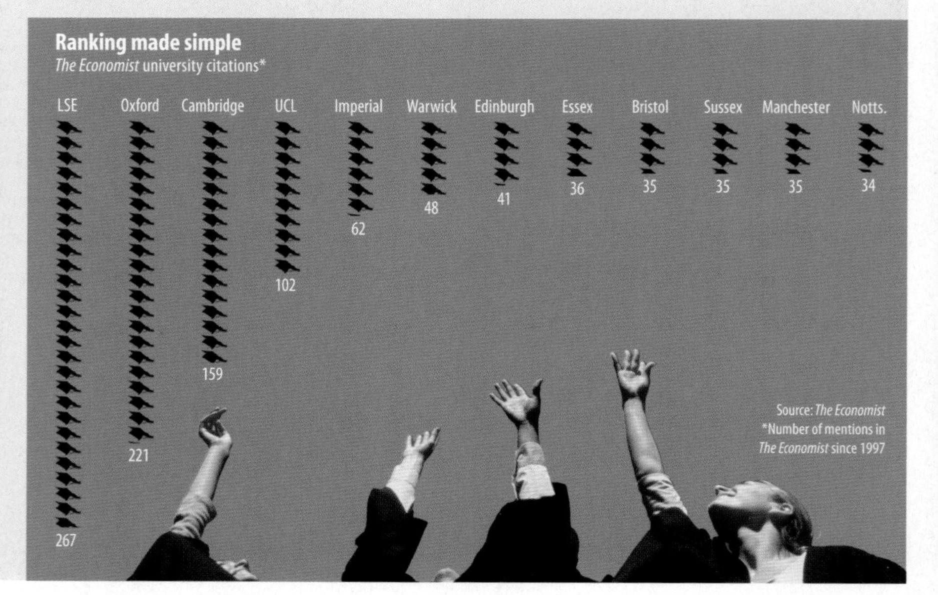

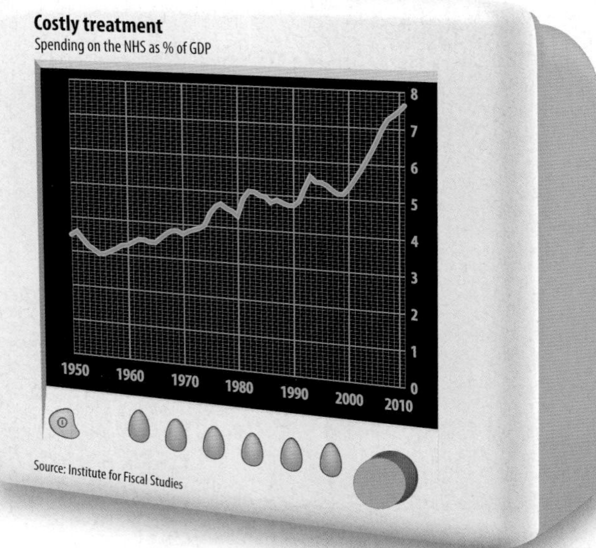

Health concerns at 60

Paul Wallace

Labour's drive to reform the NHS will falter

In July 2008 the National Health Service will celebrate its 60th anniversary. Its essential features—a tax-financed health-care system free at the point of use—have proved enduringly resilient, surviving even the privatising instincts of Margaret Thatcher's government in the 1980s. A millennium poll showed that almost half the British public regarded the establishment of the NHS as the most important achievement of the 20th century.

Yet voters have been far from happy with the condition of the health service. For decades after the NHS was founded in 1948 it provided basic but cheap medical care on terms set by hospitals and doctors. But as the British grew more prosperous they became increasingly dissatisfied with a service that had fallen behind the standard set in many other rich countries.

As prime minister, Tony Blair raised the stakes by pledging a wholesale reinvention of the NHS. His ambition was a service that would retain its traditional values of free medical care for all while offering higher quality and giving patients more of a say. Mr Blair made sure that the NHS got record increases in funding: its budget has risen by 7% a year in real terms for the best part of a decade. After an initial period when he mistakenly relied on targets and admonitions, Mr Blair realised that choice and competition were a better answer than command and control. He drove through reforms to give patients a right to decide where they were treated. And he gingered up competition among its hospitals, not least by turning to private providers to treat publicly funded patients.

The NHS's 60th birthday will prompt an audit of what Labour has accomplished in its decade in power. The end of the fat years for the NHS's finances poses awkward questions about what exactly Labour has achieved with all the extra money. Starting in April 2008 health spending will rise by 3.7% a year in real terms until 2011, a wrenching slowdown after nine years of growth at double that rate.

The setting could hardly be more unpromising for Gordon Brown, the new prime minister, who will find it hard to convince voters that the NHS is safe in his hands, let alone that it has been reinvented. Despite all its efforts, Labour's historic huge lead as the party most trusted to run the health service has shrunk, especially since the 2005 election. This is partly because taxpayers have got poor value for money, too much of which found its way into bulging wages, making British doctors among the best paid in the world. The government's reputation also took a battering when many hospitals plunged into the red despite the spending splurge. Delays in a costly reform to computerise medical records and a flawed reform of medical recruitment reinforced the impression of a meddling administration that botched and bungled whatever it touched in health.

Mr Brown will try to restore public confidence in Labour's ability to run the NHS in three main ways. First, the government will highlight its next big goal: to cut waiting times for elective operations (such as a hip replacement) by the end of 2008 to at most 18 weeks from the time a family doctor first refers a patient to a hospital. Second, Mr Brown wants to make it easier for patients to see their family doctors in the evenings and weekends. And, third, the NHS will tackle killer bugs picked up by hospital patients—like MRSA and *Clostridium difficile*—with overdue vigour.

The reforms are quite sensible but they have a fatal flaw. For the prime minister, who never shared Mr Blair's enthusiasm for introducing market forces into the health service, is going slow on them. In particular, the drive to encourage greater private provision of NHS-funded hospital care will lose further impetus in 2008. The prime minister is shunting Mr Blair's boldest reform into a siding.

> Health spending will rise by 3.7% a year in real terms until 2011, a wrenching slowdown after nine years of growth at double the rate

As a short-term political tactic, Mr Brown's approach may well make sense. It is hard for the public to feel confident about how Labour is handling the NHS when its staff are so dissatisfied. And one of their biggest gripes has been the threat of private health-care groups moving in on their territory. But there will be a long-term price to pay. For it is exactly that threat which has the potential to unleash real change in the NHS, as Mr Blair belatedly realised. His vision of turning the NHS into a publicly funded health-care market may have run into difficulties, but that reflected the resistance of the vested interests of its staff as well as ministerial incompetence. Under Mr Brown and his health secretary, Alan Johnson, genuine progress in transforming the NHS looks set to falter in 2008. ■

2008 IN BRIEF: By autumn, England, Scotland and Wales offer vaccinations to teenage girls against the **human papilloma virus**, a sexually transmitted risk factor for cervical cancer.

Paul Wallace: Britain economics editor, *The Economist*

007 in 008

John Grimond

Back to your books, Mr Bond

Few brands are as truly global as James Bond. It is said that about half the population of the world has seen a James Bond film. And 2008 will be a vintage year, for it marks the centenary of the birth of Bond's creator, Ian Fleming.

Two events will celebrate this anniversary. The first will be the opening of a ten-month exhibition at the Imperial War Museum in London, with exhibits ranging from annotated manuscripts, including that of Fleming's children's book "Chitty Chitty Bang Bang", to a Colt Python .357 Magnum revolver given to him in 1964, from a prototype of Rosa Klebb's flick-knife to the bikini worn by Halle Berry in the film "Die Another Day".

The second event will be the publication of a new Bond novel, "Devil May Care", on May 28th. Were he to return to earth, Fleming might be surprised to know that Bond books were still being produced so long after his death in 1964. The first, "Colonel Sun", was written by Kingsley Amis in 1968 (under the pseudonym Robert Markham) and since then another 20 have been published. The new one, by Sebastian Faulks, the author of "Birdsong", "Charlotte Gray" and, most recently, "Engleby", is set in 1967, with most of the ingredients of the original Bond works: alluring girls and sinister villains engaged in characteristic activities in outlandish places.

The man with the golden pen

Fleming might have been flattered by the vigour of his literary resurrection. An enthusiastic collector himself, he bought books (now in the University of Indiana at Bloomington) "that marked milestones of progress—books that had started something". Although he had in mind discoveries, inventions and theories, he would surely have been pleased that his own books had started a global phenomenon.

Whatever his appeal to foreigners, it is hardly surprising that the British took to Bond. Outwitting antagonists of all stripes, and showing up even Americans as somewhat plodding, the secret agent is presented as the embodiment of British style, sophistication and ingenious superiority.

> Outwitting antagonists of all stripes, and showing up even Americans as somewhat plodding, 007 is presented as the embodiment of British style

In the 1950s, when seven of the original 14 Bond books were written, this was exactly what the British in general were not: it was a time of drab conformity, if not austerity, in Britain, where style, dash and excitement were in short supply, as were foreign travel to exotic places, gadgets that worked and any food other than boiled potatoes and overcooked meat. Impoverished by the war, the British were retreating from their empire, humiliated by episodes such as Suez and struggling to make their economy work. Bond offered an escape.

It is the films, of course, that have made Bond so well known (the 22nd Bond film is scheduled for November 2008), but the centenary may serve to bring attention back to the books. These were derided at the time by many literary critics and have grown in reputation only slowly since. Some Bond-haters dismissed them as containing too much sex, snobbery and violence. Others called them commercial, scoffing at what would now be described as the product placement, though John Betjeman, Fleming's near contemporary, was engaged in much the same practice in his poems of the same era. The difference is that Betjeman was mentioning Hillman saloons and Ovaltine, whereas Fleming wrote of supercharged Bentleys and Bollinger Champagne.

Fleming did not produce great literature; that was not his aim. But he had the gifts of a good journalist—he started his career working for Reuters—writing sharp, vivid prose, almost entirely free of clichés. Many still find the pages irresistible to turn. ■

John Grimond: writer at large, *The Economist*, and married to Ian Fleming's niece

Also in this section:
Eurotrends for 2008 46
Germany's party friction 51
Sarkozy steps up 54
Sour grapes in France 56
Italy's unease 56
Michel Platini: The future of football 57
Spain's next transition 58
Remapping Europe 58
Putin's power pyramid 60
Redefining Turkey 61
Eastern Europe's fading halo 62
Nicolas Sarkozy: France in a challenging world 63

Europe

A plateful for Brussels

David Rennie *BRUSSELS*

Plenty of tricky issues for the EU's "big beasts"—and little Slovenia—to sort out

Within the European Union, most serious disputes usually boil down to one of three things: a fight about money, an argument over the distribution of power, or an external crisis (remember the EU's agonies in the run-up to the American-led invasion of Iraq). In 2008 the EU will at last emerge from a long row about power, caused by the death of the grandiose "Constitution for Europe" (killed off three years ago, by Dutch and French voters in referendums). Instead, the union faces a pair of rows about money, and a tough test of its foreign-policy mettle over the question of Kosovo.

The constitution's failure prompted two years of squabbling about drafting a slightly more modest replacement treaty. The election of a dynamic new leader in France, Nicolas Sarkozy, proved the key in resolving such institutional fights in the summer of 2007, and governments have now agreed on the final text. In 2008 EU leaders will work to ratify the treaty through low-key parliamentary votes, avoiding (where possible and in the face of noisy complaints) further pesky referendums, so that it can come into force in time for European Parliament elections in 2009. The treaty beefs up the role of the EU's foreign-policy supremo, or "high representative", and creates the new post of an EU president, elected by national governments to represent them abroad and chair EU summits. The jockeying over filling those two posts will be intense in the coming year.

The new treaty's impact on foreign policy will prove minimal, at least at first. More people will be watching to see if a foreign-policy dynamic forms around the union's "big beasts": France, Germany and Britain. Mr Sarkozy came into office vowing fewer "hang-ups" about American power, and in his first few months took a fresh line on issues such as Iran's nuclear programme and NATO. Angela Merkel, the German chancellor, is instinctively Atlanticist, but may prove hamstrung by her left-right grand coalition. Britain's prime minister, Gordon Brown, remains a frustrating mystery to Brussels. Some senior EU officials fear Europe's foreign policy will tread water in 2008, because Russian and American presidential elections frame the year like bookends.

The EU will begin 2008 facing a tricky external crisis, in the former Yugoslav province of Kosovo, which is set to declare unilateral independence from Serbia, or something very close to it. EU governments will be divided over recognising the fledgling nation, with countries like Britain and France in favour

> The EU will begin 2008 facing a tricky external crisis, in Kosovo

2008 IN BRIEF
Liverpool, home of the Beatles, and Stavanger, home of Norway's oil industry, are Europe's **Capitals of Culture**.

David Rennie: Brussels bureau chief, *The Economist*

2008 IN BRIEF

For the first time growth and employment surpass agriculture in getting the lion's share of the **European Union budget.**

and several southern members instinctively opposed—some out of solidarity with the Serbs (Greece), others because they have their own restive minorities and hate the legal precedent of allowing part of a sovereign state to break away (Spain and Slovakia). As if maintaining internal unity were not strain enough, the EU will be caught between America, which supports Kosovo's right to independence, and Russia, which insists Kosovo cannot secede if the Serbs say no.

In a final twist, the storm will rumble on the watch of Slovenia, a small ex-Yugoslav nation of 2m people, which takes over the EU's six-month rotating presidency on January 1st 2008 and so will be charged with finding a common European position. One of a group of ex-communist states that joined the EU in 2004, Slovenia volunteered to be the first newcomer to hold the presidency. It may come to regret that moment of enthusiasm.

Amid such high geopolitics, the EU may almost feel relief to be grappling too with rows over money. The coming year has been set aside for a formal debate on how to reform the EU budget, which now runs at over €100 billion ($140 billion) a year. In the enlarged EU, older, richer members of the club face either a bigger future budget or a dwindling share of the pot.

Real change could be in the air, an impression boosted by Mr Sarkozy, who has signalled a new French willingness to start talking about hefty reforms of the common agricultural policy (CAP). Though significantly improved over the years, the CAP still contains many market-distorting absurdities (and benefits wealthy France more than any other EU nation). Brussels reformers see recent rising world food prices as an opportunity to accelerate moves to a system based more purely on supply and demand. France takes over the rotating presidency in the second half of 2008, and Mr Sarkozy has vowed to discuss serious CAP reform then. Less reassuringly, he also called for ill-defined barriers to agricultural imports not produced to the EU's high (and highly costly) environmental and food-safety standards.

A second spending row turns on EU promises to tackle climate change. The promises were made at a summit in the spring of 2007. In the coming year those must be translated into national targets (with different countries taking different shares of the burden).

Under the agreement, by 2020 EU greenhouse-gas emissions must drop by at least 20% from 1990 levels (more if countries like America join the emissions-cutting effort). By the same date 20% of EU energy needs must come from renewable sources like wind, water or solar power. And plants must provide 10% of transport fuels by 2020, as long as such biofuels are environmentally sustainable. That caveat will get a lot of attention, amid questions about how green biofuels really are.

Given the diversity of energy interests in the EU, stand by for much haggling. Newer member-states will not easily be denied their chance to grow and develop as western Europe did, despite the carbon impact. In Austria and Latvia more than 60% of electricity is generated by renewable power (lots of rivers and dams); in Cyprus the proportion is 0.1%. It matters that carbon emissions are to be measured against 1990 levels: that is bad for ex-communist countries whose factories barely functioned in that tumultuous year. Polish officials have noted that their country has lots of forests, which soak up carbon. France loves nuclear power, which produces no greenhouse gases, but is not counted as renewable.

Who pays the bill for the EU's expensive green promises will be one of several battles to watch in 2008. ■

Trendy talk

Beppe Severgnini *MILAN*

With an Italian accent

Trend-spotting has become a fashionable sport in America. Why should Europe be left behind? Here are a Milan-based traveller's predictions for the Eurotrends to watch in 2008.

Transnational lovers. They are Europeans, lived abroad as students, fly easyJet and e-mail each other all the time. The e-generation is coming of age, and thinking of settling somewhere. Transnational couples are taking over all those nice, mid-sized cities—Bologna, Budapest, Dublin, Helsinki, Seville—and leaving the classic, the crowded and the obvious (London, Paris, Rome) to tourists.

Big tourism in small places. Eastern Europe has experienced massive growth in low-cost air travel. The trend will soon peak, but those new travellers are likely to come back, and they'll want better places to stay. Expect, on Europe's edges, new, smart and cheaper accommodation—small designer hotels, modern bed & breakfasts, farms with broadband.

More children. A tiny baby-boom in Milan points the way: in September 2007 almost 600 children were born, 16% more than the average in the past four years. Eight out of ten of the new babies were born to Italian couples. Milan is a fast-ageing city in the country with one of the lowest birth rates in Europe. Maybe in uncertain times a baby is a certainty and an investment. Like in the old days.

On your bikes. Good old-fashioned bicycles, being green and healthy, are increasingly fashionable again. Now it's time for a two-wheeled business revolution. Selling, renting and fixing bikes already provides jobs and entrepreneurial opportunities in northern Europe; other flat parts of the continent will soon follow.

Fewer coats. Miuccia Prada has said it loud and clear: "We keep churning out warm coats, but people don't need them any longer." Eating al fresco, more conversation, outdoor sports, out-of-season holidays—climate change has already affected daily life in Europe. Now it will change the way we dress. Get ready. Office belly-buttons are here to stay. ■

Beppe Severgnini: columnist for *Corriere della Sera* and author of "La Bella Figura" (Broadway)

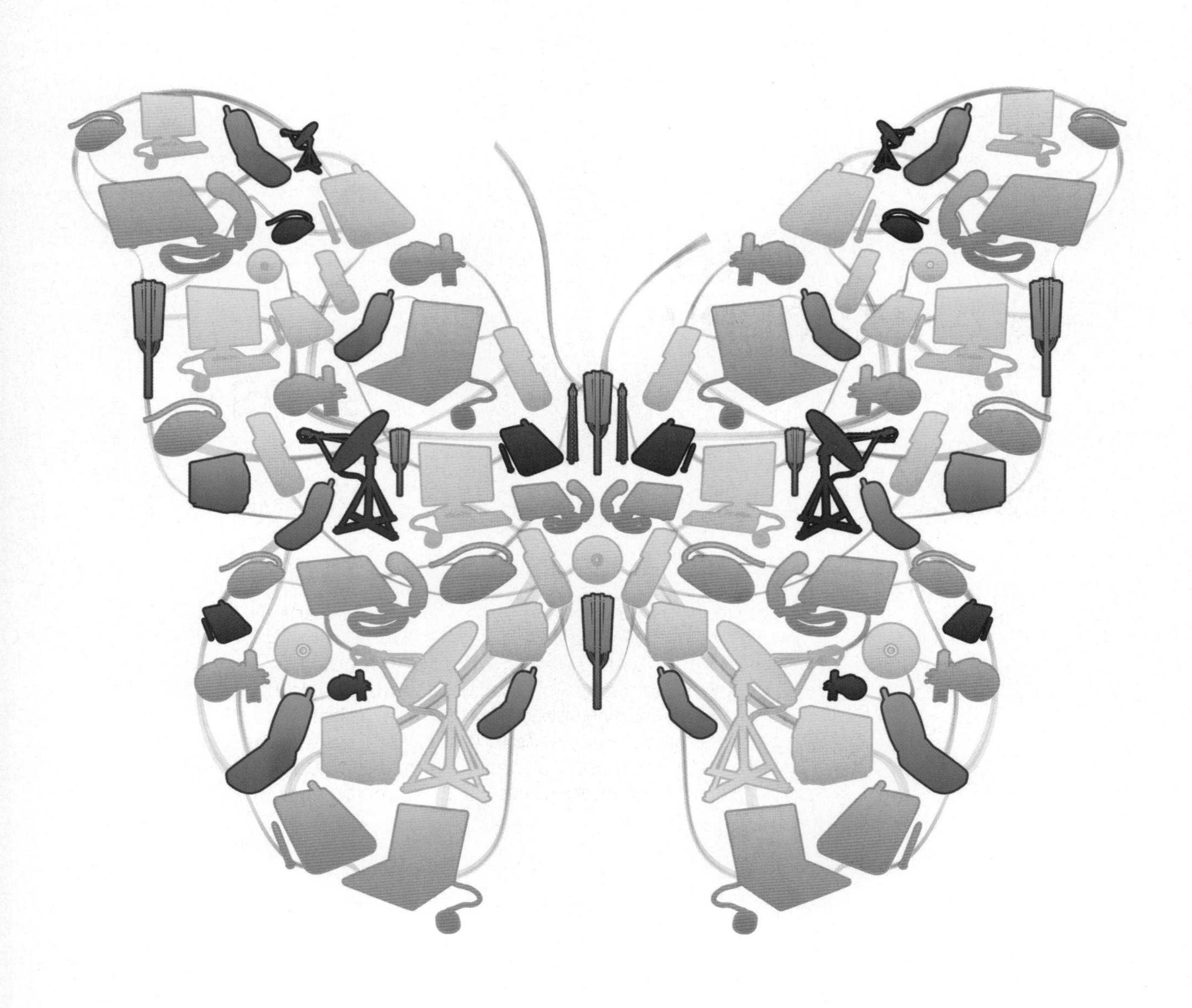

www.nokiasiemensnetworks.com/environment

Germany's double act

Brooke Unger *BERLIN*

Economic traction, political friction

The matriarch thinks ahead

Foreign policy dominated the first half of Angela Merkel's term as Germany's chancellor; raw politics are likely to overshadow the second. A series of state elections starting in January will test the popularity of the three parties in the country's "grand coalition" government and shape their strategies for national elections, which must be held by September 2009.

The coalition was the unwanted consequence of the 2005 elections, which gave neither Ms Merkel's conservative Christian Democratic Union (CDU) nor the left-leaning Social Democratic Party (SPD) a clear-cut victory. It wrangles over issues as varied as snooping on suspected terrorists and nuclear energy. There have been some advances: starting on January 1st corporate tax rates will fall from the top of the European scale to close to the average, along with a broadening of the tax base. The retirement age is to increase gradually to 67. The coalition has been fiscally responsible, aiming to eliminate the federal deficit by 2011. But pre-election tensions will make further reform difficult.

In the states the CDU and SPD are rivals, not partners. All four states set to vote in 2008 are governed by the CDU or its Bavarian ally, the Christian Social Union (CSU), the third member of the grand coalition. They are expected to win re-election everywhere, except perhaps in the city-state of Hamburg, but with reduced majorities. That might not displease Ms Merkel: Christian Wulff, the minister-president of Lower Saxony, and Roland Koch, his counterpart in Hesse, are her two main rivals for leadership of the CDU. A minor humbling would shore up her position. The CSU will probably continue its unbroken 45-year rule of Bavaria, the second-most-populous state.

> The CDU might form its first coalition with the Greens, a trial run perhaps for a national alliance

The SPD suffers from divided leadership and its association with unpopular reforms enacted by Ms Merkel's predecessor, Gerhard Schröder. Its best chance of victory is in Hamburg, but the city-state could set an ominous precedent: if the Free Democrats do not win enough votes to enter the Bürgerschaft (Hamburg's legislature), the CDU might form its first state-level coalition with the Greens, a trial run perhaps for a national alliance that would exclude the SPD after the 2009 elections.

The election results may fuel worries about the decline of both big parties, which some Germans fear will bolster the extremes. In the 1970s 85% of the electorate voted for the two big parties and the CSU; in the last election only 53% did, notes Manfred Güllner of Forsa, a pollster. The current beneficiary is the SPD's enemy, the Left Party, a new fusion between east German ex-communists and ex-Social Democrats who think their party has betrayed its leftist principles. It is now Germany's third-most-popular party (by a whisker) and in Bremen's elections in 2007 won its first seats in a western German state legislature. In 2008 it expects to win representation in Hamburg and possibly in Lower Saxony and Hesse as well. The SPD refuses to govern with it at national level.

Ms Merkel has thrived as the matriarch of an unhappy family that struggles to keep up appearances. Her approval ratings are around 70%. She has been buoyed by Germany's economic upswing, which may be dampened by America's wobbly mortgage market and the strong euro. Until now, exports and investment have taken the lead, pushing down unemployment to its lowest levels since the early 1990s, but living standards have stagnated. That should change in 2008. Higher employment income should push the rise of private consumption close to GDP growth of 2.5%.

A second stage of reform of the federal system may just squeak through. The first devolved powers from the federal government to the 16 states. The second would limit states' indebtedness and allow them more scope to raise (and lower) taxes. The coalition—especially the SPD—is too nervous to sanction further reform. Indeed, the temptation will be to spend some of the government's healthy tax revenues on softening the impact of earlier reforms.

If anything can distract politicians' attention from their electoral fates it is likely to be the issue of how to treat minorities. A third of children under six are from migrant families; their parents are more likely than average to be poor and unemployed. Germany's shortage of skilled labour makes immigration a pressing economic issue. The discovery in September of an alleged plot by two converts to Islam and a Turk to bomb American installations makes the integration of foreigners already in Germany seem a matter of life and death. This demands changes to education, immigration law and law enforcement, few of them easy for the unwieldy federal system and a divided coalition to enact.

The grand coalition still looks likely to survive until 2009 but its best days are probably behind it. ■

Brooke Unger: Germany correspondent, *The Economist*

RID DRIVE.

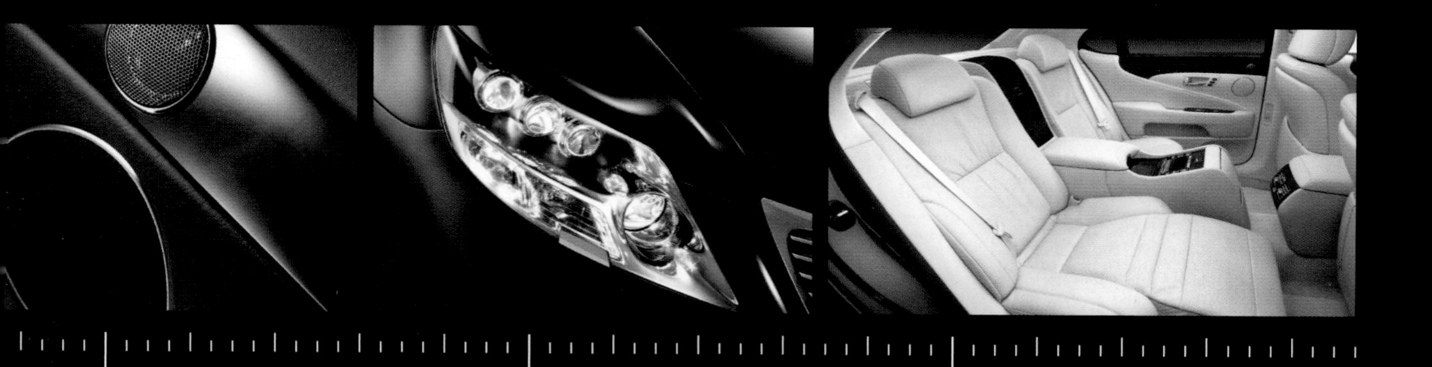

MARK LEVINSON
REFERENCE SURROUND
SOUND SYSTEM WITH 19
CUSTOM-MADE SPEAKERS

THE WORLD'S FIRST
LOW BEAM
LED HEADLIGHTS

ULTIMATE COMFORT WITH
RECLINING MASSAGE SEAT,
DVD SYSTEM AND
CLIMATE CONTROL

us will be charged at local rate and may be monitored or recorded.

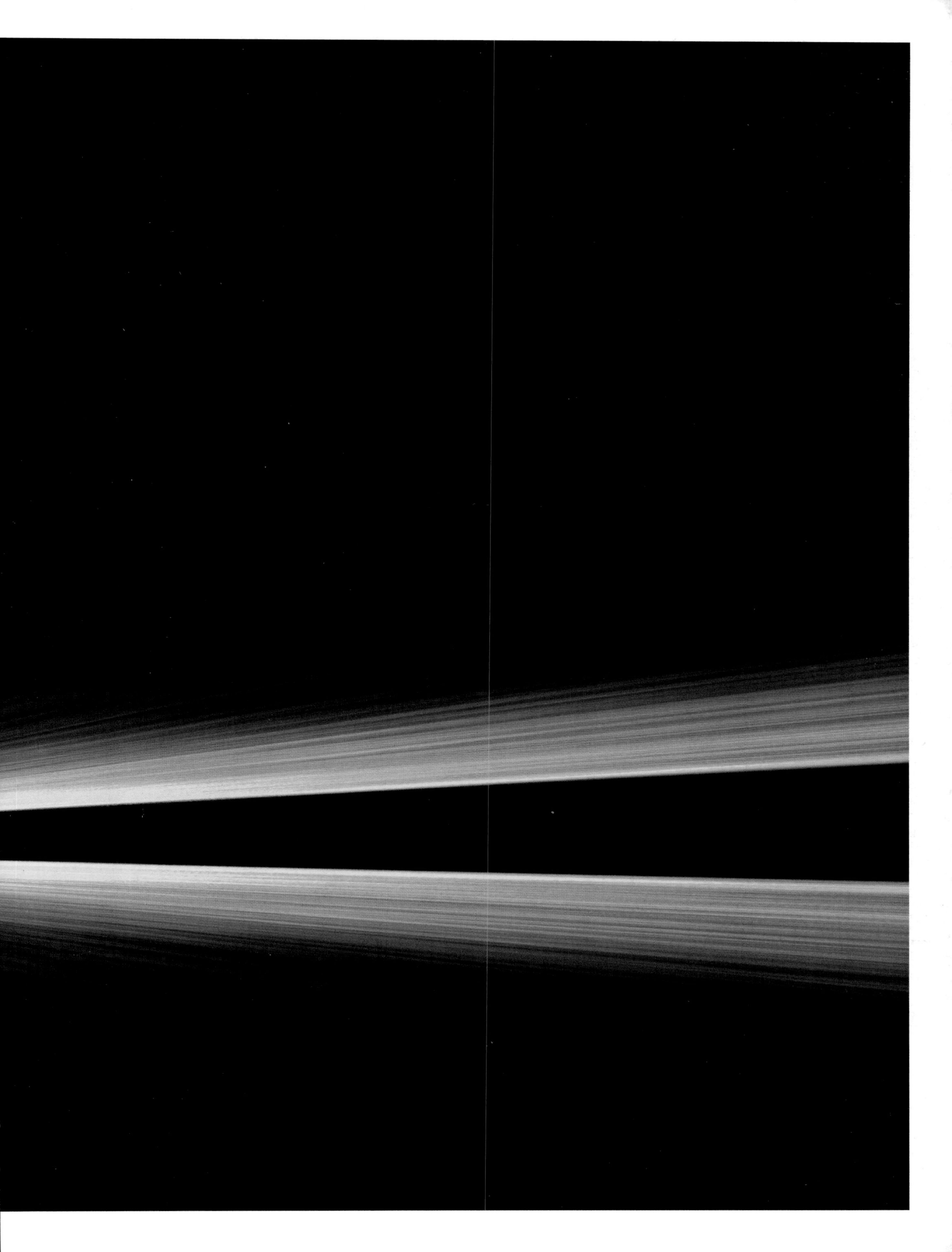

Defining Sarkozism

Sophie Pedder *PARIS*

Crunch time for France's ubiquitous new president

He will dazzle, dominate, even dismay: whichever way, Nicolas Sarkozy will be an attention-grabbing figure in 2008. After his whirlwind first months, it will be crunch time in France. The new president has amply demonstrated his talent for political inclusiveness, imagination and energy. But can he translate those qualities into real change?

Mr Sarkozy has breathed fresh air into the style and pace of government after 12 monarchical years under Jacques Chirac. A hands-on, hyperactive president, he has modernised the look of government, bringing in ethnic minorities and more women. He has disarmed the left, by recruiting some of its best thinkers. He has rejuvenated policymaking, thanks to a taboo-free, plain-talking approach. And he has started to shape a new French diplomacy designed to make France's voice count again.

So far, the French like what they see. Mr Sarkozy has enjoyed record-busting popularity. But 2008 will bring three challenges.

First, Mr Sarkozy will try to move from an early phase of uncontroversial changes, notably tax-cutting, to tougher economic reforms designed to revive French competitiveness and curb unemployment. Among them, he will end the generous "special regimes" for public pensions; tighten the unemployment-benefit rules; make rigid job contracts more flexible; introduce new ways to finance social security; streamline the bureaucracy; and deregulate certain markets, from big retail to taxis.

These changes will challenge vested interests, and so will be contested. Mr Sarkozy will try to pre-empt conflict through repeated talks, notably with union leaders. This hands-on approach will entrench the already-strong presidency of France's fifth republic, which in 2008 will mark its 50th anniversary. He will keep his prime minister, François Fillon, in the shadows. Any ministerial reshuffle—following, for instance, the outcome of the "Clearstream" smear-campaign investigation—will be dictated from the presidential Elysée palace.

Will Mr Sarkozy succeed where his predecessors failed? An enfeebled opposition and sympathetic public opinion should help. But in a year which, coincidentally, will mark 40 years since the May 1968 student uprising, there will be some protests and strikes (see picture). A one-time lawyer, Mr Sarkozy will try to settle these by cutting deals. These will come at a price: better civil-service pay, for instance, in return for trimming numbers. This will put further strain on the public finances. The government will struggle to keep its budget deficit to 2.3% of GDP, as it has promised. The economy will not help much: GDP growth is unlikely to exceed 2.2% in 2008. In short, Mr Sarkozy will end up diluting some elements of his reforms while bringing about general improvements in economic flexibility.

The second test will be municipal elections in March. All 36,000 French communes will elect a new mayor. Two of the biggest, Paris and Lyon, could stay in Socialist hands, delivering Mr Sarkozy's centre-right its first electoral knock. Bertrand Delanoë, the Socialist mayor of Paris, remains popular in the capital.

If Mr Delanoë holds Paris, he will be well placed to stand for the leadership of the Socialist Party in the autumn, when François Hollande will step down. Other contestants will include Ségolène Royal, Mr Hollande's ex-partner and defeated presidential candidate, as well as younger rising stars such as Manuel Valls. The party will struggle, however, to unify behind a new leader, as rivals squabble over how to modernise the left.

A global player

Mr Sarkozy's third challenge will be to reassert France's influence abroad. He will apply a mix of Atlanticist thinking (tough on Iran, sympathetic to Israel), Gaullist tradition (a strong Europe) and pragmatism-cum-opportunism (remember the rescue mission to Libya). With his foreign minister, Bernard Kouchner, he will take a lead on Iran, pushing for tighter sanctions and firmer negotiations, while not ruling out support for a military option. He will take a tougher stance towards Russia and China; demand more transparent, less corrupt relations with Africa; and press for help for Darfur. He will try to launch a new Mediterranean Union. Not short on ambition, he will attempt to carve out a role for France as mediator in Israel-Palestine, and even Iraq.

In a year which, coincidentally, will mark 40 years since the May 1968 student uprising, there will be protests and strikes

2008 IN BRIEF Italy regains a classical treasure when New York's Metropolitan Museum of Art returns the 2,500-year-old **Euphronios krater**, a jewel in the Met's crown since 1972—but almost certainly a looted one.

Sophie Pedder: Paris bureau chief, *The Economist*

In July, France will take over the European Union's rotating presidency. Despite Mr Sarkozy's Atlanticist leanings, he still thinks France is strong only when Europe is too. Warmer relations with America, he will argue, should not preclude fortifying Europe, notably with a stronger common defence policy. To soothe American scepticism, and revive British enthusiasm, he could even spring a real surprise: the re-entry of France into NATO's integrated military command, which De Gaulle pulled France out of in 1966. His rejection of reflexive French anti-Americanism does not mean that Mr Sarkozy will start taking orders from America. But the French will drop opposition for the sake of it.

His European friends will find, though, that Mr Sarkozy can still be a prickly partner. He will rail against the European Central Bank's monetary policy. He will contest negotiations over Turkish entry (though he may drop France's constitutional obligation to hold a referendum on new members). He will ruthlessly pursue French interests on industrial matters, on which he is an unapologetic interventionist. This will particularly test his ties with Germany, and exasperate Brussels.

In short, in 2008 the world will get full measure of the dynamic, restless Mr Sarkozy. He will be omnipresent, determined to leave his mark. At home, the pressure to achieve results will grow, mainly because he has set his ambitions so high. He wants to transform France into a less elitist, more entrepreneurial society, which works hard, buys its own homes, embraces globalisation and shrugs off its complex about money—unFrench aspirations from a rather unFrench French president. ■

Sour grapes in France

Quelle horreur!

For all its Puritan origins, America in 2008 will become the world's biggest consumer of wine, overtaking Italy and the previous champion, France. The reason is not just that Americans will be drinking more—up by 29% in non-sparkling wines in five years—but that the French will be drinking less (7% down on 2003).

On an individual basis, however, the French still win hands down: 58 litres of wine, both still and sparkling, for each adult in 2008, compared with a modest 13 for an American counterpart. Rather more worrying for France's winemakers is that, just as domestic consumption is in decline, so, thanks to New World competition, is their share of the export market. ■

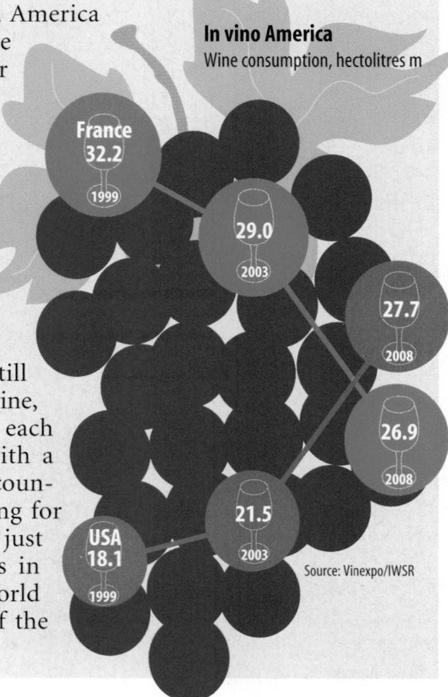

Then there were two

John Hooper *ROME*

New parties, same old problems for Italy

To qualify for an ample pension, Italy's lawmakers must put in at least two-and-a-half years in parliament. Ever since Romano Prodi's centre-left government, which came to power in April 2006 with a wafer-thin majority, began showing unexpected powers of survival, cynics have predicted it will fall as soon as potential government rebels secure themselves a comfortable old age. If so, Mr Prodi will see out 2008. But he could fall at any time, especially now the would-be mutineers know there is a substitute leader at hand.

In 2007 the two biggest parties of the centre-left—largely made up of former communists and progressive Christian Democrats—merged to form the Democratic Party. In October supporters elected as its leader Walter Veltroni, a 52-year-old former deputy prime minister who had spent the previous six years as mayor of Rome. His success in that job, and his ideological position roughly in the middle of the new party, made him a natural choice.

> Italy will continue its slow, relative decline

John Hooper: Rome correspondent, *The Economist*

The threat posed by the Democratic Party and its relatively young leader will force the centre-right to follow suit. Silvio Berlusconi's Forza Italia and the "post-fascist" National Alliance, led by Gianfranco Fini, will merge to form a rival Freedom Party. Less clear is whether the two big new parties can agree on an electoral law to keep out of parliament the smaller groups that have long held disproportionate sway in Italy.

While it endures, Mr Prodi's government will continue to pass sensible reforms and its finance minister, Tommaso Padoa-Schioppa, will strive to keep a tight rein on the public finances. But it will depend for its survival on the communist wing of the governing alliance, so ministers will not dare to impose the sweeping, liberalising measures the Italian economy needs.

The energy and transport sectors will remain mostly unprivatised. Public services will be run for the benefit of the trade unions rather than the taxpayers. What rationalisation there is will come in the private sector as small and medium-sized manufacturing companies give up the vain struggle to produce more cheaply than rivals in the Far East. Some will collapse. A growing number will move upmarket, where they cannot be outpriced.

The Italian economy, as in previous years, will grow by less than the European Union average. Italy will thus continue its slow, relative decline. More young, educated Italians will flee abroad in search of the prospects they lack in their own country. And those who stay will seethe with frustration over the parties and politicians they identify as the main obstacles to change.

Italy is a country in which evolution has usually been preferred to revolution. But, every so often, exasperation boils over into the sort of upheaval seen in the early 1990s. It just might happen again in 2008. ■

Not just another business

Michel Platini, president of UEFA, European football's governing body, argues that the sport deserves special treatment by competition authorities

For tens of millions of Europeans, the passion of football is part of their daily lives, whether as players on the pitch, spectators in the stands or watching on television at home. And this coming summer they will be watching avidly as 16 nations compete in Switzerland and Austria in the finals of UEFA's EURO 2008, culminating in the final in Vienna on June 29th.

At a time when Europe is seeking to define and unify itself and to form an identity around a common set of values, nothing contributes more to this quest than the love for our sport across the continent. How many children have put down new roots in their host country by playing football, long before settling down at school? I would suggest hundreds of thousands.

The values championed by football are a powerful force for social integration and civic education. These values include the principles of financial solidarity, openness and opportunity. These are values not only of European football but of European society as a whole.

Nevertheless, as football becomes increasingly commercialised and is often seen (by some at least) as just another "business", it is all the more crucial that we do not lose sight of the special characteristics that make our sport so attractive in the first place. For example, you cannot have an exciting sporting contest without some element of uncertainty. This means that careful measures have to be taken to protect the competitive balance between teams.

A sporting chance

"Normal" businesses may like predictability. Sport, however, thrives on uncertainty. In football, a predictable match is nearly always a dull match. So the governing body—the custodian of the game—has to ensure that football does not become dull; that it remains exciting. It must do so both to protect the sport and, hardly less important, to protect the interests of the public.

This leads to the question of how sport's rules and regulations should be treated under the law, in particular under European competition laws. It is encouraging that both UEFA and the European Commission are largely promoting the same objectives: a level playing field, equality of opportunity and, above all, the protection of the interests of a public that wants to see varied and exciting sporting competition.

We believe that the law needs to be applied in a nuanced way, taking into account the particular characteristics or the "specificity" of sport. Balanced measures and regulatory policies are needed to preserve and enhance the quality of competition and to deliver wider benefits, such as improving the training and education of young players. The naked operation of the "free market" will not accomplish these tasks, so it is up to the governing body to do it.

It is almost ironic that European economic law is cited when it comes to criticising regulatory policies adopted by UEFA. For example, the central marketing of TV rights (and redistribution of the revenue) is designed to promote competition, not to restrict it. Similarly, our rules on the training of local players and squad size limits are not an unjustified interference with economic liberty but are intended to enhance competition and improve player training in the process. Are we really suggesting that the governing body for football in Europe should not be concerned with these matters?

UEFA intends to strengthen sport's rules and regulations to protect football. We are not going to abandon our sport to some purist free-market dynamic that will simply kill it off. Furthermore, we are optimistic that both judicial and political authorities will be supportive of us in our task, when they appreciate exactly what we are trying to achieve.

We are not going to abandon our sport to some purist free-market dynamic that will simply kill it off

We need to protect and strengthen ethical sporting values—values that champion fair play, respect for referees and opponents, and fair competitions. We must defend the European sports model based on financial and social solidarity between rich and poor, as we are convinced that this is the best way to protect the future of football.

Football remains the most popular sport played and followed across Europe. Today's top professionals are watched live on television by millions of European citizens every week. To maintain a good image for the game we must start at the top: we have a policy of "zero tolerance" towards violence or racism, both on and off the pitch.

At the same time, we must nourish the grass roots. Through our "HatTrick" project we will have helped to build over 3,000 mini-pitches and invested over €300m ($420m) between 2004 and 2008 in our member associations. This is nearly all financed by UEFA competitions, so protecting their future is vital.

We must not have the sort of football where money can buy everything, including success. Let the fascination of sport prevail over the fascination for money. ■

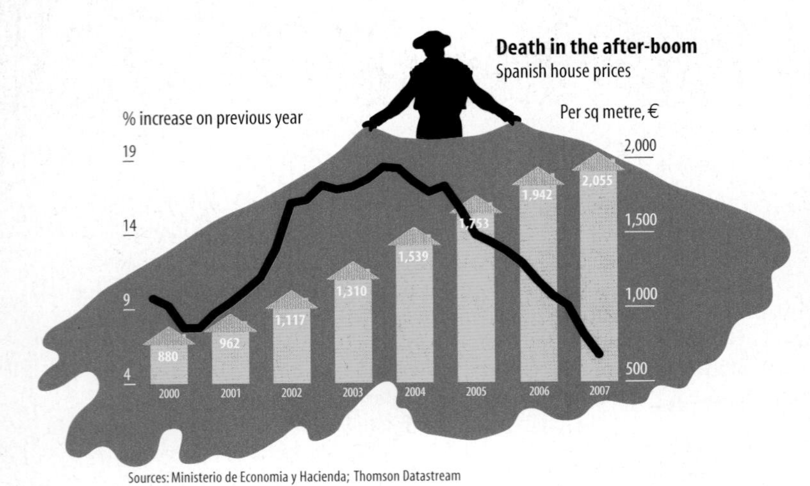

Sources: Ministerio de Economia y Hacienda; Thomson Datastream

The second transition

Thomas Catan *MADRID*

Prepare for some pain in Spain

In the wake of Spain's heady transition from dictatorship, the incoming Socialist leaders vowed in 1982 to alter the country so radically that "even its own mother will not recognise it." A quarter-century later, it seems fair to say she would have a hard time doing so. What was an isolated, backward country when General Franco died in 1975 is today a thriving, self-confident place with growing international influence.

Mr Zapatero will win a second term at the general election in March

But Spain now faces another big transformation. It must thoroughly overhaul its economy, its education system and its work habits if it is to avoid the sclerosis of some other European nations. Will 2008 be the year that Spain embarks on this "second transition", or the year it begins its gentle decline?

The signs are not encouraging. Spain's two main political parties spent much of 2007 in a dismal slanging-match: over the violent Basque separatist group ETA, over the devolution of powers to the regions, and over the unresolved legacy of Spain's 1936-39 civil war. Spain's Socialist prime minister, José Luis Rodríguez Zapatero, squandered political capital in his first term fighting anachronistic "culture wars" with the Spanish right. The opposition People's Party, meanwhile, has hammered Mr Zapatero for his now-abandoned peace talks with ETA, accusing him of surrendering to terrorists—yet it attempted an identical feat while in power. The opposition's fixation on (an enfeebled) ETA has played well with its base but failed to win it new converts. Barring a change of luck, Mr Zapatero will win a second term at the general election in March.

He will not have much time to celebrate. After growing at twice the euro-zone average since 2000 the economy will slow in 2008 as higher interest rates hurt Spain's debt-laden households. House prices will stagnate, ending a decade-long property boom.

In the short term, the pain in Spain should be mild. The economy will continue to grow in 2008, albeit at a slower pace than the 3.8% expected in 2007. But over the long term the economy faces serious issues.

Growth remains too dependent on construction and consumption, both of which will sag in 2008. So far, Spanish companies have compensated by boosting their exports. But they, too, will feel the pinch of scarcer credit and a strong euro in 2008. The flood of foreign takeovers by Spanish companies will slow to a trickle. Spain's current-account deficit—the euro zone's largest, at 8.8% of GDP—will remain dangerously high.

Spain has become too expensive to compete in low-tech, low-wage industries against new members of the European Union, let alone India and China. The next government therefore urgently needs to revamp Spain's antiquated education system to prepare for the changes ahead. It must make labour markets more flexible and foster competition in sheltered markets.

None of this is easy. It involves taking on powerful interests and the benefits will not be felt for some time. But bold moves are vital if Spain is to continue its successful trajectory. The next government needs to summon the courage to tackle the future rather than the past. ■

2008 IN BRIEF

Barcelona, one of Spain's traditional homes of bullfighting, **ends the corrida**, to the dismay of fans and the delight of animal-lovers.

Thomas Catan: Spain correspondent, the *Times*

To coin a phase

Making mischief with maps

Map-making and politics go together the world over: witness sovereignty disputes from the Middle East to various rocks off the coast of Japan. So why should the European Union be any different? Take the new euro coin, adopted by Slovenia in 2007 and to be rolled out across the euro zone in 2008. Etched into the map on its surface for the first time is Cyprus (long divided between quarrelling Greeks and Turks). But the geographically astute will notice that Cyprus has somehow moved hundreds of kilometres westward, and the politically aware will note that this means the map can exclude Turkey, whose candidature for EU membership alarms many an existing EU state.

Some EU map-amenders might like to go further. *The Economist* has already suggested doing away with Belgium, and many Belgians seem to agree. The Schengen agreement will in 2008 have eliminated border controls between all but three EU nations, so why not eliminate the borders too? That, of course, would confirm for British Eurosceptics the notion of an EU "superstate". What they really want is for Britain to be off the EU map. ■

2008 IN BRIEF

For three months, starting in June, the Spanish city of Zaragoza hosts **Expo 2008**. The theme of the international exhibition is "Water and Sustainable Development".

Putin's pyramid

Arkady Ostrovsky *MOSCOW*

Russia's politics will be increasingly unstable

By March 2008 Russia will have a new president and parliament. But the power will stay in the hands of the same man: Vladimir Putin. After much speculation, Mr Putin has decided to hang on to power one way or another.

One way is for him to become prime minister, which he has said is "entirely realistic". He could use the majority of his United Russia party in parliament to turn Russia into a parliamentary republic where the president plays a largely ceremonial role while real power is wielded by the prime minister. Alternatively, Mr Putin could select a loyal president who would keep the Kremlin seat warm for a while and then quietly step down, clearing a way back for Mr Putin. Viktor Zubkov, the Soviet-style apparatchik appointed as prime minister by Mr Putin in 2007, fits the role of a temporary president. He is loyal (he was Mr Putin's deputy in St Petersburg's mayoral office), quite old (66 to Mr Putin's 54) and has no visible ambitions of his own.

This neat, if brazen, plan allows Mr Putin to stay in power while not formally breaking the constitution, which demands that he leaves office after two terms. Whatever Mr Putin decides, people will support him. And it is not just because he controls the media, the parliament, the economy and just about every other sphere of life. It is also because oil money is flowing in and people's lives are generally improving. And if none of it looks democratic, it does not seem to bother the vast majority of Russians.

Arkady Ostrovsky: Russia correspondent, *The Economist*

Rich Russians
Numbers of $ millionaires and billionaires

Sources: Merrill Lynch/Capgemini; *Forbes*

Yet Mr Putin and the people around him seem twitchy. Why else would the Kremlin be sending troops to squash opposition protests which pose no threat? And why would state companies, which have only recently taken over many private assets, be itching to sell some of their shares on international markets? The answer is that the system which has emerged in Russia under Mr Putin is profoundly unstable.

> Nationalism, already strong, will become the dominant force in Russia

The eight years under Mr Putin have not legitimised the property accumulated by his loyal friends who control Russia's largest companies. Having undermined property rights as well as whatever might act as a counterbalance to the Kremlin's power, Mr Putin has built a political construction that resembles a pyramid which rests on its tip, rather than on its base. A transfer of real power to even a hand-picked successor could upset the balance and jeopardise the safety of Mr Putin's friends. Which is why he decided (or was persuaded) to stay.

In the short term this might calm the nerves of Mr Putin's closest allies as well as some investors. But it will not make Russia any more stable and will only increase the pressures that already exist.

Enemies here, enemies there

First, there will be pressure on the Kremlin from outside its charmed circle. Mr Putin draws his main support from a small group of former KGB colleagues who rose with him and occupy powerful political posts as well as the commanding heights of the economy. This stifles social mobility. Ambitious regional politicians have almost no chance of getting lifted into the higher echelons of power. The dominance of United Russia, supported by the apparatus of the state, eliminates the hope for a multi-party system developing any time soon. Nor is there much hope for any kind of economic reform.

Within the Kremlin itself, rivalry between factions backed by different financial interests is fierce. Until now, Mr Putin has masterfully claimed all the credit for the oil-fired boom, while transferring the blame for anything that goes wrong to the government. If he becomes prime minister, he may have to bear some responsibility for the inefficiency of the system he created.

To divert attention from such problems, the Kremlin will try to find enemies both inside and outside the country. The number of "extremists" persecuted by the security services will increase. To justify its hard line, the Kremlin will call for national unity in the face of a growing threat from the West. Nationalism, already strong, will become the dominant force in Russia—indeed, the Kremlin will adopt it as its main policy. In the process it risks creating a monster it will be unable to control. ■

Beyond Ataturk

John Peet

Turkey will struggle to redefine itself

What lies in store for Turkey after the unexpected drama of 2007? The drama featured hotly contested presidential and parliamentary elections, a constitutional crisis, hints of military coups, a threatened invasion of Iraq and new roadblocks on Turkey's path towards the European Union. In 2008 some big questions will linger over the country's future direction, reflecting both the divided nature of Turkish society and souring attitudes to the West.

The old cosmopolitan, liberal elite, based mainly in Istanbul and Ankara, clings fiercely to the legacy of Kemal Ataturk, who in the 1920s dragged the remnants of the Ottoman empire into the 20th century. Ataturk was interested more in modernity and secularism, the twin pillars of his new republic, than in democracy. This explains the special status accorded to the army, guardian of Ataturkism, which has staged four coups in four decades to kick Islamists and other undesirables out of government.

In contrast stands a new, younger and more conservative Turkey, with its roots in the Anatolian hinterland. These Turks are more interested in growth and rising living standards than in secularism. Indeed, many are devout Muslims. They form the backbone of the Justice and Development (AK) party, led by Recep Tayyip Erdogan, the prime minister, and Abdullah Gul, the president. The traditional ruling classes, including the army, regard these two men, who have Islamist backgrounds and also wives who sport the Muslim headscarf, with deep suspicion.

Identity and style

Tensions should ease in 2008. Mr Gul is now safely installed in the Çankaya palace. Mr Erdogan is back in power for a second term after his party won a bigger share of the vote in 2007 than in 2002. The constitutional clash of April 2007, when the army threatened to intervene, has been settled in favour of the AK party and democracy. The hawkish army boss, Yasar Buyukanit, has more or less made his peace with Messrs Gul and Erdogan.

> Public opinion in Turkey has shifted markedly against the EU

Even so, Turkey will run into three big problems in 2008. The first is over secularism. The government will come under growing pressure from its grassroots to relax or scrap bans on the Muslim headscarf in public buildings, and to let graduates of religious-training schools attend state-funded universities. Such moves will trigger protests from Ataturkists. But after AK's big win in 2007, new laws are likely to water down Turkey's strict secularism.

That will please millions of Turks. More worrying for many of them will be economic slowdown. Under Mr Erdogan the economy has boomed, after many years when Turkey lurched from one crisis to another. That reflects the rare competence of the AK government, but also an unusually benign world economic climate. As the outlook for the global economy worsens, Turkey, with a relatively high-cost but low-skilled workforce, will be especially exposed. This will be Mr Erdogan's biggest headache in 2008.

The third problem will be Turkey's relationship with other countries, notably in Europe and America. Turkey's friends and neighbours are keenly aware of its strategic significance: a fast-growing, mainly Muslim democracy that straddles the crossroads of Europe, Asia and the Middle East. Yet although talks on EU membership are proceeding slowly, the Europeans, influenced by the negative views of French, Austrian, Dutch and German voters, are increasingly hostile to the very notion of Turkey joining their club. In 2008 Turks will need a lot of patience to keep alive their hopes of eventual membership. As it is, public opinion in Turkey has shifted markedly against the EU.

It has also shifted against America. Turkey is a rare American (and Israeli) ally in the region, as well as a NATO member. But the prospect of a largely autonomous Kurdish region in northern Iraq, where Kurdish guerrillas can base themselves to make attacks on Turkey's south-east, infuriates the Turkish armed forces. Under pressure from the Americans, Mr Erdogan will restrain the army from a full-scale invasion that could destabilise all of Iraq. But even smaller military incursions will make the Turkey-Iraq border tense. After an eventful 2007, Turkey is not going to be wholly out of the headlines in 2008. ■

John Peet: Europe editor, *The Economist*

Unoriginal sins

Edward Lucas

For eastern Europe the EU's "halo effect" is set to fade

2008 IN BRIEF
After two centuries **Russia withdraws** its last troops from Georgia, except probably from the disputed territory of Abkhazia.

The ex-communist countries of eastern Europe will start the year with some good news: on January 1st most of them will join the Schengen passport-free area, removing the last obstacles to frontier-free travel within the European Union. That will help remove the lingering feeling that the eight new member-states from the region that joined in 2004 are second-class citizens.

The EU's decision will be followed by yet more good news in the spring, when Congress will vote to give the citizens of many ex-communist countries visa-free travel to America. That will remove another lingering feeling: that their help in Afghanistan and Iraq was taken for granted. As other allies depart from Iraq, the east Europeans—notably Poles, Romanians, Georgians and Bulgarians—will stand out as America's most resolute European friends.

White-hot speculation has sent prices and rents soaring

The dying months of the Bush administration will also be marked by another attempt to establish some kind of "legacy" in eastern Europe, by setting Georgia, along with Croatia, Albania and Macedonia, further on the road to membership of NATO. That will infuriate the hawks in the Kremlin, who will use it as an excuse to edge closer to America's rivals and bugbears such as China and Iran.

But the big story of the year will be a different one: of popping bubbles and slowing economies. In 2008 the truth will start to hurt: the ex-communist countries have botched reform, made sham improvements and fudged hard choices. For four years, that has been covered up by the "halo effect" of joining the EU, and by exceptionally favourable external conditions.

As liquidity drains away from global markets, the ex-communist countries' lack of competitiveness will become increasingly exposed. Fast wage growth means that they are no longer sources of cheap, unskilled labour. Simple manufacturing and services are moving elsewhere—to Morocco and Ukraine, for example, where workers are more plentiful. Employers in industries that add lots of value, such as sophisticated services and high-tech manufacturing, are worried too: they complain that east European universities are not turning out the graduates they need. These disadvantages will be underlined in 2008 by the lack of progress in other areas, such as roads (especially in Poland, the biggest country in the region) and bureaucracy (almost everywhere).

The sharpest pain will be in the economies that have seen the most furious growth, notably the Baltic states, and particularly in property, where white-hot speculation has sent prices and rents soaring way above comparable cities in western Europe. The foreign banks that own most of the ex-communist world's banking system will find themselves bailing out local subsidiaries that have lent rashly. Their shareholders' willingness to suffer for local managers' imprudence will provide a big cushion. If that fails, disaster looms for countries such as Latvia, whose inflation hit 11.4% in September 2007 and where the current-account deficit was over 22% of GDP.

Rocketing growth has fuelled inflation, killing the ex-communist countries' hopes of joining the euro any time soon (though in 2007 Slovenia squeaked in). The good news from the 2008 slowdown will be that the best-run countries will have at least some chance of getting inflation down to the low single digits needed to be allowed into the single-currency zone. That may be unwelcome news in parts of rich Europe, where many feel that the euro area has too many wobbly members already.

Wise politicians in the region will use 2008 to restart reforms, chiefly of an education system which is all too often fossilised and ridden with cheating. But they will be the exceptions: squabbling, self-indulgence and short-termism are the defining characteristics of post-communist politics now. Western Europe may be little better—but it is richer and can afford bad government. Regaining eastern Europe's competitiveness will require the hard choices that usually stem from a real crisis; 2008 is unlikely to provide it. ■

Edward Lucas: central and eastern Europe correspondent, *The Economist;* author of "The New Cold War" (to be published in February by Palgrave and Bloomsbury)

The bloom will soon be gone

France in a challenging world

Nicolas Sarkozy, president of France, sets out a busy foreign-policy agenda for the coming year

"To predict developments in the world is a complex exercise that The Economist *undertakes each year with much talent. As head of state, my approach is necessarily different: I must ask myself not only what 2008 has in store for us but equally what we, the world's decision-makers, can do—and must do—to have a positive influence on those developments."*

In 2008 several crises will be top of the global agenda, and for each the status quo is neither desirable nor possible. The world has a responsibility to do its utmost to find a peaceful resolution to these conflicts.

Most important is Iran. The prospect of a nuclear-armed Iran is an unacceptable security risk. The international community must pursue its policy of increased sanctions—while offering an opening to Iran if it chooses to respect its obligations. To this end, "the Six" (the five permanent members of the UN Security Council, plus Germany) have offered to co-operate in all areas that matter for Iran's development. This is an opportunity for the country to end its isolation and embrace nuclear power for civil purposes.

For Kosovo, while I remain convinced that the scars of history make independence inevitable, I still sincerely hope that Serbs and Kosovars will finally find a mutually acceptable solution. But should the international community conclude on December 10th 2007 that there is no hope for agreement, a decision will have to be made. It should include international monitoring, so that minority rights are safeguarded. European unity on this will be essential, since the long term future of the Balkans rests in the EU.

For Darfur, the international meeting in Paris in June 2007 led to two essential resolutions by the UN Security Council: one creating a joint UN-African Union force in Darfur, the other authorising the deployment of an international force in Chad and the Central African Republic. These two forces must now be deployed to respond to the security and humanitarian emergency. And, after the opening in October 2007 of talks in Libya, there will be a chance of moving towards a political solution to the conflict. The international community must be prepared to put pressure on those who obstruct a settlement.

The resumption of talks between Israel and the Palestinian Authority perhaps augurs well for peace. Clearly, much remains to be done, but with both sides showing greater political will than for a long time, there is hope.

For Lebanon, the election of a president in agreement with constitutional norms is an indispensable stage in the country's reconciliation. France has worked hard to restart the dialogue between the Lebanese parties. But it is they themselves who must move forward, together, on the path to a political solution. We expect all players in the region, including Syria, to act towards such an outcome.

In Afghanistan, the Atlantic alliance must continue its engagement, but it is important to reinforce training of the Afghan army and to increase aid. It is no doubt time, under President Hamid Karzai, to name a high-ranking person to co-ordinate international aid better.

In Iraq, there can be no solution other than a political one. This involves marginalising extremists and making progress towards a national reconciliation by which each Iraqi will be assured of fair access to the country's institutions and resources. This implies defining a clear horizon for the withdrawal of foreign troops, for it is this which will force all sides in Iraq to assume their responsibilities.

Opportunities, not just crises

Quite apart from these crises, 2008 will be an opportunity for progress on several key issues.

The first is Europe. For me, the second half of 2008 will obviously be marked by the French presidency of the EU. I want the presidency to be the occasion for Europe to advance together in such essential areas as the environment, energy and immigration. I want similar progress in defence: we must not put common European defence in opposition to the Atlantic alliance—we need both, because they are complementary. The French presidency must also prepare for the entry into force on January 1st 2009 of the simplified EU treaty. Thanks to this treaty, the union has escaped institutional paralysis.

This should now allow us to consider the future of the European project. The founding fathers had a dream for Europe; what should that dream be today? I have proposed a group of "wise men" to spend two years, to the end of 2009, reflecting on the demands of the future.

I also want progress in 2008 for a project that is a priority of my foreign policy: the Mediterranean Union. The goal is to create an area of solidarity involving the environment, cultural dialogue, economic growth and security. This union should be built on projects that are ambitious but realistic, showing all the peoples of the Mediterranean that together we can build a shared future of peace.

Last but not least, there is the challenge of global warming. At stake in a post-Kyoto accord will be new goals involving all countries on the principle of a shared, but differentiated, responsibility. Our efforts will remain futile if they are not co-ordinated with countries such as China and India. We must ensure that developing countries receive the attention they deserve. So that all can express their concerns, the new climate regime must be decided within the framework of the UN. ■

Also in this section:
The costliest campaign 66
An economic hangover 67
Nancy Pelosi: Green expectations 68
Good luck for Indian tribes 69
Poor American travellers 69
Conservatives in the court 70
Michael Bloomberg: The city club 72

United States

The Democrats' year

Adrian Wooldridge *WASHINGTON, DC*

The betting is on another Clinton presidency

This much is sure. Americans will elect a new president to replace George Bush on November 4th. The election process will be a weird mixture of the old and the new: of flesh-pressing in Iowa and guerrilla warfare on YouTube. The presidential election will dominate the nation's—and the world's—attention, though the way the new president governs will also depend greatly on the outcome of the House and Senate elections which take place on the same day.

The primary season will be unusually front-loaded. The citizens of Iowa and New Hampshire will vote earlier than ever, probably in the first half of January. Other states have been tripping over each other to move their primaries forward. The season will also feature a new do-or-die date, February 5th, when a score of states, including giant California, will hold elections. The primaries will then give way to the longest general-election campaign in the history of presidential politics—and the most expensive, too.

It is a golden rule of American politics that every election season brings at least one big surprise. Nevertheless it looks highly likely that this will be the Democrats' year. The Republican Party is in serious disarray—unpopular with the electorate, plagued by scandals, tarnished by incompetence and unsure which way it is heading. Five years ago America was evenly divided by party identification: 43% for each party. By 2007 the arithmetic had evolved to give the Democrats an advantage of 50% to 35%. By October 2007 Democratic presidential candidates had raised about 70% more money than their Republican rivals. Ohio, Virginia and Colorado are all leaning Democratic—Ohio, which tipped the election for George Bush in 2004, decidedly so. Whoever wins the Democratic primary will most likely end up in the White House.

The betting is that that person will be Hillary Clinton. Mrs Clinton enjoyed a sustained lead in the opinion polls of 20 points or more over her nearest Democratic rival, Barack Obama, for most of 2007. She proved to be an impressive performer in debates and, to a lesser extent, on the stump, always in perfect command of policy details. She was also supported by the best political machine in the country.

This is not to say that she will be a shoo-in. Mr ▶

2008 IN BRIEF

With passport-free travel to Canada, Mexico and the Caribbean no longer possible for Americans, the State Department issues a record **26m passports**, up 44% from 2007.

Adrian Wooldridge: Washington bureau chief, *The Economist*

Obama or John Edwards could make a breakthrough in Iowa (where they are running neck and neck with Mrs Clinton). The Republicans may be able to rally around a "Hillary slayer". Yet both Mr Obama and Mr Edwards come across as too lightweight (America tried lightweight in 2000 and came to regret it). Al Gore, should he change his mind and enter the race, is a proven loser (except when it comes to Nobel prizes and Oscars). The potential Hillary slayers on the right all have significant weaknesses. Rudy Giuliani, who tops Republican polls, has plenty of skeletons in his closet, including two previous wives and a pack of problematic cronies.

The possibility of Mrs Clinton's return to the White House will dominate the political debate more than anything. If she wins, she will break all sorts of records. She will be America's first female president. She will be the first president married to a former president (who will in turn be America's first male "first lady"). She will be the second Clinton in a row to take the keys to the White House from a Bush. If Mrs Clinton is the candidate elected in November, members of the Bush and Clinton families will have been president for 24 years on the trot.

> The Democrats will not march as far to the left as George Bush did to the right

The battle for control of Capitol Hill will be even more one-sided than the battle for the White House. The Democrats will comfortably maintain a working majority in the House of Representatives: polls show the public prefer Democratic candidates for the House by 7-12 percentage points. The Democrats will also expand their majority in the Senate from what has been a measly margin (provided by two independents who normally vote with them).

The defence will not hold

The Republicans will be defending 21 seats in the Senate compared with the Democrats' 12. Several of these will be open seats thanks to a rash of retirements, including Pete Domenici of New Mexico and, belatedly, scandal-soiled Larry Craig of Idaho. They will have much less money than the Democrats. And they will be defending a tarnished brand, thanks to out-of-control public spending, presidential incompetence and a rash of sex-and-money scandals.

Even so, the Democrats will be lucky if they hit the 60 seats needed to give them a filibuster-proof majority. But they will win a majority of six or seven seats (including picking up seats in once-Republican states such as Virginia and Colorado). This will make it much easier for the Democratic president to enact their agenda.

What will this agenda be? The centrepiece at home will be health-care reform. Abroad the focus will be on repairing America's fraught relations with the rest of the world (Mrs Clinton has already pledged to make her husband a roving goodwill ambassador).

Anyone who expects a dramatic lurch to the left will be disappointed. At least, the Democrats will not march as far to the left as Mr Bush and the Republicans did to the right. Mrs Clinton's health-care reforms, for example, are modest and market-based. And on foreign policy she has carefully refused either to pledge herself to removing American troops from Iraq or to tie America's hands when it comes to the problem of Iran. The November election, for all its drama and passion, will usher in a period of pragmatic caution rather than tub-thumping ideology. ■

The $1 billion campaign

Robert Guest *WASHINGTON, DC*

The costliest ever—but so what?

The presidential race in 2008 has a long way to go, but two things are certain. First, it will be the most expensive election ever. Second, this fact will cause widespread hand-wringing.

The two main parties' nominees will burn through $500m each by November. The losing candidates for the Democratic and Republican nominations will raise hundreds of millions more. The two parties' national committees will spend at least $800m between them, though some of that will go to support congressional candidates. Political Action Committees and independent campaign groups will spend about the same. *Fortune* magazine predicts that, all told, 2008 will be the first $3 billion campaign. And if New York's mayor, Michael Bloomberg, runs as an independent candidate, he will spend another $1 billion of his own money wooing voters.

Whether the final tab is $2 billion or $4 billion, most pundits will wail about the corrupting influence of money on politics. Many will urge tighter restrictions on how candidates may raise and spend money, and on independent groups too.

But campaign-finance reform will go nowhere in 2008. Parties and partisans easily found loopholes in the last attempt to restrict the flow of campaign cash, the McCain-Feingold Act of 2002. The new Supreme Court has shown itself wary of politicians making laws to restrict speech about themselves. And there are plenty of studies to suggest that the evils of costly campaigns are exaggerated.

Politicians seldom take their cues from donors, finds John Samples of the Cato Institute: they attract money from donors who approve of their policies. John Coleman of the University of Wisconsin argues that voters in the most expensive elections end up better informed than those in less hotly contested ones, and attack ads often give useful information. As for the scarily huge headline figures, George Will, a columnist, points out that the $1 billion the Republican and Democratic nominees will spend is only half as much as Americans spend every year on Easter candy. ■

Robert Guest: Washington correspondent, *The Economist*

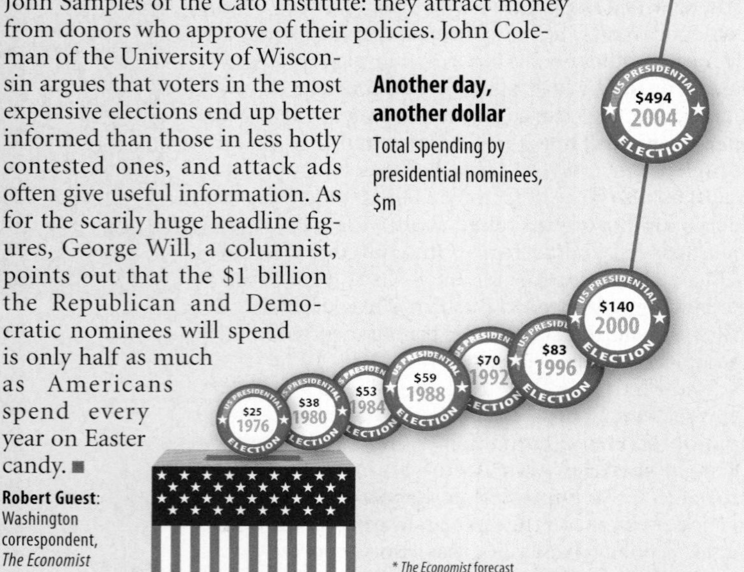

Another day, another dollar
Total spending by presidential nominees, $m

* *The Economist* forecast
Source: Federal Election Commission

After the binge

Zanny Minton Beddoes *WASHINGTON, DC*

A hangover for America's economy

Crudely put, the fate of the American economy next year will be determined by three F-words: foreclosures, foreigners and the Fed.

Record rates of mortgage defaults and repossessions will be the most visible symbol of a deepening housing bust. That slump will drag the economy down. Just how far will depend on America's central bankers and the resilience of the rest of the world economy.

The housing downturn will deepen in 2008. The pace at which new houses are being built is down by more than 40% from its peak in January 2006. That collapse has dragged down the economy's growth rate by almost one percentage point over the past year.

But despite builders' cutbacks, the stock of unsold homes has soared as demand has fallen even further. By August 2007 the supply of unsold new houses was big enough to cover eight months' worth of sales. In the much bigger market for existing homes, the backlog was ten months of supply. Long before credit markets seized up in the summer of 2007, that glut was beginning to drag down prices.

Over the coming year things will get worse. Some 2m Americans will face sharply higher loan payments as their adjustable-rate mortgages reset. Many of these borrowers have little or no equity in their homes. A large fraction will be forced into foreclosure, adding to the supply of homes for sale. More important, tighter credit conditions will further reduce the demand for houses.

All this means that house prices will slide. In the bubbliest areas, such as California and Florida, prices could halve over the next few years. Nationally, the decline will be more gradual. (Unlike shares, house prices tend not to plunge suddenly, as most homeowners try to sit out the bust.) Even so, average national house prices will end 2008 at least 10% below their peak.

That is grim news for builders. But the bigger question is what impact such a price decline will have on consumer spending. (Residential construction makes up about 5% of America's GDP; consumer spending contributes almost 70%). There are plenty of reasons to worry. America has had regional housing booms and busts but little recent experience of a national slump. At some $20 trillion, housing wealth makes up around a third of all household assets. In recent years consumer borrowing has soared, as people have tapped equity in their houses. The latest research suggests that housing wealth may have a bigger effect on spending patterns than other financial wealth, in part because of people's ability to borrow against it.

Tighter credit and falling house prices will prove a poisonous combination. The weakest borrowers will simply be unable to borrow and spend as before. Even those who do not face a credit crunch will feel poorer and so spend less. The spectre of weaker consumer spending and tighter credit will weigh on firms' willingness to create jobs and invest. In other words, you have more than enough ingredients for recession.

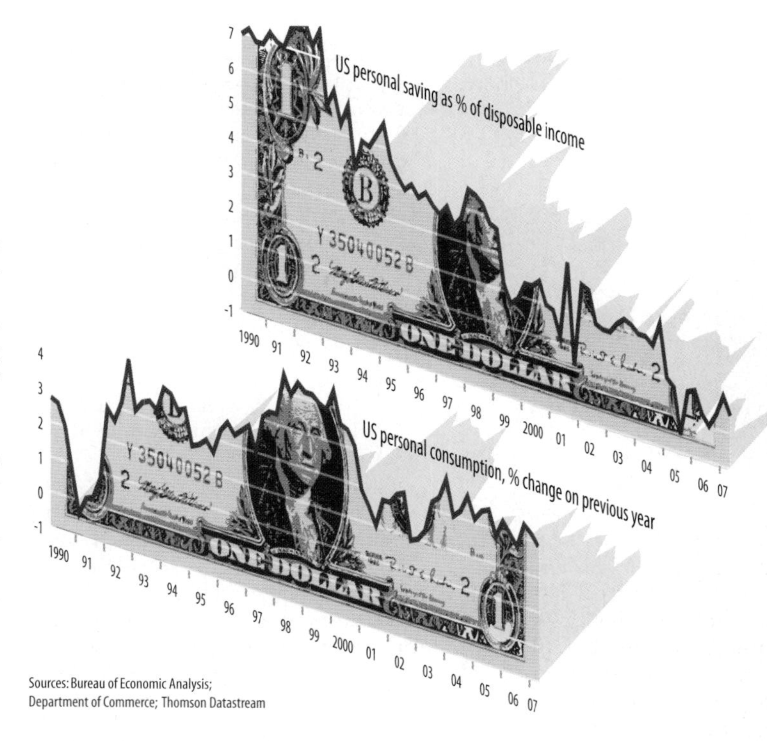

Sources: Bureau of Economic Analysis; Department of Commerce; Thomson Datastream

Even those who do not face a credit crunch will feel poorer and so spend less

Recession is not a certainty, however, because of two counterweights. The more important is monetary policy. America's central bankers cut short-term interest rates by an aggressive half-percentage point to 4.75% in September 2007, to "forestall" the impact of financial turbulence on the economy.

More rate cuts will follow and during 2008 the federal funds rate will fall below 4%. But with underlying inflation, at 2%, at the high end of the central bankers' comfort zone, short-term rates will not be slashed as dramatically as they were between 2001 and 2003, when the federal funds rate fell to 1%.

And lower interest rates will cushion the economy less fully than they did after the stockmarket bust. Then, low interest rates boosted spending in part by buoying house prices. Since the economic weakness in 2008 will result from the bursting of the housing bubble, lower interest rates will now have less impact.

The second pillar

Fortunately, monetary policy will not be the economy's only source of support. In 2008 America ought to gain from economic strength abroad. Exports—whose share of overall output is twice as big as that of residential construction—were growing at double-digit rates in the summer of 2007. With a cheaper dollar, that boom will continue in 2008—provided firms and consumers in the rest of the world open their wallets.

All told, with a degree of good luck, America's economy could survive 2008 without a recession. But one rough year will not be enough. The hangover from America's housing binge will last well into 2009. ■

2008 IN BRIEF

New York's 13,000-strong **taxi fleet will go greener,** with 1,000 hybrid vehicles (up from 400 in 2007) plying for trade. From October all new taxis entering the fleet will need to achieve at least 25 miles per American gallon, almost double the rate of the old yellow cab.

Zanny Minton Beddoes: United States economics editor, *The Economist*

Green expectations

America will rise to the challenge of global warming, believes **Nancy Pelosi**, the speaker of the House of Representatives

During a visit to Greenland in May 2007, I toured Disko Bay by boat to see first-hand the impact of global warming. According to local Inuit leaders, such a tour would have been impossible in years past. Disko Bay would have been a solid sheet of ice, easily crossed by dogsled, but impassable for our small watercraft. No longer. My boat tour itself was a by-product of global warming.

Global warming is a fact, not a theory, and it has the potential to reshape our planet for all generations to come. The catastrophic consequences of unchecked climate change are clear: severe weather; coastal flooding; drought; ecosystem disruption; and deaths due to heat waves, storms, infectious diseases and pollution. And global warming's impact will fall hardest and soonest on those in the poorest nations.

It has taken years of effort, but at long last, in the face of overwhelming scientific evidence, global-warming deniers have been laughed out of the debate. Yet they have been replaced by an equally dangerous impediment to action—the global-warming defeatists who claim that climate change is under way but that the price of action is too high.

The Stern review, a British government study, made clear that the price of combating global warming pales in comparison with the cost of complacency. The study, the most comprehensive review of the economics of climate change, argued that taking action now will require a serious commitment and financial investment. With just 1% of global GDP each year, we could achieve meaningful reductions in greenhouse-gas emissions. On the other hand, as the "Stern Review" said, failing to take serious action would shrink the global economy by at least 5%, and as much as 20%, each year.

In the coming year, all of us around the world must decide to see global warming as a challenge, and also as an opportunity. We can start to address global warming with innovation and with market-based solutions that will grow economies around the world and create the next generation of good-paying jobs—including "green-collar" jobs.

We have placed global warming and greenhouse-gas reduction as one of our highest priorities in Congress

We have already seen the powerful potential of green jobs in America. For example, when a steel plant closed in Pennsylvania, many Americans lost their jobs, as they have in manufacturing industries across the country. But today, 1,000 of those men and women are back at work on the site of their former steel mill—building wind turbines.

Reducing greenhouse-gas emissions also has the enormous benefit of reducing pollutants that contribute to asthma, heart attacks and neurological problems. If we take action, people in every nation of the world will be healthier.

A climate change in Washington

Though President George Bush and his administration have failed to recognise the urgency of this issue, this indifference is not shared by the vast majority of the American people, or by the majorities in the United States Congress. Since assuming the majority in January 2007, Democrats in the House and Senate are setting the legislative agenda for America, and we have placed global warming and greenhouse-gas reduction as one of our highest priorities in Congress.

One of my first acts as speaker was to create the Select Committee on Energy Independence and Global Warming. We have also passed bold and sweeping energy legislation that is unencumbered by old ways of thinking. We are reducing excessive subsidies for private oil and gas companies and instead investing in energy efficiency and renewable energy. We are requiring that 15% of our electricity comes from renewable energy resources. And we are making substantial commitments to energy efficiency, biofuels, training for green jobs, research into climate change and renewable energy, and much more. These are the solutions of the future.

A significant component of our initiatives must be international action. Whereas each country can take significant steps to slow down global warming, the world must work together to forge a strong agreement to prevent catastrophic climate change. I am hopeful that America will be an active and constructive participant in these efforts.

In my recent travels as speaker I have met presidents, prime ministers and kings, but I have been most impressed and inspired by my encounters with young people. At a time when some world leaders question the value of dialogue and progress, young people all over the world are engaged in their own international conversations, on campuses and through e-mail, instant messaging and blogs. They have hope and ideas for the future, and want to know if their leaders will take steps to end global warming and preserve the planet—God's beautiful creation. I believe that in the year to come we can and we will. ■

The new buffalo

Joel Budd *LOS ANGELES*

Good odds at the casino for the Indian tribes

In 2008 gamblers will lose more money in Indian casinos than in Atlantic City, Las Vegas, Reno and Macau put together. Tribes that two decades ago lacked paved roads will throw up glitzy new hotels and extend their cavernous gambling rooms. They will pay for political campaigns and keep several states solvent. And, along with their power and profits, their troubles will grow.

Indian gambling began to take off in 1987, when the Supreme Court ruled that states had no right to restrict gambling on Indian reservations if they allowed it elsewhere. Today about half of all tribes run gambling operations. Some are ramshackle bingo halls. Others, particularly close to big cities such as Los Angeles and New York, are as absurdly opulent as casinos anywhere. The "new buffalo", as the casino has been wryly labelled, has upended Indian country. Tiny, coastal tribes such as the Agua Caliente band of Mission Indians and the Mashantuckett Pequots have become stupendously rich. More famous tribes such as the Navajo remain mired in poverty—although the Navajo, too, will build a casino in 2008 if they can raise the debt.

Lawyers will pore over family trees, seeking evidence that people are or are not members of a tribe

In 2008 the biggest casinos will become bigger still. If an agreement signed in 2007 is not overturned by voters, five Californian tribes that had been limited to 2,000 slot machines each will install new ones until they have as many as 7,500—twice as many as the MGM Grand in Las Vegas. The Foxwood resort in Connecticut, which now has over 7,000 slot machines, will unveil a spa, a concert hall and yet another casino.

Such rapid growth will bring cries of outrage from other tribes. In California some will complain that the new deals provide an unfair advantage. In 2004 a group of tribes signed an agreement with the state that levied an annual fee for each new slot machine, with the fees increasing on a sliding scale. Since, beyond a certain threshold, slot machines tend to earn less as their number increases, this helped to keep the casinos fairly small. The new agreements, by contrast, impose a percentage tax on profits from the extra machines. That will not prevent rapid growth in 2008.

This will not be the only dispute. Lawyers will pore over family trees, seeking evidence that people are or are not members of a tribe—and thus entitled to a share of casino profits. Those who are excluded will sue. Tribal members will also debate whether to relax the "blood quotient" that decides membership. If they do so, profits will be spread more thinly; if they do not, many children will be pushed away from the pot.

The tribes will also argue over whether they ought to be allowed to build casinos away from the reservations. They will argue, too, with unions about whether tribal sovereignty allows them to prevent workers from organising. Such disputes will spill over into the political arena, and into campaign finance. The gambling tribes spent twice as much as the tobacco industry on the 2006 elections. They are likely to keep that up in 2008.

Leaving Las Vegas

As the gambling tribes grow in prosperity, politicians will ask more questions. Is it time to exert more control over Indian casinos? How can state treasuries get more of their profits? Most of all: since gambling has become so widespread, should it not be legalised altogether? ■

Joel Budd: West Coast correspondent, *The Economist*

Home and away

Ariel Ramchandani *LONDON*

Watching the pennies

Americans, victims of a soft-centred dollar, will have a hard time travelling abroad in 2008: London, with posh places charging up to £4 ($8) for a café latte, will quickly strain the credit card. So, too, will Paris and Rome. In short, Europe will be out. And, amazingly, Canada too; not just because an American now needs an expensive passport to get there but also because the grilled salmon to go with the view of the Niagara Falls could cost C$30—which in 1997 meant $22. Ten years later it meant $30-plus.

So where is the savvy American traveller to go? The obvious answer is South America. Though even the Argentine peso has risen against the dollar, Buenos Aires offers not just European-like architecture but a steak dinner for a mere $5. More exotic would be India: the entrance fee to the Red Fort in Delhi is 100 rupees ($2.50), quite a bargain compared with the £16 to visit the Tower of London.

You can, of course, always have a wonderful holiday within the United States, but there will still be American Europhiles determined to cross the Atlantic. Perhaps their money-saving answer in 2008 will be to arrange a house-swap—and invite the Europeans to enjoy the land of the weak dollar. ■

Ariel Ramchandani is a poor American student

2008 IN BRIEF

In October would-be Americans face a **new citizenship test**, stressing an understanding of American values rather than rote learning.

Cautious conservatives

Robert Guest *WASHINGTON, DC*

George Bush's appointments to the Supreme Court will nudge it to the right, but not very right

For such a staid body, the Supreme Court arouses fiery partisan passions. When President George Bush nominated Samuel Alito to replace the retiring Justice Sandra Day O'Connor in 2005, liberal lobbies predicted calamity, wailing that this notoriously right-wing judge would strip basic protections from workers, women, minorities and the disabled in favour of unchecked power for corporations and special interests. Nothing of the sort has occurred, nor will it.

Many conservatives rate Mr Bush's two picks for the court, Mr Alito and Chief Justice John Roberts, as the brightest point of a disappointing presidency. Since both are young and have appointments for life, they will shape American law for decades after Mr Bush has retired. But neither is likely to wreak radical change.

Awaiting his day in court

Mr Roberts is a solid conservative, but so was the chief justice he replaced, the late William Rehnquist. The real change is from Mrs O'Connor (an inconsistent conservative) to Mr Alito (a consistent one). But both new judges say they favour narrow rulings and hesitate to tear up settled precedents. The evidence from their first full term suggests they mean it.

Even so, 2008 will see important rulings in several areas. One is the question of what to do with the hundreds of terrorist suspects imprisoned in legal limbo in Guantánamo Bay. The Bush administration argues that as "unlawful combatants" in the "war on terror", they can be held until that war ends, which could be a very long time. Also, since they are not on American soil, they cannot challenge their detention in American courts.

The Roberts court struck down part of this argument in 2006, ruling that the detainees must have some way of contesting their detention. Congress duly created military tribunals to hear their cases. The constitutionality of those tribunals is being challenged. And so, in *Boumediene v Bush*, is the part of the Military Commissions Act that bars the detainees from using ordinary courts. Following revelations about how poorly these commissions resemble due process, the Supreme Court will demand that the administration allows the Guantánamo prisoners the right of *habeas corpus*, but it will stop short of shutting the prison down.

Another fight is brewing over gun control. At issue is the District of Columbia's ban on the private ownership of handguns, one of the nation's strictest. A federal court struck it down for breaching the second amendment: "A well regulated militia, being necessary to the security of a free state, the right of the people to keep and bear arms, shall not be infringed." In their appeal, DC lawyers will argue that the right to bear arms does not apply to individuals, but only to members of a state militia. This is an old argument, but the Supreme Court has never ruled on it. It will find that the constitution does indeed include an individual right to bear arms, but will craft the ruling so that, although it makes gun control harder, it will not make it impossible.

Another fight is brewing over gun control

The most intriguing death-penalty case before the court in 2008 will be *Medellin v Texas*, concerning a Mexican on death row in the Lone Star state. José Medellin, like at least 49 other Mexicans, was tried in the United States without access to a Mexican diplomat. America has signed the Vienna Convention on Consular Relations, guaranteeing foreign criminal suspects consular contact, but many local sheriffs do not know this. The Bush administration has ordered Texas to reconsider Mr Medellin's case, but Texas refuses. The Supreme Court will order it to uphold America's treaty obligations.

Picking precedents

Critics will say that this represents craven kowtowing to foreign law, though no one forced America to sign the Vienna convention. The debate will feed a broader controversy about whether the Supreme Court should heed foreign precedents when interpreting American law. Advocates of this view, including Justice Anthony Kennedy, argue that foreign precedents are a useful measure of evolving global mores. Opponents retort that a judge who thinks he can pick and choose precedents from anywhere to buttress his arguments is allowing himself vast latitude to make up the law as he goes along.

Mr Kennedy's views matter because, sandwiched between four conservatives and four liberals, he is almost always on the winning side. On some issues he leans right. His distaste for racial quotas, for example, ensures that their use by public bodies will be further curtailed. On others he leans left: he was instrumental in ruling the death penalty for juveniles unconstitutional. He will ensure that *Roe v Wade*, which stops states banning abortion, is not reversed in 2008. But given the incrementalism of the new judges, and the impossibility that the Senate will ever confirm another judge who would overturn *Roe*, that was never much of a danger. ■

Robert Guest: Washington correspondent, *The Economist*

The city club

Cities won't wait for national governments to solve their pressing problems, argues **Michael Bloomberg**, the mayor of New York City

For the first time in history, the majority of the world's people are living in cities. As mayor of America's largest city, a place we humbly call the capital of the world, I believe this development holds real promise. Although it's true that growing cities face enormous challenges, in working with urban leaders from around the world I have seen how cities are increasingly becoming incubators of change and drivers of innovation.

Not only are more cities embracing bold action, we're sharing our best strategies. A new urban global community is emerging in which cities are collaborating with each other on common problems while simultaneously competing with each other in the global marketplace. The days of sitting back and waiting for national governments to act are becoming a memory, especially as cities are faced with challenges that require immediate action.

Urbi et orbi

Population growth can exacerbate the most common headaches of city life, such as traffic jams, overcrowded buses and trains, and air pollution. Growth can also strain vital services, including water supply, energy production and waste management. The cities that take bold steps now to pre-empt these problems will prove increasingly attractive to both families and businesses. In New York we have developed a comprehensive long-term growth strategy that we call PlanNYC, and the year ahead will be a critical test of whether our partners in state government have the willpower to implement some of its major components, including congestion pricing—a traffic-reduction plan that we developed after studying the experiences of London, Stockholm and Singapore.

Congestion pricing is also a tool in combating global warming. Here, too, collaboration among cities will continue to grow. In developing the climate-change strategies that underpin PlanNYC, we drew on the experiences of Berlin for our renewable-energy and green-roof policies; Hong Kong, Shanghai and Delhi for our innovative transit improvements; Copenhagen for our pedestrian and cycling upgrades; Chicago and Los Angeles for our plan to plant 1m more trees; Amsterdam and Tokyo for our transit-oriented development policies; and Bogotá for our plans for Bus Rapid Transit. In 2008, as our federal government remains at sea on climate change, we will be working to put all of these plans into effect, and we look forward to sharing the lessons we learn with other cities.

Just as with climate change, economic globalisation demands that governments look forward and adapt to a changing reality, one that places a premium on education and skills. Cities will increasingly find that attracting new jobs requires more local investment in education and training. In New York, our additional investments—predicated on governance reforms that have strengthened accountability and standards—have led to significant increases in test scores and high-school graduation rates, which will help our students compete in this new marketplace.

Competition for jobs and talent will also lead cities to step up their efforts to offer the best possible quality of life: safe streets, convenient transit, exciting nightclubs and theatres, and beautiful parks. This kind of competition will allow cities to attract the best and brightest, provided nations are smart enough to let them in. In the United States, our broken immigration system is hurting America's ability to attract the top talent. In the year ahead, even if no comprehensive reform bill is passed, we must at least bring service improvements to our customs and immigration departments, so that all visitors are treated as guests, not potential terrorists.

In working with urban leaders from around the world I have seen how cities are increasingly becoming incubators of change and drivers of innovation

Preventing terrorism requires a far more sophisticated approach than rudely hassling international travellers. The best intelligence tells us that terror networks are intensifying their efforts to strike, and their primary targets remain cities—because they seek to cause maximum death and destruction. Not every attack can be prevented, but we know from experience that effective policing and intelligence-gathering at the local level can thwart plots and save untold numbers of lives.

In New York, we have dedicated 1,000 of our best police officers to counter-terrorism and intelligence duties, and they have cracked numerous plots in the past six years, including one to blow up the Brooklyn Bridge. We have also posted some of our officers to terror targets overseas, where they work closely with local and national authorities. Local action cannot be a substitute for national leadership, but sophisticated local efforts—and communication and co-operation among cities across the world—will increasingly prove essential.

Growing levels of both collaboration and competition can produce big benefits for cities, if urban leaders confront their challenges head-on. And we must. More than half the world's people are counting on us. ■

Also in this section:
Remittances back home 74
Canada picks its battles 75
Felipe Calderón Hinojosa: Mexico's road 76

The Americas

Who'll dance with Chávez?

Michael Reid

A test of Latin America's new-found resilience

After four years of economic growth averaging 5% a year, Latin America faces a testing time in 2008. A downturn in the United States will hit Mexico, Central America and the Caribbean hard. South America's prospects turn more on the growth of China's economy, which has underpinned the prices of its commodity exports. Tighter credit means that investors will pay more attention to the policy differences that distinguish countries in the region. But investment and domestic consumption remain strong in many Latin American countries, inflation and public finances are more or less under control, and debt ratios are more manageable. So the region will have a chance to display its new-found economic resilience.

None of the larger countries faces a national election and so the incentives for centrist governments to push forward with reforms will be greater: for all the progress of recent years, businesses in Latin America still battle against red tape, creaking infrastructure, and a poorly educated workforce. Some of this will take a generation to fix. But reforming government finances to boost public investment can be done more swiftly.

The radical populist governments in the region will find the going harder in 2008. Venezuela's Hugo Chávez will begin the year with new constitutional powers and a new currency (the *bolívar fuerte* or "strong bolívar", with three fewer zeros than its debauched predecessor). The constitutional changes will almost certainly include the abolition of presidential term limits and the advent of full presidential control over central-bank reserves and over new local-government bodies.

Unless the oil price falls steeply, Mr Chávez will once again defy those of his opponents who have repeatedly predicted a sharp slowdown in Venezuela's economic growth. Oil-fuelled public spending combined with price controls will prevent the opposition gaining traction, whatever the long-term damage inflicted by the president's "21st-century socialism". Despite its name, the new currency is likely to be devalued at some point in 2008—and to be worth ever less on the black market. Even so, Mr Chávez will increasingly tighten his grip, tacitly encouraging opponents to leave by measures such as imposing a socialist curriculum on private schools.

> The influence of Mr Chávez's radical brand of leftism will decline somewhat in 2008

South America's leftward drift will ▶

2008 IN BRIEF

The five-island **Netherlands Antilles** disbands in December after 54 years (and a year later than planned). Curaçao and the Dutch half of St Maarten become self-governing parts of the Netherlands; three tiny islands become Dutch municipalities.

Michael Reid: Americas editor, *The Economist;* author of "Forgotten Continent: The Battle for Latin America's Soul" (Yale)

Homeward dollars

Michael Reid

Migrant money will fall, but will matter as much as ever

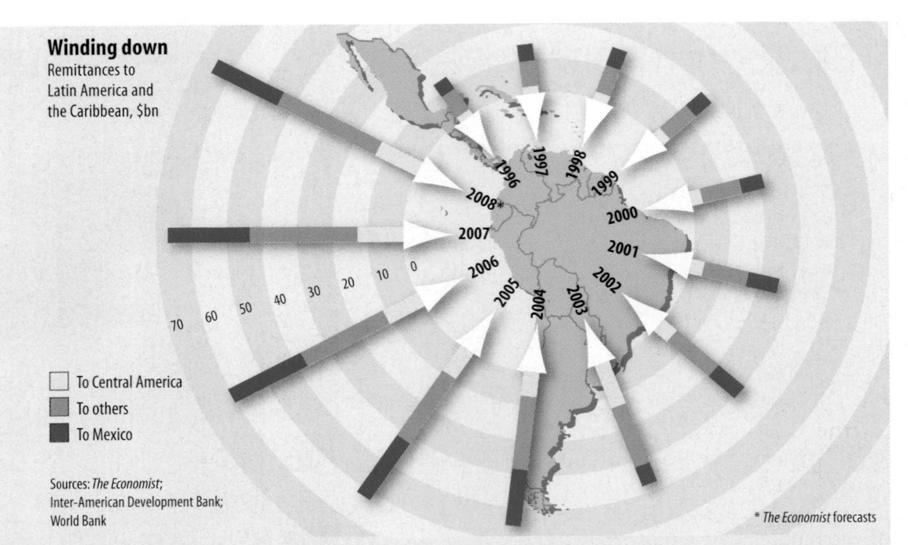

There has been one recent constant in Latin American economics: the reported flow of remittances from workers outside the region leaps up each year, to the point that it has outstripped foreign direct investment and foreign aid combined. But it is probable that 2008 will see the first-ever drop in remittances to Latin America since figures began to be collected a decade or so ago (see chart).

Blame that fall mainly on the tougher approach to immigration in the United States. Fences on the more populated parts of its southern frontier with Mexico, together with all the other security paraphernalia installed in recent years, have obliged migrants to try riskier ways of crossing the border, for example by traversing the Sonoran desert. At the same time a crackdown by local authorities, especially in states that have not traditionally received Latinos, means that life has become more uncertain and more uncomfortable for illegal migrants from Latin America.

Add the decline in housebuilding in the United States, a traditional magnet for migrant labour, and strong growth over the past three years in formal-sector jobs in Mexico, and the balance of incentives has begun to shift in favour of staying at home. Job growth in Mexico may falter in 2008 but tougher controls and the slowdown in the United States economy have already had their effect.

The estimated sharp increase in remittances in recent years in part reflects past undercounting by central banks. Donald Terry of the Inter-American Development Bank reckons that remittances to Latin America will have increased by only 10% in 2007, compared with 15% or so in each of the previous three years (once undercounting is stripped out). Remittances to Mexico are flat, he says, while those to Central America are still rising, as is the amount of money sent back from Spain and other European countries.

The Bush administration in 2008 will appease the Republican base by forcing employers to sack illegal migrants. That will eventually produce a backlash—but not until the United States economy grows more strongly again. Remittances will still cushion some Latin American governments in 2008, but they will no longer fuel economic growth. ■

▶ see Fernándo Lugo, a former Roman Catholic bishop and supporter of liberation theology, elected president of Paraguay in April. That will end 60 years of uninterrupted rule by the Colorado Party, currently the world's longest-ruling political party. But Mr Lugo will seek closer relations with Brazil's social-democratic president, Luiz Inácio Lula da Silva, than with Mr Chávez.

Indeed, the influence of Mr Chávez's brand of leftism will decline somewhat in 2008. Cristina Fernández de Kirchner, who succeeds her husband, Néstor, as Argentina's president in December 2007, will face a difficult year: inflation risks getting out of control but reining in Argentina's overheating economy will be unpopular. Bolivia's socialist president, Evo Morales, will be more pragmatic in 2008, perhaps agreeing with Chile to develop his country's natural gas for export. Ecuador's president, Rafael Correa, who also fancies himself a 21st-century socialist, will find it hard to impose his will on a fractious country.

More quietly, Brazil, the region's powerhouse, will continue its steady progress, with its economy growing by between 4% and 5%. In Mexico President Felipe Calderón will spend much of the year negotiating the liberalisation of the state-owned energy monopolies. If Mr Calderón succeeds—and he probably will—Mexico will have a reasonable chance of reversing the precipitous fall in its oil production. Peru's President Alan García, having reinvented himself as a "neoliberal", will seek to use his role as host of both the EU-Latin American summit in May and the APEC summit in November to boost his country's trade links with Europe and Asia. In Colombia, President Álvaro Uribe will hope that 2008 turns out better than 2007, when scandals linking some supporters to right-wing paramilitaries helped stall a free-trade agreement with the United States. And in the Dominican Republic, Leonel Fernández seems set to win a third term in May. A moderate social democrat, he has twice presided over rapid economic growth, once in the mid-1990s and then again since 2004.

Municipal elections in Brazil and Chile in 2008 will also demonstrate that democracy has become uncontested in the region. Except, of course, in Cuba, where Raúl Castro will be hoping for a rapprochement with a Democratic president in Washington in 2009.

The bicentenary of independence from Iberia will be a regional theme for the next 20 years. The celebrations will begin by marking the establishment of juntas in Caracas and Buenos Aires in 1808 after Napoleon toppled the Spanish monarchy. They were the forerunners of independent government in a region with a long, if often truncated, constitutional tradition. More than is often recognised, that is something to celebrate. ■

2008 IN BRIEF The Dominican Republic offers **Santo Domingo's commuters** a metro system, only the second in the Caribbean (after Puerto Rico).

Canada goes greener

Jeffrey Simpson *OTTAWA*

Farewell Kandahar, hello Kyoto

Canada will decide in 2008 to withdraw its 2,300 troops from Afghanistan's troubled Kandahar province. Some or all might be deployed in a less violent part of Afghanistan before their two-year mission ends in 2009. But they are not staying in Kandahar, where more Canadians have been killed or wounded than in any operation since the Korean war.

Public opinion will not stand for a prolongation of the mission, as Stephen Harper's Conservative government now understands. Mr Harper has only a minority government, and the other three parties in parliament have no wish for Canada to stay beyond 2009. Notoriously pacifist and isolationist Quebec especially wants out. Fighting in Afghanistan while also campaigning in Quebec, where the Conservatives must gain ground to capture a majority government, would be like skiing uphill.

The Americans and British in next-door Helmand province want the Canadians to stay put: the Canadians have done well, and if they leave, who will replace them? Germany, France, Italy, Turkey and other NATO partners are lodged in relatively safe parts of Afghanistan. Even so, their people are unhappy with the Afghan fight. It is hard to imagine these countries trading places with the Canadians in Kandahar.

Meanwhile, the Canadian public sees that the opium trade is booming, Pakistan's border is open to Taliban fighters, and the Afghan government is said to be corrupt. Coffins draped in the maple-leaf flag do not help. Mr Harper has said he would not extend the Canadian mission without parliamentary approval—and since a majority of MPs are from parties that want the mission ended, it will end.

Though the Conservatives remain stuck in minority territory, voters have not warmed to other parties. The opposition Liberal leader, Stéphane Dion, a brainy, boring man who tries to make a virtue of being underestimated, has left Canadians cold.

The result, paradoxically, is a stable minority government, since no party thinks it can gain ground in an election. A recourse to the ballot box that looked almost certain in early 2007 now will not occur until 2009. At which time, Canadians will be judging their politicians on environmental issues, especially climate change. Canada ratified the Kyoto protocol on climate change, and then compiled the worst emissions record of those countries that accepted the protocol.

These days, however, politicians can't paint themselves and their parties green enough, fast enough. Even Mr Harper, a renowned climate-change sceptic, has become a convert, although he lacks much passion in talking about the challenge, which leads his critics to wonder about the sincerity of his commitment.

But Mr Harper seldom talks about anything with much passion, not being a very emotional man. He is the biggest control freak Canadians have seen as prime minister. He centralises everything through his office, giving ministers almost no margin for manoeuvre or initiative, tightly scripting every public event, controlling all messages to the public, running foreign policy by himself, and earning the reputation of a decisive but distant sun king of a leader. Asking him to lighten up is akin to telling George Bush to stop back-slapping.

> Canada ratified Kyoto, and then compiled the worst emissions record

The federal government is rolling in money and every provincial government is in surplus, courtesy of the continuing strength of the Canadian economy, which, so long as commodity prices remain high, could again top the G7 growth tables in 2008. No other G7 country will cut taxes, pay down debt and spend more in 2008. Barring a serious slowdown of the United States economy, to which the Canadian economy remains tied, Canada's virtuous circle should continue. With high commodity prices, the only flaw will be weak manufacturing, where productivity is 20% lower than in America.

Of course Canadians, being Canadians, will still find plenty to grouse about in 2008. But the economy will flourish, the Quebec separatist threat will remain faint, the budget will show a healthy surplus, unemployment will remain at record lows, the currency will be strong and the greening of politics will continue. Other countries should be so lucky. ■

2008 IN BRIEF

Ice hockey's coming home: for the first time in its history, the **Ice Hockey World Championship** is held in its motherland—Canada.

Jeffrey Simpson: national affairs columnist, the *Globe and Mail*; co-author of "Hot Air: Meeting Canada's Climate Change Challenge" (McClelland & Stewart)

Green enough?

Mexico's road

Felipe Calderón Hinojosa, president of Mexico, sets out his plans for modernising reforms

Latin America faces a critical choice. It is a choice between the past and the future, between returning to authoritarian systems and strengthening democracy, between protectionism and more open markets—and between the wastefulness of populist measures and a responsible balance in public finances.

At this crossroads, Mexico has chosen democracy, a social market economy, the rule of law, respect for human rights and responsible public policies. This goes hand in hand with a commitment to sustainable human development: we know increased opportunities and capacities of the present generation should not be gained at the expense of future generations. That is why we also have an unprecedented commitment to the environment.

Mexico has enormous potential, thanks to its geographical position, its trade agreements, its resource wealth and its young workforce. But these natural advantages have not been sufficient to generate more dynamic economic growth. Since the outset of my administration in December 2006, we have been determined to put Mexico on the road to development.

A priority is to ensure law enforcement and stop criminal groups. I have explained to Mexicans that it is a complex issue with no short-term solutions which will require time, money and, unfortunately, even human lives. Some results are beginning to be felt: violence has decreased in the areas of the country where special operations against crime have been applied. More than 10,000 people linked to drug trafficking and some 20 of the most important drug-trafficking leaders have been arrested. Ten of the most dangerous leaders of organised crime have been extradited to the United States. In 2007 Mexico confiscated the world's largest amount of money from illicit activities ($205m in cash) and seized the biggest haul of cocaine in any country.

These results have enabled us to change Mexicans' perception of insecurity. Some months ago, more than half considered security to be the country's main problem. Today that proportion has been reduced to a quarter. To continue advancing on this path, we have submitted an initiative to Congress to reform our criminal-justice system. Among other changes, trials with oral cross-examination may very soon be established in Mexico.

On the economic front, we are pursuing structural reforms with a new dynamism. We began with an issue that is as complex for Mexico as it is for other nations: pension reform for civil servants. This involved a change from a "pay as you go" system to a system of individual savings accounts for retirement, alleviating pressure on public finances. This reform achieves a saving that in the medium term will be equivalent to 25 percentage points of GDP. Even more important, the plan will ensure fair pensions for beneficiaries and rebuild the institution that provides health services to civil servants and their families.

Congress has also approved a tax reform which will enable the state to collect extra resources worth up to two percentage points of GDP a year, for two basic purposes. The first is to strengthen government social programmes and thereby honour the age-old obligation to help the Mexicans who have least. The second is to reduce the dependency of government finances on oil revenues.

In the political sphere, progress is being made on electoral reform, which was approved by consensus in the legislative branch. This will strengthen electoral institutions and increase citizens' confidence.

In the next few years we will promote other structural reforms, such as the modernisation of our telecommunications to expand their coverage and encourage greater competition

Still more to come

In the next few years we will promote other structural reforms, such as the modernisation of our telecommunications to expand their coverage and encourage greater competition in this industry, in addition to promoting the integration of new technologies. We will also take steps towards modernising the energy sector. And we have presented an ambitious National Infrastructure Programme for 2007-12, which will increase investment in this area from 3.2% to 5% of GDP to build highways, ports, airports, energy and other projects. We will allocate half of the tax collected through the fiscal reform to this purpose.

We are determined to become one of the world's best destinations for investment, since greater investment is the base for economic growth and job creation. In the first half of 2007 the inflow of foreign direct investment reached a record $13.2 billion. And in spite of the weakening performance of the American economy with which we are strongly linked, more than 825,000 registered new jobs were created between January and October.

These good results, and the changes that are in prospect, strengthen our conviction that in 2008 the world will view Mexico with renewed optimism. ■

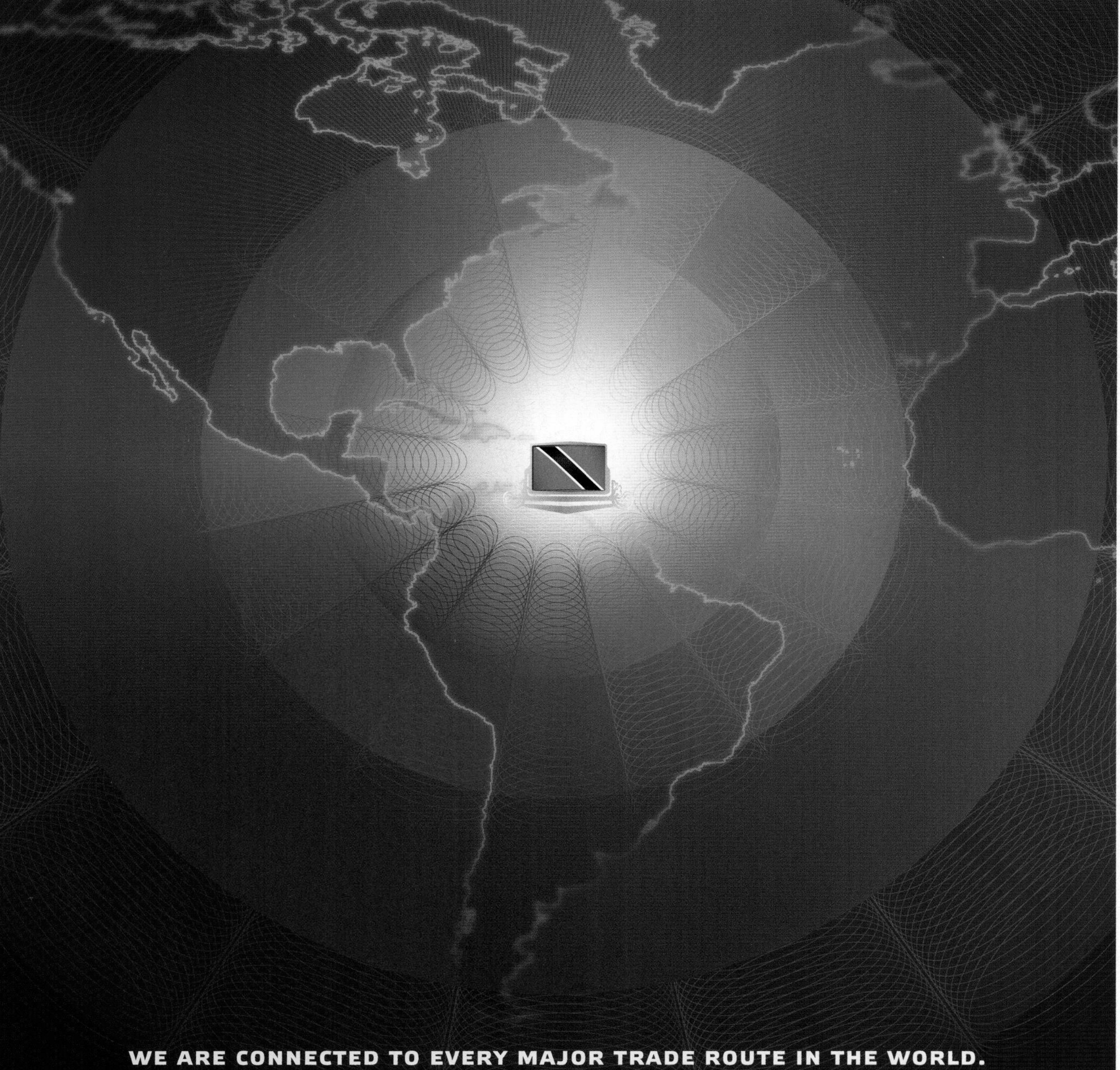

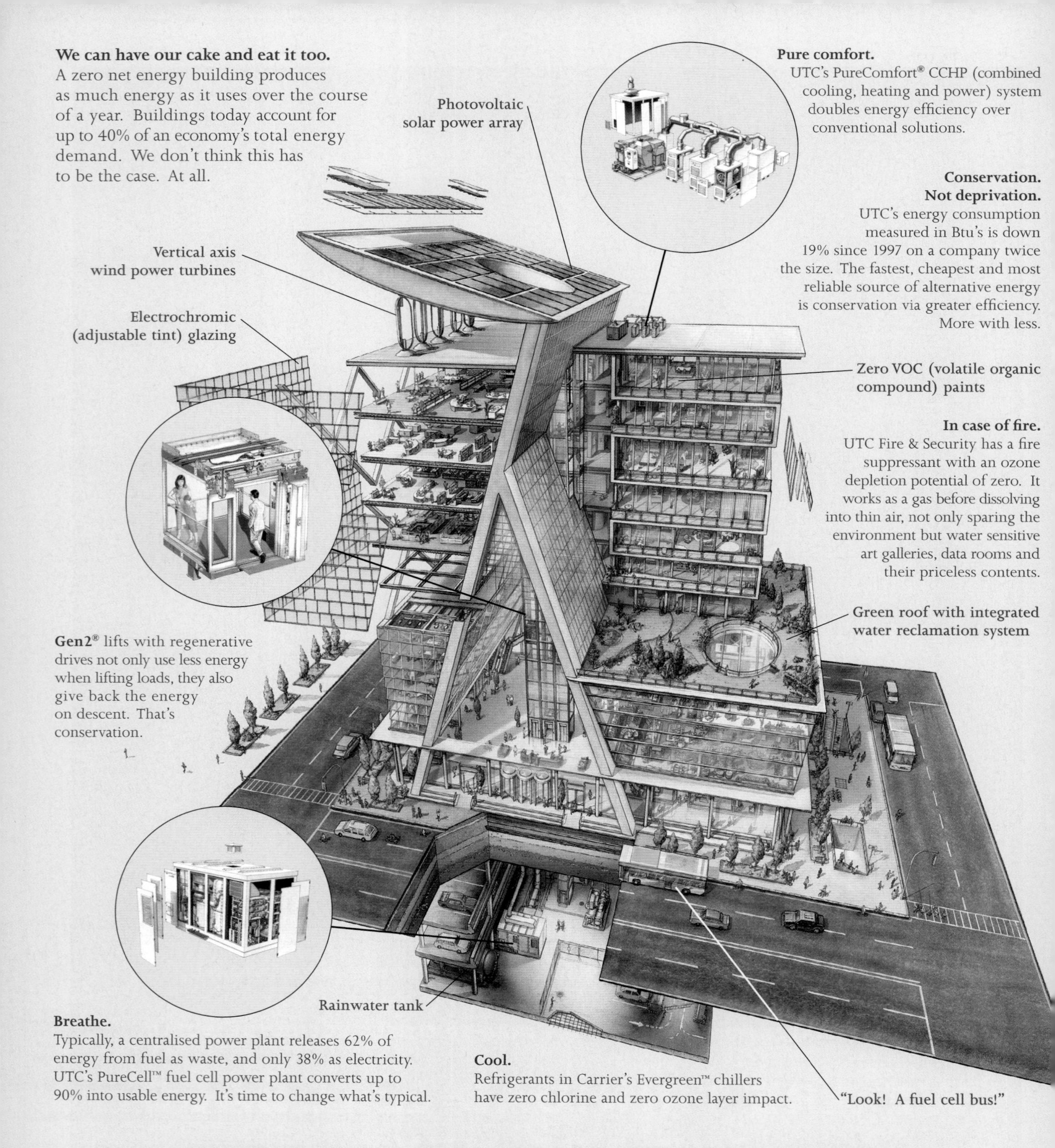

We can have our cake and eat it too.
A zero net energy building produces as much energy as it uses over the course of a year. Buildings today account for up to 40% of an economy's total energy demand. We don't think this has to be the case. At all.
Photovoltaic solar power array
Pure comfort.
UTC's PureComfort® CCHP (combined cooling, heating and power) system doubles energy efficiency over conventional solutions.
Conservation. Not deprivation.
UTC's energy consumption measured in Btu's is down 19% since 1997 on a company twice the size. The fastest, cheapest and most reliable source of alternative energy is conservation via greater efficiency. More with less.
Vertical axis wind power turbines
Electrochromic (adjustable tint) glazing
Zero VOC (volatile organic compound) paints
In case of fire.
UTC Fire & Security has a fire suppressant with an ozone depletion potential of zero. It works as a gas before dissolving into thin air, not only sparing the environment but water sensitive art galleries, data rooms and their priceless contents.
Green roof with integrated water reclamation system
Gen2® lifts with regenerative drives not only use less energy when lifting loads, they also give back the energy on descent. That's conservation.
Rainwater tank
Breathe.
Typically, a centralised power plant releases 62% of energy from fuel as waste, and only 38% as electricity. UTC's PureCell™ fuel cell power plant converts up to 90% into usable energy. It's time to change what's typical.
Cool.
Refrigerants in Carrier's Evergreen™ chillers have zero chlorine and zero ozone layer impact.
"Look! A fuel cell bus!"

IMAGINE THAT. YOU CAN DO WELL IN THE WORLD WITHOUT HURTING IT.

We double traditional energy generation efficiency by doing it on site and capturing otherwise waste heat and transmission losses. We install lifts needing up to 75% less energy than comparable equipment a decade ago. Routinely. The first zero net energy building is coming. Want to get in on the ground floor? Learn about other innovative parts of United Technologies at utc.com/curious.

You can see everything from here.

CARRIER | HAMILTON SUNDSTRAND | OTIS | PRATT & WHITNEY | SIKORSKY | UTC FIRE & SECURITY | UTC POWER | NYSE: UTX

Also in this section:
Taiwan heads to the polls 80
The global temptation for Chinese companies 81
More empty-nesters 82
The economy's Year of the Rat 82
Shanghai's hot stockmarket 83
Opportunity in e-commerce 84
China climbs the charts 85
Winning Olympic gold 85
The Dalai Lama: Be nicer to your neighbours 86

China special section

The challenge to Beijingoism

James Miles *BEIJING*

China prepares for the games—and its critics

In readiness for the Olympic games, Beijing is putting the finishing touches to a colossal makeover: the world's biggest airport terminal, skyscrapers, subway lines and lavish stadiums. It is guaranteed to impress the world. But the leadership is nervous. The games will be a magnet for China's critics. At a time of growing unease around the world about everything from the safety of China's products to its policies in Africa, there are plenty of them.

"A new Beijing, a new Olympics" is one of China's slogans for the games. The English translation of this is tailored to suit a foreign audience. It refers to a "great Olympics", not a new one, to avoid upsetting those who might fear an end to what they quaintly regard as a century-old tradition of international camaraderie. But there is no cause for alarm. What China means by new is an Olympics taken to new heights of razzmatazz. Hollywood's Steven Spielberg has been recruited to help design the opening and closing ceremonies. Beijing is justifiably confident that its purpose-built Olympics infrastructure, including a $430m stadium resembling a bird's nest of steel, will be ready in time.

Psychologically, however, China is less well-prepared. Hollywood has already shown it can be a fickle partner, with some of its thespian elite lashing out in 2007 against Mr Spielberg's involvement. Their allegation was that China's large oil investments in Sudan were helping to sustain the government-orchestrated bloodshed in Darfur. Stung by this, China began to support UN intervention in the Darfur crisis.

> The Olympics will focus global attention on China's poor record of environmental protection

But China's critics in the West will not be sated. In the build-up to the games on August 8th they will step up their attacks on issues ranging from China's human-rights record to the status of Tibet and Taiwan. It will be the most politically contentious Olympics since Moscow staged the games in 1980, not long after

2008 IN BRIEF

The size of China's **working population** stops growing—so economic growth will depend in future on workers improving their productivity.

James Miles: Beijing bureau chief, *The Economist*

the Soviet invasion of Afghanistan. Foreign activists and Chinese citizens overseas with axes to grind will flock to Beijing to try to stage public protests. If mishandled by the Chinese police (who have been instructed to stop demonstrations as politely as possible), these incidents could seriously embarrass the hosts, multinational companies sponsoring the games and foreign dignitaries.

Patriotic fervour and a surging economy will help to keep a lid on unrest by domestic malcontents. But China's security forces will be vigilant. An unexpected bout of food-price inflation in 2007, which looks likely to continue in 2008, will anger the urban poor. Some of Beijing's political dissidents will take advantage of the spotlight on China to highlight their grievances.

Troubling for China too will be political uncertainty in two countries of vital concern to its security interests: Taiwan and America. Elections in Taiwan in early 2008 (see below) will fuel debate there about the island's relations with the mainland. In America, presidential candidates will use an appearance of toughness about China (particularly its massive trade surplus with America) to appeal to voters.

The Olympics will focus global attention on China's poor record of environmental protection and its huge contribution to global warming. The prime minister, Wen Jiabao, will begin a second five-year term of office in March and is certain to make a big issue of the environment in his annual address to parliament that month. Beijing will introduce draconian—albeit temporary—restrictions on cars and industries in an effort to reduce the city's haze in time for the games.

2008 IN BRIEF

Instead of lifting all its quotas, as planned, the EU monitors China's **textile exports** to Europe throughout the year.

Beijing's other environmental crisis—a critical shortage of water—will be somewhat alleviated in 2008 when it will begin receiving water piped in from four reservoirs in neighbouring Hebei province. The 300km (190-mile) pipeline will eventually form part of a channel bringing water from the Yangzi river basin hundreds of kilometres farther to the south. Environmentalists are unhappy. They fear that the scheme will damage the Yangzi's ecology and that the water will be undrinkable. But China's leaders like grandiose displays of engineering and technological prowess: the coming year will also see the first walk in space by Chinese astronauts, following the launch of a lunar probe in 2007.

Mind games

China will make few concessions to its critics abroad. President Hu Jintao, despite rewriting the Communist Party charter to reflect his calls for a fairer society, shows little enthusiasm for political reform. But rapid social change from the embrace of market economics will continue to erode the Communist Party's grip. Although the party's instinct will be to tighten controls on media freedom in the build-up to the games, the spread of advanced information technologies will make it ever harder to stem the tide of uncensored information.

A successful Olympics will give the party a bit more of a swagger, but success will depend on curbing its instinct to lash out at its critics. The games will not usher in democracy to China, but they will help to acclimatise both the leadership and the public to the world's concerns about how the country is developing. ■

Make love not war

Dire straits

James Miles

Taiwan heads, turbulently, to the polls

Taiwan will get a new president in 2008. But China—which has heaped abuse on the outgoing one, Chen Shui-bian, since he took office in 2000—will not be overjoyed. Mr Chen's successor, no matter from which party, will not decisively reverse the island's drift towards a more assertive independence from the mainland.

Taiwanese politics, boisterous at the best of times, is entering a period of unusual turbulence. Elections to the island's parliament, the Legislative Yuan, will be held on January 12th. The power of the ruling Democratic Progressive Party (DPP) has been severely curtailed during Mr Chen's presidency because of its lack of a parliamentary majority. It will be a close—and fierce—contest between independence supporters and advocates of closer ties with China.

The presidential polls will be held just two months later. Mr Chen is constitutionally obliged to step down. The DPP's nominee to succeed him is Frank Hsieh, a former prime minister who appears less suspicious of China than Mr Chen. The main opposition party, the Kuomintang, is fielding Ma Ying-jeou, a former mayor of Taipei who also wants to reach out to China. Again it will be a close-fought race. Even if the more pro-China Mr Ma wins, he will be cautious in his dealings with the mainland for fear of being accused of selling out Taiwan.

At the same time as the presidential election, Mr Chen plans to hold a referendum on whether Taiwan should apply for United Nations membership using the name Taiwan instead of the island's formal title, the Republic of China. The outcome will have no impact on Taiwan's application. As a member of the Security Council, China can always block it.

But just holding a referendum will infuriate the leaders in Beijing, who see it as yet another move to downplay Taiwan's links with China. America fears it might provoke China into a dangerous rage.

This will not lead to war in 2008—China has too much to lose. But the likely outcome is a protracted sulk by China that will cloud any prospects for post-election breakthroughs in cross-strait ties. ■

Chery-picking

Charles Lee *HONG KONG*

The global temptation for Chinese companies

The world will become more familiar with Chinese corporate names in 2008. For starters, there is Lenovo, a personal-computer maker from Beijing which bought IBM's PC division in 2005. The company is one of only 12 official worldwide Olympic partners. At the Beijing games its logo will be omnipresent. But the organisers of the Beijing Olympics have also chosen more than two dozen other Chinese firms as local partners, sponsors and suppliers. This sundry roster includes state-owned behemoths such as China Mobile as well as the more obscure Yanjing Beer and Dayun Motorcycle.

A higher international profile, alas, hardly assures cross-border success. No Chinese company has yet joined Japan's Toyota or South Korea's Samsung on the global A-list, and none is likely to do so in 2008. But it will not be for lack of trying. Besides Lenovo, Chinese players have challenged the existing industry order—with mediocre to poor results—in television (TCL), home appliances (Haier), telecommunications equipment (Huawei) and oil (CNOOC). More will follow.

Among the immediate beneficiaries of the Olympics, Air China and Li-Ning are worth watching. Chinese authorities are expecting some 1.7m visitors to Beijing for the event. Air China is an official partner of the games and will have its hub at the capital's airport upgraded to a huge new terminal in March 2008. That will allow it to add flights and expand market share on Beijing-bound routes. Already China's largest international carrier, it will attract more overseas passengers when it joins the Star Alliance network in late 2007. In the longer term, there is even the possibility of a full merger with Hong Kong's blue-chip Cathay Pacific Airways—the two airlines set up a 17.5% cross-shareholding arrangement in 2006. As the country's air-travel market becomes ever more buoyant, Air China should soar with it.

For Li-Ning, China's favourite home-grown sporting-goods brand, the Olympics should be a once-in-a-lifetime marketing bonanza. Founded by the gymnast of the same name who won three gold medals in the 1984 Los Angeles Olympics, the company is in fierce competition with Nike and Adidas to win over China's growing legion of recreational athletes (it lost the deal for a Beijing-games partnership to Adidas). Li-Ning has been expanding its retail network and splurging on sponsorships. It plans to have 5,000 stores by the end of 2007 and has enlisted Shaquille O'Neal, an American superstar, to promote its basketball products in China. If Li-Ning can use the Olympics to subdue its foreign rivals at home, that would lay the foundation for going global.

Among the immediate beneficiaries of the Olympics, Air China and Li-Ning are worth watching

Olympics or no Olympics, some Chinese companies are eager to take on the world. China is now the world's second-largest car market after America. A few leading firms—Chery, Geely, Great Wall—are leveraging China's cost advantages to speed into foreign markets. Chery, the biggest exporter of Chinese cars, founded in 1997, has captured 7.2% of the domestic market and now exports to more than 50 countries, mostly in the developing world. In July 2007 it formed an alliance with Chrysler, which plans to sell Chery-made vehicles under its own brand in the United States, Europe and Latin America.

Is Chery the next Hyundai? It took the best South Korean and Japanese firms decades to join the global elite. Chinese companies may learn faster. But most have taken only baby steps onto the world stage, and they are tripping up. Chery and its brethren, for instance, have been accused of pirating the designs of entire cars from European and Japanese competitors. What is more, in a PR nightmare, Russian crash tests of Chinese cars crumpling like paper have been plastered on YouTube.

Along with the deep-pocketed but often clueless state-owned giants, China is producing a growing crop of innovative private firms. Nine Dragons Paper, led by China's richest woman, may become the world's largest paper producer in 2008. Suntech Power, a New York-listed company founded in 2001, is already the world's fourth-largest solar-cell maker.

For all the temptation to take on the world, most Chinese companies will be too busy for that. In 2008 they will focus mainly on trying to expand in their booming home market. ■

Sign of the times

2008 IN BRIEF

Shanghai hosts **The Fair** (formerly the Millionaire Fair) in October, with global brands vying for custom from a country that boasts the world's third-biggest number of consumers of luxury goods.

Charles Lee: editor, *Business China*, Economist Intelligence Unit

No kids, more money

Watch out for China's empty-nesters

China's "little emperors", the offspring of the country's one-child policy, are growing up. And, as they leave home, the number of working-age "empty-nesters" is rising rapidly. Already there are some 265m Chinese aged between 40 and 64 with no dependent children. In 2008 their ranks will swell by another 7m or so, increasing by more than 50m over the next ten years—in other words, their numbers will be growing on average by 1.8% a year, compared with only 0.2% for the population as a whole.

The empty-nesters will find themselves with money to spare. As more mothers return to work, this group will see "a huge rise in disposable income", according to Clint Laurent of Global Demographics, a Hong Kong firm specialising in population forecasting. Most of them already own the basic household appliances—a television, a fridge, a washing machine—so how will they spend their spare cash?

Partly by pampering themselves. The empty-nesters will be a big market for skin-care products, health products and restaurants. And they will travel. First, many will want to explore their own country (already, two- and three-star hotels are flourishing). Then the world will beckon. ■

New class

Chinese aged 40-64 with no dependent children, m

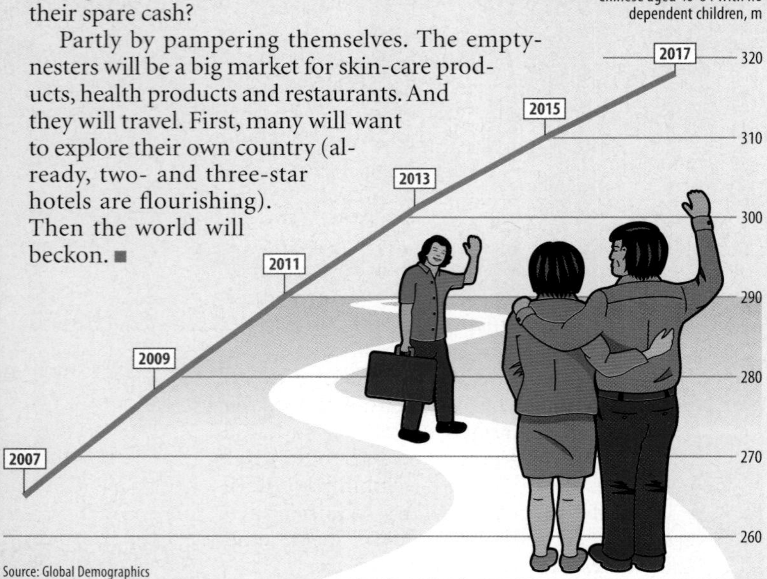

Source: Global Demographics

Smelling a rat

Steven Sitao Xu *BEIJING*

Worries about China's economy are overblown

A sizzling stockmarket and double-digit growth made 2007, the Year of the Pig, an excellent one for China's economy. The upcoming Year of the Rat also looks promising. The boom will surely go on—if for no other reason than that China will not let anything spoil the Olympic party.

But what happens after the games? Many pundits worry that the economy could come down to earth with a bump. China has been growing too fast for too long, they say, boosted by its artificially weak currency. They note that inflation has already picked up. And demand for China's exports will suffer from the slowdown in America—where a protectionist backlash against China could turn ugly.

Steven Sitao Xu: director, China corporate network, Economist Intelligence Unit

In reality, China is strong enough to power ahead regardless. But it will need to recalibrate crucial policies if it is to maintain its momentum.

Inflation is a worry: at risk, potentially, is not only China's price-competitive cachet but its deflationary role in the world economy. China, some fear, could change from being a deflation exporter to an inflation exporter. In 2007 surging prices of pork and eggs prompted the government to take action to stabilise prices (the leaders in Beijing are starkly aware that food prices are linked to social stability). Many suspect that things may be worse than the official figures suggest, since essential living expenses, such as health and education, are not adequately reflected in the calculation of inflation.

> Start with tax cuts and more spending on public goods

But there are good reasons to believe that China can keep a lid on inflation. First, productivity is rising fast. Surging inflation in China should be felt abroad; yet in America the import-price index of Chinese goods has risen by only 3-4% in the past year, according to the United States Labour Department, and after stripping out the dollar's mild depreciation against the renminbi the index has been more or less flat since 2003. Chinese products remain as cheap as ever despite higher input costs. The only logical conclusion is that the economy is undergoing a marked productivity improvement.

Second, the government has room to loosen the labour market, which has been notably tight in the coastal areas. For example, it can phase out the residential-permit system. Labour relocation alone could inject 9m workers every year into the industrial economy for the next 20 years.

Even if its export markets splutter in 2008, China has pots of cash and plenty of scope to boost demand at home. For the future it anyway needs to wean itself off its over-reliance on exports and investment.

China's export growth has consistently outpaced import growth in recent years. A widening trade surplus has already caused a protectionist backlash abroad. A plausible solution would be to boost consumer demand by cutting taxes and significantly increasing state spending on areas that benefit consumers directly, such as health and education. The trick is to do this without resorting to an expansionary fiscal policy, which would needlessly increase financial risks. Instead, the government would do better to change the composition of spending from fixed-asset investment and administration to things that all Chinese people can consume.

The Year of the Rat, which represents the start of a new cycle in the Chinese calendar, will be important for China's sustainable development. China must work a bit harder to ensure its future success. After 30 years of reform, a degree of reform fatigue may begin to set in. Thus far, China has done much more than expected to integrate the country into the global economy. The real test in 2008 is the extent to which the government is willing to "store the wealth within the people". To translate this ancient Chinese principle into practice, the government should start with tax cuts and more spending on public goods. China has ample ability to unleash domestic demand in 2008 and beyond. ■

Flashing red

Thomas Easton *SHANGHAI*

Sooner or later, the world's hottest market will burn up

It's crazy in Shanghai

The scene on the trading floor of the Shanghai Stock Exchange appears to be strikingly out of character for a market that is on fire. Situated in an iconic square building at the heart of Shanghai's costly new financial district, it has a vast trading floor filled with orderly rows of obsolete, box-like terminals. Clustered in one corner are a dozen clerks, heads resting on desks, dozing peacefully.

On a purely objective level, the lack of activity on the exchange is the result of trading becoming fully electronic. But why, then, does the trading floor exist at all? A rather more worrying interpretation of the Potemkin village set-up is that it does speak of something more than merely a shift to electronic trading. The Shanghai market itself is a kind of façade—not really a market, at least in the Western sense where prices are set by broad forces of supply and demand, but rather a place where China's government can provide the appearance of a modern economy, complete with a signature statement of modern finance and business: an equity exchange.

The result is an odd trading venue where companies are tied to shares but the shares do not carry genuine ownership rights, such as the authority to determine management (often directly controlled by the central government) or dividends. And, perhaps most importantly, it is not a trading venue where people believe shares are as likely to go down as to go up. Currently, they believe they can only go up.

This confidence has its roots in a spate of initial public offerings of government-controlled companies, each of which was deliberately priced to leap on opening day. Wealth made from flipping offerings proved to be contagious, particularly given the lack of alternatives. With few exceptions, China bans its citizens from investing abroad. At home, the choice is between savings accounts paying less than inflation or real estate with uncertain property rights.

The flood of money into shares has pushed stock prices so high that even China's remarkable growth cannot justify them: 65 times trailing earnings on the Shanghai exchange in October 2007, and 75 times earnings on the exchange in Shenzhen, which caters to smaller companies. The valuations are even more jarring because earnings are often inflated by corporate investment in the stockmarket, a circular logic that can just as easily come unwound. Similar distortions are also rife throughout the balance sheets of public Chinese companies as a result of recently adopted accounting rules that require assets to be revalued at prevailing prices, though the markets to set prices, for example in real-estate holdings and exotic securities, often do not exist.

In a normal stockmarket, speculators can deflate bubbles by shorting shares. That is illegal in China. In a normal stockmarket, investors can reap large rewards by having their investments bought in a heavily fought acquisition. In China, an acquisition must survive central planning (and often doesn't). Most of all, in normal markets, share prices are based on how a substantial amount of the shares in a company trade. In China, shares in many of the benchmark companies are held by the company or the government and do not trade. Prices are determined by just a few shares being batted back and forth.

> Only a few people need change their opinions for the market to unwind

If only a few shares are determining the overall valuation, it means only a few people need change their opinions for the market to unwind. Normally, a counter-balancing force for a sudden panic comes from contrarian-minded investors who believe an objective understanding of information provides a reason to buy shares as their prices become more reasonable. Put simply, crashing prices are an opportunity, not just a problem. But finding objectivity in the Chinese market is no easy task because information disclosure is wretched. Companies, and the investment banks that coddle them, distribute information to favoured investors but not to the market at large. For its part, the Chinese government broadly abets this process, granting selective permission to favoured foreigners wanting to invest.

These insiders are comforting friends for China to have, but they are insidious forces for a genuine market. Instead, China needs disinterested outsiders—and insiders—free to do research, free to buy and free to sell. Yet the market in China has become an example of moral hazard gone wild. Historically, this is not uncommon. Markets work in nasty ways and countries frequently try to control them. Critics are faulted for misunderstanding the local "culture" or for missing the crucial fact that this time, really, is different. And then, inevitably, there is a crash. ■

2008 IN BRIEF

To avoid food scandals during the Olympics, China uses hi-tech methods, including satellite-tracking, to **monitor food hygiene**.

Thomas Easton: Asia business editor, *The Economist*

E-commerce with Chinese characteristics

Jack Ma *HANGZHOU*

A million internet entrepreneurs will bloom, predicts the boss of China's biggest internet company

In 2008 it will become clear that e-commerce will have a much larger impact in China than in the West. China will generate new models of internet business which will spill over to the West. And e-commerce will lead China's economy into a new era in which innovation, customer focus and responsible business practices—rather than relationships with people in power—become the main determinants of success.

When Western e-commerce was born in 1995, China could only watch with admiration. The thought of clicking a mouse to buy products online—often from complete strangers—seemed an impossibility in China. If you were lucky enough to have a phone line, internet connection was slow and expensive. Banks were inefficient, making payment difficult and time-consuming. Sending a package meant waiting in long lines at the post office. And consumer culture had not yet taken off, hindered by low disposable incomes and an inefficient, state-run retail system.

The most significant trend in 2008 will be the emergence of a new class of entrepreneurs

It was businesses—not consumers—which drove e-commerce's early years in China. The most agile enterprises began to take notice of the internet as a channel for finding buyers and suppliers. As China entered the World Trade Organisation in 2001, a new "widget economy" was developing along the east coast of China, fertile ground for a multitude of small and medium-sized companies which made a living from trade. The internet proved to be the best way to connect these otherwise fragmented buyers and sellers, replacing trade shows and magazines as the medium of choice for sourcing products.

By 2003 two trends were converging to bring consumer e-commerce out of its long slumber. China's first generation of internet users had graduated from universities and turned their attention from online games to online shopping. With ever-increasing disposable income and more products than ever to choose from, a healthy consumer culture had developed, and the physical retail infrastructure was unable to keep pace. Second, international e-commerce companies began major investments in China. The ensuing competition between foreign and local companies helped educate the market, attracting more online shoppers.

New modes of business arose to meet the unique needs of China's consumers. Rating systems and escrow payment services developed to resolve the issue of trust between buyers and sellers. The integration of real-time chat into marketplaces allowed people to get to know each other before making transactions, a necessary function in a society in which relationships are still one of the most important channels through which trust flows.

In 2007 the leading consumer marketplaces counted 50m users and, for the first time, the value of daily online transactions surpassed the cash taken by major physical retailers in China, such as Wal-Mart. Moreover, users of online-payment systems exceeded the number of credit-card holders, showing that China's e-commerce is taking a very different path from the West's, which relied heavily on credit cards.

Whereas C2C and B2C models have remained largely distinct in the West, in China they will continue to blend together, with consumers visiting single marketplaces to buy from individuals, small retailers and large retailers alike. Credit systems will take new forms as individuals and companies develop track records, giving banks reliable information to make loans to businesses and consumers.

The most significant trend in 2008 will be the emergence of a new class of entrepreneurs. Niche manufacturers will link up with niche retailers, cutting out middlemen and out-competing larger, less specialised firms. A growing number of entrepreneurs will buy in volume from China on sites like Alibaba and sell to consumers on Western sites such as eBay.

China's e-commerce is creating economic opportunities in China and around the world. A new class of businesspeople is emerging and the transparent nature of e-commerce means businesses are becoming more responsible as they further integrate into the world economy. This new generation of entrepreneur provides the best chance we have to encourage economic development at a grassroots level in China, and around the world. ■

2008 IN BRIEF

A spate of books is released in the Olympic year, starting in January with Mark Leonard's "What does China think?" (Fourth Estate).

Jack Ma: chairman and CEO, Alibaba Group

The new champions

Pam Woodall *HONG KONG*

Guess who'll be rising up the statistical charts in 2008

Sports fans care passionately about their home team's position in the league. Likewise, countries feel the same about their economic ranking. The past year has been a bumper one for international leapfrogging in all sorts of league tables—and usually it was team America that got thrashed, more often than not by China. China's exports jumped ahead of America's; and China's ICBC overtook Citigroup as the world's biggest bank by market value (though not by assets or profits).

In 2008 it will be Germany's turn to see China surge past. China will shove Germany off its pedestal as the world's biggest exporter. It will also overtake Germany as an importer, putting China in second place behind the United States. And China's GDP (measured at market exchange rates) will push ahead of Germany's to make China the world's third-biggest economy, behind America and Japan.

China will continue to overtake America in all sorts of fields. In 2008 Chinese demand will for the first time become the main driver of world economic growth, with the increase in its domestic spending in current dollar terms contributing more to global growth than American domestic demand. China will overtake America as the country with the largest number of internet users. But there is one crown that America will be glad to lose: China will become the world's largest emitter of greenhouse gases in 2008 (some claim it had already achieved this by the end of 2007). However, America's emissions per person are still more than four times China's.

If share prices in Shanghai continue to soar and more Chinese companies carry out IPOs, it will push China's total stockmarket capitalisation ahead of Japan's and second only to America's. Chinese firms will increasingly dominate international corporate rankings. Already, by late 2007, three of the world's six biggest companies by market capitalisation were Chinese. In 2008 PetroChina could even eclipse ExxonMobil as the world's largest company by market value, if it goes ahead with its plan to sell shares on the Chinese mainland and if prices soar above those currently listed in Hong Kong. Many will claim that this is not a true "market value" since the bulk of PetroChina's shares will still be in government hands. But the mere suggestion that a Chinese firm outranks any in America will add to the impression that China has truly become a global giant. ■

China will overtake America as the country with the largest number of internet users

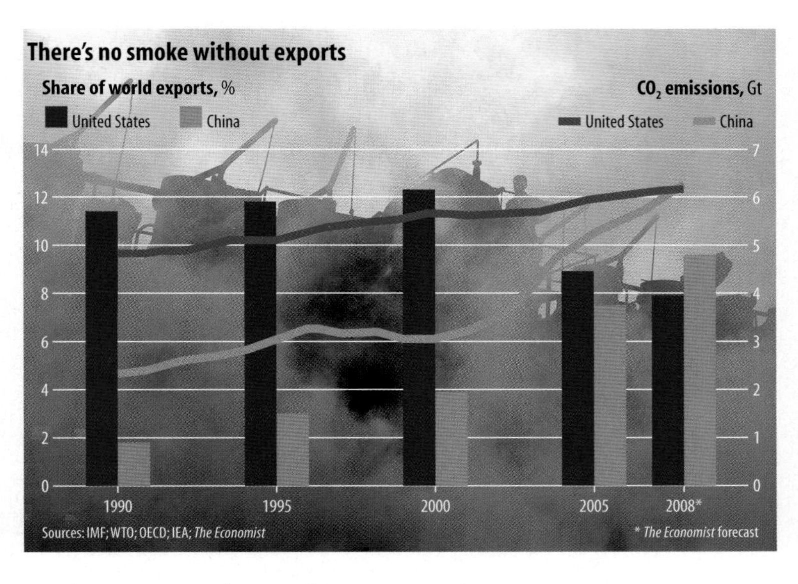

Pam Woodall: Asia economics editor, *The Economist*

Win-win Olympics

Matthew Glendinning

Team China will strike gold in Beijing

Whisper it softly, but China will top the gold-medal table at the Olympics. Softly, because the Chinese authorities want to cool public expectation—and take pressure off their athletes.

At the Athens Olympics in 2004, China won 32 golds, just three behind the United States. But on home territory and with another four years of sports development behind it, China will have the edge (see table for our forecast). "It's no secret we're underdogs," says Jim Scherr, the chief executive of the United States Olympic Committee. "They're blowing us out of the water in the gold-medal race."

Olympic golds	Atlanta 1996†	Sydney 2000	Athens 2004	Beijing 2008*
China	16	28	32	45
United States	44	40	35	41
Russia	26	32	32	32

*The Economist forecast †Germany came third in Atlanta with 20 gold medals
Source: International Olympic Committee

Perhaps not out of the water, where the American swimming team excels. But the Chinese will dominate more technical sports such as shooting, diving, table tennis and badminton. Shooting alone could win the hosts five or more golds.

Despite the strength of the United States on the track, Beijing 2008 will also see China claim gold in events like the 110-metres hurdles, in which Liu Xiang, who won gold in Athens, is a national hero with commercial appeal to match any of his Western counterparts.

A hangover from the planned economy, China's costly, centrally funded sports academies with names like Shanghai Sports School Number 2—the alma mater of Liu Xiang—have groomed champions. But after Beijing 2008, sport too will become part of the market economy. The sports schools will be sold off and run as sports clubs, joining basketball, football and volleyball in China's commercial sporting mainstream. ■

Matthew Glendinning: sports and business writer

In 2008, be nicer to your neighbours

The **Dalai Lama**, Tibet's exiled spiritual leader, urges the world in general—and China in particular—to show more compassion in the year ahead

As we face the challenge of ever-expanding populations, increasing demands for energy and food, as well as huge disparities in wealth, we have to embrace globalisation and accept people from all countries as neighbours and collaborators, not rivals. In this interdependent world, war is outdated. Destroying other countries brings no benefit, but creates humanitarian suffering, trade disruption and environmental problems that everyone must bear.

In 2008 there will be efforts to put an end to ongoing violent conflict in several parts of the world. The drive to achieve economic growth will also go on, while awareness of the perils of climate change and the need to protect ourselves from its unpredictable effects will become more acute. This will surely focus attention on the powerless and dispossessed, who will be the first to suffer and the least able to help themselves.

People need goods and services to meet the essential requirements of existence, not to mention those things that bring dignity and comfort to human life. Yet for all the innovation and creativity of our economic activity, we have not succeeded in securing these essentials for all human beings. The yawning gap between the "haves" and "have nots" is going to create a great deal of suffering for everyone.

We watch, hear and read every day about breathtaking manifestations of affluence, alongside deaths due to starvation, poverty, malnutrition, and preventable or curable diseases. Shouldn't we ask ourselves whether something is wrong with our choice of goals or our motivation, or both? I believe we have to find ways of bringing compassion to bear in our economic activity.

Compassion and love are fundamental to relations between human beings. Therefore the interdependent society in which we live has to be a compassionate one, compassionate in its choice of goals, and compassionate in the pursuit of those goals.

When we focus only on our own requirements and disregard the needs and interests of others, we are likely to provoke hostility. This is especially true when we view our own happiness and needs predominantly in terms of material wealth and power. All human beings yearn for freedom, equality and dignity, and have a right to achieve them. Therefore, in today's shrinking world the acceptance of universally binding standards of human rights is essential.

Tibetans love their own culture and their way of life, but Chinese officials regard their urge to preserve their identity as a threat to the unity of China

I do not see any contradiction between the need for economic development and the need to respect human rights. The right to free speech and association is vital in promoting a country's economic development. In Tibet, for example, there have been instances where unsuitable economic policies have been implemented and continued long after they have failed to produce benefits, because citizens and government officials could not speak out against them. And it is the same elsewhere.

A middle way for Tibet

We praise diversity in theory, but too often fail to respect it in practice. If someone is different from us, we are inclined to interpret the difference in negative terms and perceive it as threatening. The Chinese government's attitude to the people of Tibet is a case in point. Naturally Tibetans love their own culture and their way of life as best suited to their distinct environment and situation, but whenever they show active interest, respect or faith in it, Chinese officials regard their urge to preserve their identity as a threat to the unity of China. Such an inability to embrace diversity is a major source of dissatisfaction that can give rise to conflict.

The Chinese leadership places great emphasis on harmony: an excellent goal. But in order to achieve it, there must be trust. Trust flows from equality and compassion. Suspicion creates restraint and is an obstacle to trust. Without trust, how can you develop genuine unity or harmony?

I believe we can find a way for both Chinese and Tibetans to live together with dignity, freedom and in the spirit of good neighbourliness. I am convinced that we can achieve a "middle way", if we engage in a process that respects our differences and acknowledges that we have the ability and the means to solve our problems and help each other.

In 2008 close attention will be focused on China as it hosts the Olympic games. I feel strongly that as the world's most populous nation, with its long history and ancient civilisation, China deserves this privilege and honour. However, we must not forget that the Olympics are a free, fair and open contest in which athletes of all recognised nations, no matter how small, are welcome to compete on an equal footing. Freedom, fairness, openness and equality are not only the principles enshrined in the Olympic games but among the highest human values, a measure against which all nations should be held to account. ■

Also in this section:
Hard slogging for India's economy 88
India's unquiet periphery 89
Two-party politics in Japan 90
Japan's green wish 90
Asia's forests 91
Australia's coal question 92
Surin Pitsuwan: A new miracle for tigers and dragons 94

Asia

Much more than China

Bill Emmott *BEIJING, DELHI AND TOKYO*

The continent's great powers know they need to be friends as well as rivals

"Asia is one." When the Beijing Olympics are transfixing the world, it will seem as if that sentence is wrong and that Asia is simply China. Other countries will try to draw your eyes away from the Middle Kingdom to their own domestic events: to India, if its Congress party-led government is forced to hold an early general election; or to Japan, if the hands of the Liberal Democrats' new prime minister, Yasuo Fukuda, turn out to be not quite as safe as was assumed when he was chosen in September to clear up the shambles left behind by Shinzo Abe—and if he too is forced to go early to the polls. Asia's serial troublemaker, Kim Jong Il, always has the potential to grab attention to himself and to North Korea, though this time he may do so by revealing his preferred successor (Kim will turn 66 in 2008) rather than by exploding a nuclear device. Yet while these and other individual countries jostle for the spotlight in 2008, bear those first three words in mind: "Asia is one".

They represent a bigger, more enduring trend than all those single-country events, important though those will be. The great powers of the region are coming to look at it in the way that cartographers do, as a single space, whether for military strategy, diplomacy or economic relations. This region stretches from Iran in the west to Japan in the east, a space in which India is as much an Asian actor as are China, Singapore, Thailand or Japan, and in which the commercial and political interests of the big powers range across the whole continent.

This has never happened before, at least not in modern times. That is not for want of dreaming. "Asia is one" was the opening sentence of a book published just over a century ago by a Japanese art historian called Kakuzo Okakura, entitled "Ideals of the East". He caused a stir at the time, as a scholar from the first Asian country to modernise successfully, one that was about to be the first to defeat a European power, Russia, in war. Okakura's ideas influenced Asia's first Nobel literature laureate, Rabindranath Tagore, a poet from Bengal, who in turn even influenced Sun Yat-sen, the father of the Chinese republic that replaced the Qing emperors in 1911. They were all, in their different ways, pan-Asianists, seeking unity among Chinese, Indians, Japanese and others to forge a single idea of Asia, in a spirit of rejection of the European colonialists.

> Pan-Asian thinking is on its way back—for benign reasons and for less friendly ones

It didn't happen. Asians proved to be as divided from one another as they were united in the desire to be rid of the Europeans. Once the imperialists left, they turned in on themselves or into their local neighbourhoods, whether as South ▶

2008 IN BRIEF

Macau is the world's **fastest-growing economy**, with growth of around 25% a year, thanks to massive investment in casinos and tourist arrivals from China.

Bill Emmott: writer on international affairs and author of "Rivals" (to be published in April by Harcourt in America and Penguin in Britain)

Hard-slogging India

Simon Cox *DELHI*

Will the economy's run rate slow?

In September 2007 India's burly batsman Yuvraj Singh struck six sixes in a single over for only the fourth time in cricketing history, en route to India's triumph in the "Twenty20" World Cup. In the same month, India's currency strengthened past 40 rupees to the dollar for the first time since 1998, and its Sensex stockmarket index passed the 17,000 mark. The country's press was quick to draw parallels between its hard-hitting cricketers and its hard-charging economy.

But the analogy may run deeper. The breathless, 20-over version of cricket gives a player no time to build and sustain an innings. Batsmen swing, cheerleaders strut, and prodigious feats of scoring are followed by the quick tumble of wickets. After his string of sixes, Mr Singh had to miss the next match with tennis [sic] elbow. Might India's economy suffer a similar strain in 2008?

Optimists argue that the Indian economy is laying the foundations for a long stay at the crease. They are impressed by the unusual source of India's growth as well as its speed. Investment in "fixed" assets (such as roads, bridges and office blocks) contributed more to India's 9.4% expansion than private consumption in the 2006-07 fiscal year, which ended on March 31st. The question is whether this will add to the economy's capacity quickly enough to forestall inflation—or whether these outlays will first put intolerable pressure on India's stretched resources.

In so far as economists can gauge such things, India can probably sustain growth of no more than 8% a year before the strain starts to show in higher prices. It could go a bit quicker if the government first made room by spending less on unearned sinecures and misdirected subsidies. The government hopes to cut the combined federal-and-state deficit from almost 10% of GDP five years ago to about 5.2% in 2007-08 (if you ignore the liabilities it keeps off its balance sheet, such as arrears on fertiliser subsidies).

But 2008 may bring an early general election, which is never an auspicious time for fiscal restraint. And in April the government's vast retinue of employees expect to hear the proposals of the sixth pay commission, which sets salaries once every decade or so. Following the last such commission, about 600 billion rupees ($15 billion) was added to public pay and pensions, nearly ruining some states. After Mr Singh's magical innings, one old hand pointed out that most of his strokes "were proper cricketing shots, and could only have been essayed by someone who was well-versed in the basics." Alas, India's growth of 9% or more is not yet as grounded in the fundamentals. ■

Howzat?

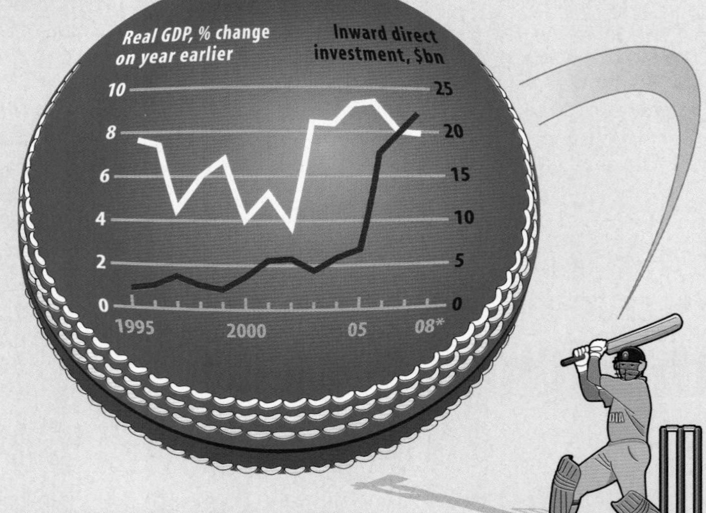

Sources: Central Statistical Organisation; Reserve Bank of India
*Economist Intelligence Unit forecasts

Simon Cox: India business and finance correspondent, *The Economist*

Asia, North-East Asia, the Association of South-East Asian Nations or merely Indochina. But that is now changing. Pan-Asian thinking is on its way back—for benign reasons and for less friendly ones.

One symbol of that change will come in February when Kishore Mahbubani, Singapore's best-known diplomat of recent decades and now dean of the Lee Kuan Yew School of Public Policy, will publish a book called "The New Asian Hemisphere". This will be notable because during the 1990s Mr Mahbubani, and the "minister mentor" for whom his school is named, were prime advocates of a more limited idea of "Asian values", one with a strictly East Asian focus and an authoritarian view of human rights. The new Asia, however, represents a much larger political and economic space, connecting together the world's largest democracy, India, and its largest dictatorship, China.

But such unity is also bringing suspicion and rivalry. With India achieving rapid economic growth and increasing its trade, and with China extending its interests and influence deep into and across the Indian Ocean in search of African and West Asian resources to fuel its growth, Asia's two aspirant great powers are becoming more conscious of each other's breath on their necks. President George Bush's civil nuclear deal with India, conceived in 2005 but uncertainly awaiting implementation in 2008, was an attempt to exploit that inherent rivalry by strengthening India to balance China. Japan's security alliance with Australia in 2007 was another recognition of this change, as were the four-way military exercises conducted by Japan, America, India and Australia in September. In 2008 Japan will confirm that it is providing much of the finance for an ambitious industrial and transport project connecting Mumbai, Delhi and Kolkata, to further shore up its links across the hemisphere to India.

Now that they are thinking on this larger, continent-wide scale, Asia's great powers are seeking to stress their friendships with one another as well as preparing for an adversarial power game. They may be inherent rivals, but they also know that conflict would be a disaster and that their rivalry needs to be managed rather than being allowed to escalate. So when the oddly named East Asia Summit holds its fourth annual meeting in December 2008, pulling together countries as far apart as India, China, Japan and New Zealand, it will be more serious and substantive than in previous years. Asia is one—for good and for ill. ■

2008 IN BRIEF

At the age of 75, Japan's Yuichiro Miura attempts to regain his title as the oldest man to **climb Everest**. Others, even older, may try to foil him.

An unquiet periphery

James Astill *DELHI*

India should do more to help its troubled neighbours

South Asia has long been a rowdy neighbourhood. But the view from the Secretariat building, the elegant south Delhi seat of India's foreign ministry, will be particularly riotous in 2008. In Pakistan and Sri Lanka, there will be war; in Bangladesh, there will be protests against army-backed rule; in Nepal, a return to war will be a constant threat. Only tiny Bhutan, a Himalayan recluse whose foreign policy India dictates, will be a peaceful fellow resident of the subcontinental hood.

Who will preside over the mayhem in Pakistan? The hope was that it would be a civilian—for the first time since General Pervez Musharraf seized power in 1999. General Musharraf had himself re-elected president in October, in uniform. He planned to divest himself of it shortly after, provided that the Supreme Court accepted the legitimacy of the October poll. The court, however, may have had other ideas, and in early November 2007, as its ruling loomed, General Musharraf suspended the constitution. Emergency rule has thrown Pakistan's political outlook into deeper confusion.

India has a poor record of meddling in the politics of its troubled neighbours

The general election that had been planned in Pakistan for January 2008 may be delayed by a year or more. In a free election, the Pakistan People's Party (PPP) of Benazir Bhutto, a former prime minister who returned (to a huge welcome horribly marred by two deadly bombs) from eight years of self-imposed exile in October 2007, and the Muslim League (Q), which backs General Musharraf, might each win about a third of the votes. The Muslim League (N) of Nawaz Sharif, another former prime minister, and smaller Islamist and regional parties would account for the rest.

If an election happens—and assuming General Musharraf is in charge—a long-mooted partnership between the PPP and ML(Q) might be the best hope for stability, though the November "coup" made it less likely. The political troubles will distract the president from an ongoing campaign to defeat a Taliban insurgency along the Afghan border. There is no hope of victory in 2008.

Sri Lanka's government, under the populist president, Mahinda Rajapakse, will prosecute a war in 2008 that is partly of its choosing. Officially, a ceasefire has been in place since 2002 between the government and the Tamil Tiger rebels who control the country's north. But over the past year it has broken down. Having shelled the Tigers out of another fief, in eastern Sri Lanka, the government will try to conquer the north.

Government forces will gain ground; losing the east has weakened the Tigers. But the government will not end Sri Lanka's ethnic strife because it does not understand it. It calls the Tigers terrorists, and so they are. Yet they also reflect the grievances of many Sri Lankan Tamils against a bullying Sinhalese majority, the government's main constituency. So long as the Tamils' basic demands—including autonomy for the north and a proper share of state patronage—are not met, Sri Lanka's troubles will endure.

Bangladesh's will worsen in 2008. Its technocratic administration, installed by the army in January 2007, promises to hold elections in December 2008. It will break its promise. At the army's behest, it has arrested the country's main political leaders, Khaleda Zia and Sheikh Hasina Wajed. The charges against the two women—of corruption and extortion, respectively—may or may not be deserved. But, in the absence of other leaders, their parties demand their release. This gives the army a choice: democracy and the two begums (as the feuding Mrs Zia and Sheikh Hasina are known) or no begums and no democracy. It will choose the latter in 2008. Public disaffection with the government will increase during the year. Violent protests are all but guaranteed.

2008 IN BRIEF

With political parties now legal, the Kingdom of Bhutan, the only country to measure its "**gross national happiness**", holds its first general election.

Mao still lives

Nepal, which recently ended a civil war, will enjoy little of a peace dividend in 2008. A key part of the peace process—the election of an assembly to write a new constitution—was due in November 2007, but was postponed. Armed Maoists within the transitional government were to blame. They fear they would wither in a democracy. Under pressure from India, they were persuaded not to quit the government.

Neighbourhood watch

Alas, India is rarely so helpful. It is rightly proud of its more stable democracy; yet India has a poor record of meddling in the politics of its troubled neighbours. It has held back somewhat of late. But India still spurns opportunities to do good. In particular, it could do more to expand its miserly trade with Pakistan and Bangladesh. For both countries, this would bring much-needed relief. And India would profit. ■

James Astill: South Asia correspondent, *The Economist*

The enduring caretaker

Dominic Ziegler *TOKYO*

The ruling party regains its balance, but Japan's politics enters an untested era

In a country that expects its politics to be predictable, flux or even chaos will be the mark of 2008 for Japan. That much is assured by the ruling party's loss in 2007 of its majority in the upper house of the Diet (parliament). The Liberal Democratic Party (LDP) and its allies had ruled unchallenged for all but nine months of the previous half-century, and the humiliation did for the prime minister, Shinzo Abe, whose disastrous term lasted but a year.

Smelling blood, Ichiro Ozawa, leader of the opposition Democratic Party of Japan (DPJ), will now attempt to use his party's new upper-house majority to bring down the government and force a general election, as early in 2008 as possible. The win that Mr Ozawa expects would be ground-shaking, because it would herald the arrival of proper two-party politics in Japan.

Yet Mr Ozawa will find chaos to be a fickle mistress, and in 2008 she will favour Yasuo Fukuda, the LDP's new "caretaker" prime minister. Mr Fukuda was shoved into the breach at a time when an LDP in disarray sought unflashy competence. At 71, Mr Fukuda's age counted for him and his party: better that he lead the LDP through this horrible patch than younger men with ambitions still before them.

In the coming year, however, Mr Fukuda will prove remarkably durable. He will win his first battle against the bruising Mr Ozawa, over the role of Japan's armed forces abroad in the "war on terror", with deftness and conciliation. Turning to domestic matters, he will challenge the DPJ's contention that Japan has no more appetite for market-based reforms. Mr Fukuda will argue that with an ageing population, new sources of growth must be found. At the same time, he will show concern for the victims of change.

> Mr Fukuda will prove remarkably durable

Mr Ozawa will not be helped by Japan's entering its eighth year of an economic recovery that will slowly spread to the depressed regions on which the DPJ counts for support. He will fail to land a knockout blow at least until Mr Fukuda presents a spring budget, one that will attempt to plug the government's deficits while providing reassurance over pensions and other areas of financial insecurity. The prime minister may even survive to host the G8 summit in Hokkaido in the summer, which Japan hopes will produce a breakthrough on climate change (see below).

Sooner or later, though, there will be a general election during the year. In it, the DPJ will learn that the 2007 upper-house result was a vote against the ruling party, not a vote for the opposition. It will gain seats, but not enough to unseat the LDP's coalition, ensuring continued stalemate and frustration, but more for the DPJ than for the LDP. So a final prediction for 2008: the autocratic Mr Ozawa, who 14 years ago stormed out of the LDP vowing to bring it down, but whose health today may not be strong, will be outlasted as a party leader by the "caretaker" Mr Fukuda. ■

Dominic Ziegler: Tokyo bureau chief, *The Economist*

A wish to lead

Dominic Ziegler *TOKYO*

Japan wants to show the way on climate change, but how?

Two attacks from China in 2008 will launch a national hand-wringing debate in Japan about the country's weak leadership in Asia. The first will be an invasion of giant Nomura's jellyfish, horrifying blobs two metres wide that spawn and thrive in China's polluted waters before drifting on the currents to Japan, breaking fishermen's nets and spoiling catches. The second will be the relentless publicity surrounding Beijing's Olympic games. Whoever will be prime minister of Japan next summer, people at home will urge him to use the G8 summit—which will be held at a lakeside resort in Hokkaido, the least trashed of Japan's four main islands—to prove that Japan, not China, is Asia's natural leader, starting with environmental matters and climate change.

The logic of the Japan-boosters is unassailable. Having cleaned up after its own industrial revolution, the country has unbeatable knowledge of environmental technology and energy efficiencies; it can share these with dirty neighbours, starting with China. And as host to the first international commitment on carbon emissions, which produced the Kyoto protocol, it has the moral standing to lead the region into a post-Kyoto world.

Its dirty fellow Asians, notably China and India, also note that Japan probably has oodles of cash to spread around to combat climate change. But Japan's relations with its nearest neighbours are still bedevilled by problems of acknowledging its rapine wartime past. It will take a strong, confident Japanese leader to overcome those problems. Or indeed any lasting leader at all—which is why Japan's year of political confusion is more likely to be felt by its neighbours than by ordinary Japanese themselves. ■

Falling here, rising there

Peter Collins *BANGKOK*

Ways will be sought to save Asia's dying forests—and new forests will spring up

A year of tree-hugging is in prospect. The world's governments will meet in 2008 to discuss replacing the Kyoto protocol on climate-change prevention, which expires in 2012. A key issue will be how to include "avoided deforestation" in Kyoto's successor—in other words, schemes in which polluters pay for the conservation of forest that would otherwise doubtless have been chopped down.

The relentless felling of the world's tropical forests may be causing one-quarter of all carbon-dioxide emissions. The Kyoto protocol's clean-development mechanism, under which polluters in rich countries pay for projects that cut emissions in poorer ones, does include projects to plant new forests. But schemes to stop existing forests from being chopped are excluded, despite their enormous potential for reducing emissions. Countries with lots of vulnerable forest, like Indonesia, want this to change because it could provide billions of dollars for conservation.

The Asia-Pacific region will, overall, gain about 6,000 square km of forest in 2008

To pilot the idea of giving credits for avoided deforestation, the World Bank wants to get started in 2008 with its $250m Forest Carbon Partnership Facility. This will, first, help about 20 countries compile inventories of their forests and the carbon locked up in them, and work out the opportunity costs of not cutting them down. Then, pilot projects will be set up in which the bank pays their governments in return for measurable progress in stopping the chopping.

For all the huge potential of such schemes, designing them so that they genuinely reduce logging, not just shift it elsewhere, will be tricky. Furthermore, places like Indonesia's Aceh province, whose forests currently face few threats, will be tempted to say to the rich world: "Pay up, or the trees get it."

While the climate experts expend much hot air discussing how to save the trees, swathes of moist tropical forest across the Asia-Pacific region, as elsewhere, will continue to be cleared. Studies by the United Nations Food and Agriculture Organisation (FAO) suggest that Indonesia alone will lose a further 2% of its forest next year, or 19,000 square km, an area bigger than Connecticut. Other misgoverned Asian countries, like Myanmar and Cambodia, are losing tree cover at similar rates. In many such countries there are impressive conservation laws on paper (that is, dead trees) but in practice illegal logging, often by "untouchable" cronies of politicians, continues unhindered.

Loggers wrench out the most valuable hardwoods, the dipterocarp family: these grow up to 50 metres high and provide a protective canopy for the plants and animals below. They leave behind shadeless "secondary" forest, which dries out and becomes prone to fire, releasing huge amounts of carbon dioxide. Often blazes are set deliberately as farmers move in to clear the land for planting. The annual "haze" caused by out-of-control fires during Indonesia's mid-year dry season spreads smoke across much of South-East Asia.

However, the news is not all bad. The FAO's research suggests that the Asia-Pacific region will, overall, gain about 6,000 square km of forest in 2008. That is quite a turnaround from the 13,000 square km net loss of forest each year in the 1990s. The main reason is China's huge reforestation effort. This accelerated after terrible floods in 1998 convinced the government that it must restore tree cover, especially in the mighty Yangzi's basin. Vietnam is reforesting quickly and India, which has almost as much forest as Indonesia, is gaining a bit each year.

New trees, and some new virtues

Asia's new forests will, besides preventing floods and landslides, soak up carbon dioxide. But they are less diverse than those still disappearing. Some are plantations of eucalyptus for papermaking, or other fast-growing species such as poplar, used for building materials. Others are fruit orchards. Nevertheless, even in plantation forests, nature subversively reinvades and populates them with a variety of other species.

In some places—Thailand is one example—there are projects to restore something pretty close to the original, diverse tropical forest. Nature does this by itself if left undisturbed. But conservationists are lending a helping hand by planting fast-growing "pioneer" tree species which provide a high canopy of foliage. This in turn speeds the regeneration of the original moist forest. Not only has Asia-Pacific's forest area begun to regrow, but after centuries of shrinking there are even grounds for hope that some of its rich diversity can be maintained. ■

2008 IN BRIEF

Singapore hosts its first **Formula One** car race—and it may be the first to be held at night.

Peter Collins: South-East Asia correspondent, *The Economist*

All the wood in China
Forest change rates by country or area
Annual increase/decrease

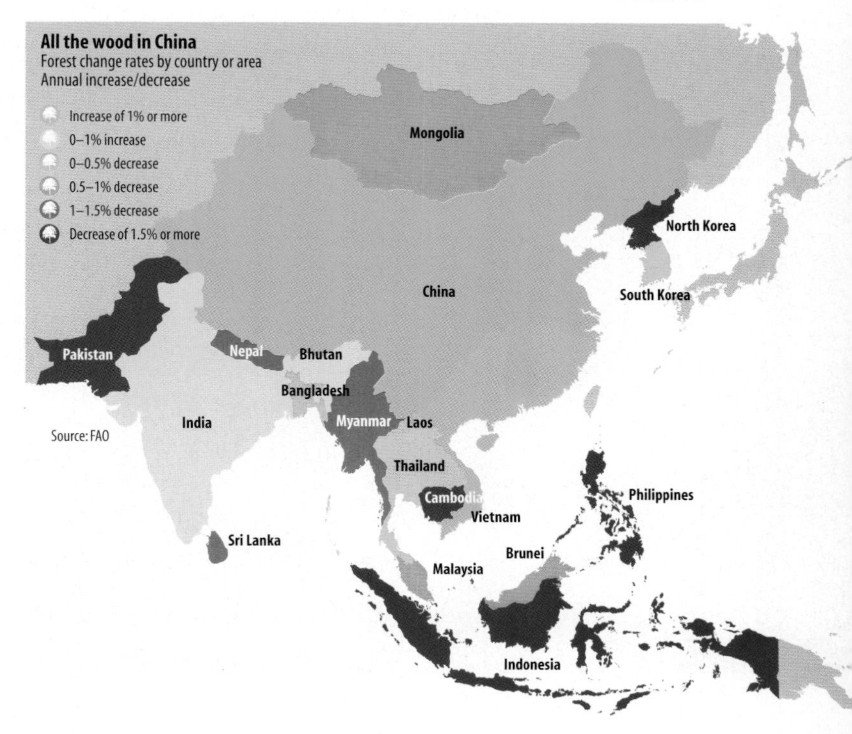

Source: FAO

Australia's coal question

Robert Milliken *SYDNEY*

Can Innamincka provide an alternative?

The hotspot for Australia in 2008 will not be Canberra, the political capital, or Sydney or Melbourne, the big eastern cities where the business world's movers and shakers hold sway. Instead, eyes will turn to Innamincka (population 15) in the outback of South Australia. This unlikely place will hold the key to how Australia deals with global warming, the issue that will dominate the country's political debate. Geodynamics, an Australian company, has spent five years exploring ancient granite "hot rocks" 4.5km (2.8 miles) beneath the surface of Innamincka's red desert. Tests so far have shown them to be the hottest (250°C) of their kind on earth (with 1 cubic km of hot granite holding the stored energy equivalent of 40m barrels of oil). By early 2008 the company will know from fresh tests if the hot rocks can form a viable geothermal power source for Australia's electricity grid.

2008 IN BRIEF From February internet-savvy Asians get to register **.asia domain names** for their presence on the web.

If the answer is yes, Australia's federal and six state governments will be under pressure to help make it happen. Australia is one of the world's biggest greenhouse-gas emitters per head. Along with America, it is one of only two rich countries not to ratify the Kyoto protocol. Up to now this has been largely because of the "king status" of coal. Australia is the world's biggest coal exporter, with enough black coal reserves to last more than 200 years at current production levels (800 years in the case of its less combustible brown coal). The country derives 83% of its own electricity from coal, and governments have shown little inclination to change this.

Australia is the world's biggest coal exporter, with enough reserves to last over 200 years

Robert Milliken: Australia correspondent, *The Economist*

Spot the hot rock

Yet most Australians are ahead of their government in pushing for change. In a survey in late 2007 the Lowy Institute, a Sydney foreign-policy think-tank, found that a majority of Australians saw climate change as the country's biggest external threat (ahead of unfriendly countries developing nuclear weapons and international terrorism), and tackling climate change as the most important foreign-policy goal; 92% found renewable energy—such as wind, solar and geothermal power from hot rocks—the most convincing way to reduce carbon emissions (well ahead of nuclear power and "clean coal", where emissions are stored underground).

Investing in such renewable-energy sources will take much money and political will. But Tim Flannery, Australia's climate-change guru, author of "The Weather Makers" and 2007 Australian of the Year, is right when he says that 2008 will see a race between green energy industries to start moving into the territory now occupied by high-greenhouse-gas-emitting coal.

In any case, Canberra is awash with money thanks to a decade of fiscal surpluses (largely from Australia's flourishing trade with China). The boom will only get bigger in 2008. China's insatiable demand for Australia's minerals (it takes more than half Australia's iron ore exports alone) is matched by Australia's hunger for inexpensive electronic and other consumer goods from China. For the first time China in 2008 will be Australia's biggest trading partner, a status long shared between Japan and America.

That change will be symbolic, too, for Australia's foreign policy. For the past seven years Canberra's close relations with George Bush's presidency have overshadowed, and sometimes bedevilled, relations closer to home in the Asia-Pacific region. Such cosiness was never popular: the same Lowy Institute poll found two-thirds of Australians looked unfavourably on America under Mr Bush. So while the American alliance will remain strong, the looming end of the Bush presidency will see Canberra building on the China trading partnership to forge stronger strategic ties with Beijing.

Underpinned by the high prices China and other countries will pay for its commodities, Australia's economy will grow by at least 3% in 2008, perhaps more as farms recover from a lengthy drought. A record 150,000 immigrants will arrive, two-thirds to provide skills that business and industry leaders cannot find at home.

But this booming economy masks several worries. The skills shortage shows why the government will have to reverse a decade of under-investment in higher education: Australia is one of only five OECD countries in which spending per student actually fell between 1995 and 2002. Tackling Australia's chronic water shortage will be even more urgent. After decades of poor management the Murray and Darling rivers, the lifeblood of Australia's east-coast farming regions, have slowed to a trickle. Canberra's plan in 2007 to take control of the rivers from the four states through which they flow has stalled amid bickering and political rivalries. So 2008 will be a crunch year for the environment on several fronts. Put another way, Australia's future will be balanced delicately between a hot rock and a dry place. ■

A new miracle for tigers and dragons

Surin Pitsuwan, incoming secretary-general of the Association of South-East Asian Nations, argues that Asia's countries must collaborate against poverty

The dynamics of Asia today are a complex of relations among three emerging communities—East Asia, South-East Asia and South Asia. How these three communities relate to one another will be the great challenge facing Asian leaders in 2008 and beyond. Over a decade ago the world admired South-East Asia's tiger economies for their market-friendly and export-oriented policies, providing years of spectacular growth. Today, ASEAN's leaders need a new economic miracle to meet the challenges posed by a resurgent China and India.

China's pre-eminent status will be consolidated after the 2008 Beijing Olympics. Shanghai, for example, has ambitions to be the cultural capital of the world. In India, a talented middle class, in spite of a cumbersome state, is fostering its own economic miracle as millions of Indians seek a share in the country's growing prosperity. Meanwhile, the success of India, Japan and South Korea has demonstrated to countless Asians that development is freedom.

Yet we must be mindful that most of Asia remains home to endemic poverty. Around 100m people, nearly a sixth of ASEAN's population, live under the tyranny of poverty, and although China has made impressive growth economically the income gap between the people of urban areas and the rural hinterland remains dangerously wide. In this next phase of economic surge Asia's poor must not be left behind.

Fortunately, there is now a commitment to build an East Asian Community, from India to the Antipodes, to consolidate political, security and socio-economic co-operation. Real economic interdependence through free-trade agreements is laying the ground for a truly robust community.

Certainly, Asia is years away from developing the singular vision of the West, which, despite its diversity, shares a common and unified history. But as Asians connect within a larger pan-Asian economic framework, Asia will no longer be that "vague immensity" described by W.B. Yeats. There is a growing confidence among Asians that we are all stakeholders in the continent's future stability and prosperity. The Indonesians have a better way of expressing this nuanced sense of oneness among Asians: *bhinnika tunggal ika*—"unity in diversity", a vision of unity based on shared and inclusive humanistic ideals, not imposed by political coercion.

We must be mindful that most of Asia remains home to endemic poverty

In this new context, the rise of the Asian economy must be sustained and expanded by heavy investments in education and human capacity. We can see that Asian universities in 2008 will do well in global rankings, while the research capability of Asian institutions and industry will also grow.

As regional integration intensifies, globalisation will accelerate the integration of Asia into the world economy. It is for this reason that Asians must shape a new regional vision, encompassing the values of openness, freedom, diversity and cosmopolitanism.

To achieve this pan-Asian goal ASEAN must remain in the "driver's seat". Thus far ASEAN has played a crucial role in promoting peace and stability in Asia through its engagement with the world's major powers in regional economic and security processes. With the adoption of the new ASEAN charter at the leaders' summit in November 2007 a new dynamism is being added. ASEAN's catalytic role in the decades ahead will be to promote the integration of the three Asian communities and the welfare of their people.

Strength through the middle class

Clearly, ASEAN has to strengthen itself economically and politically before it can aspire to cement the three communities. A second "green revolution" is needed to lift farmers from poverty. The middle class has to expand to include at least a third of the ASEAN population by 2027. That will amount to perhaps 260m people—a magnet for investors and traders.

On the other hand, ASEAN has other challenges to confront in 2008. It can no longer ignore the ethnic and religious violence in the southern Philippines, southern Thailand and parts of Indonesia. Myanmar is another glaring example of how poverty can lead to political upheaval. These problems of human security require common solutions from the emerging East Asian Community.

Ecological degradation is another critical problem. Rapid industrialisation has been accompanied by serious environmental damage and cultural disintegration all over Asia. What was produced by 200 years of industrial revolution in the West has been accumulated in less than 50 years in the East. New models of sustainable development have to be devised to rebalance the relationship between the city and the countryside.

If ASEAN is unable to sustain the successes of the past 40 years, future generations will be less than kind when they sit in judgment on us. The tigers and dragons of the three communities must make haste. ■

Also in this section:
Religion v the state in Israel 96
Staying on in Iraq 97
Federalism for the Arab world? 98
Africa's need for jobs 99
Mo Ibrahim: Criteria for a continent 100

Middle East and Africa

Solving the insoluble

David Landau *JERUSALEM*

Israelis and Palestinians, talking in the shadow of Iran

"Last chance" prognostications are notoriously treacherous, and therefore impolitic. Nevertheless, many local politicians and international peacemakers insist that 2008 is in effect the last chance to reach an Israel-Palestine peace agreement. Last, they say, because if those Palestinians who want a deal don't make one soon and start implementing it, their capacity to do so may evaporate for ever. Chance, because with the Palestinians split now between Fatah pragmatists and Hamas radicals, and the wider Arab world, too, divided between Western-leaning moderates and Iran-led hardliners, this is the moment for Israel's own pragmatic majority to assert itself over the settlers—and at last repartition Palestine.

It may be the last chance, too, to stop Iran, by force if need be, from attaining nuclear-weapons capability. Speculation over whether President George Bush will leave office with Iran's nuclear programme intact is shaping up as the diplomatic leitmotif of 2008, certainly in Tehran and Tel Aviv but also around the world.

Tel Aviv's prosperous streets and crowded nightclubs seem to belie apocalyptic talk. But the good life in Israel is built on an almost obsessive escapism. Beneath is a pervasive fear for the future that troubles rich and poor alike. Israel, which is planning a 60th-anniversary extravaganza in May 2008, is the only post-colonial country whose existence is not entirely taken for granted. Not by other people, and not even by its own people.

Israelis' angst and Palestinians' exhaustion are the foundations on which the world will try once more to build a peace agreement. Tony Blair, the latest envoy of the Middle East Quartet (America, the European Union, the United Nations and Russia), embodies the high hopes and their ephemeral nature. He took on the mission late in 2007 after Hamas in Gaza had bloodily seceded from the Palestinian polity, leaving President Mahmoud Abbas, his authority shrunk to the West Bank, free to negotiate with Israel. But Mr Blair's investment of his prestige is finite. The key for him will be the ability of the moderate Palestinian leadership, with massive international help, to create institutions of government responsive to its people's basic interests.

> Israel may decide that it must act alone against Iran

The Quartet's strategy posits ignoring Hamas, holed up in Gaza, until there is a credible deal on the table, with a clearly defined time-line to statehood and a package of immediate improvements to life. Then, the theory goes, Mr Abbas and his Fatah will have the wherewithal to recover their popular support, in Gaza too.

As for the Israelis, today's peacebrokers hardly need to remind them that 2008 is scarily close to the moment when the Palestinians reach numerical parity with the ▶

2008 IN BRIEF

Iran chooses a new Majlis, but the 270-member legislature will still take second place to the Supreme Ayatollah Khamenei.

David Landau: editor, *Haaretz*

Jews across the whole territory of Palestine (the West Bank, Gaza and Israel itself). Yossi Beilin, who negotiated for Israel in 2000-01 and now leads the doveish Meretz party, says this will happen in 2010.

This mind-concentrating demography is at last penetrating the Israeli escapist mindset. Israelis were aghast to read in 2007 of British trade unions seeking to boycott the Jewish state. Foreign references to apartheid South Africa are vehemently rejected. But the realisation is seeping in that if the Jews do become the minority, while the occupation of the West Bank continues, then the South African analogy will be less easy to refute.

Ariel Sharon's unilateral withdrawal from the Gaza Strip in 2005 was intended to allay "the demographic danger" by redefining the arithmetic. But the 1.6m Gazans remain part of the equation as long as Gaza is besieged, with only Palestinian rockets and missile-firing Israeli drones crossing the barbed-wire border.

Mr Sharon probably planned to pull out of much of the West Bank too. His successor, Ehud Olmert, wants to leave almost all of it, swapping sovereign Israeli soil for the big blocks of settlements built along and beyond the old pre-1967 border.

But however obvious and inexorable the outlines of a territorial solution seem, the prospect of Israel agreeing to implement it is darkly clouded by the incessant firing of rockets from Gaza. They cause relatively little death and damage, but they make life in the towns and kibbutzim near the Strip horribly tense.

Mr Olmert will need to deliver reassuring answers in 2008 if the negotiation is to succeed. He must keep his disparate coalition together while promoting the very policy that can easily break it apart. Shas, an Orthodox party, is wary of proposals to redivide Jerusalem into its Israeli and Palestinian components. Yisrael Beiteinu, a nationalist party mainly of Russian immigrants, is uncomfortable with the prospect of forcibly dismantling scores of settlements. Even Labour, Mr Olmert's largest and most doveish ally, is being awkward. Its leader, the minister of defence, Ehud Barak, says Israel cannot pull back until it has developed and deployed an anti-missile shield—which could take years.

But Mr Olmert's position going into 2008 is a good deal stronger than a year before. Then he was still staggering under the embarrassing failure of the summer 2006 war in Lebanon. He has weathered the worst of that, and, while still not popular, should survive into 2009. Mr Barak, the Likud party's Binyamin Netanyahu and three or even four members of his own Kadima party all want his job—and Mr Olmert is famously adept at leveraging such rivalries to his benefit.

The cynics say Mr Olmert's strategy will be to negotiate over the principles of peace and fudge on their implementation. Mr Abbas, navigating between the world's encouragement and Hamas's excoriation, needs visible, tangible progress.

Enter the Persians

His strongest ally, in typically perverse Middle Eastern logic, is fire-breathing Iran. If Iran is to be defanged, by sanctions or by force of American and allied arms, successful containment of the subsequent fallout could be largely determined by the Israeli-Arab conflict. A deal over Palestine could cement an axis of Muslim moderation, leaving Tehran stricken and isolated.

That calculation is not new, of course. But the advent of 2008 gives it new urgency. For Israelis who doubt the world's determination to prevent Iran's nuclearisation, but are themselves determined not to acquiesce in it, the need to "clear the decks" of the Palestine conflict is, if anything, even starker. Israel may decide that it must act alone against Iran in 2008, possibly in the hope that its action would trigger a larger American action. An untrumpeted Israeli air and ground attack in September 2007 on a secret Syrian nuclear facility, supplied by North Korea with Iranian connivance, was read throughout the region as a signal of Israel's refusal to accept Iran's nuclear ambition. ■

A bitter shmita

Gideon Lichfield *JERUSALEM*

Israel's rowing rabbis

...on the other hand

The Jewish year that ends in the autumn of 2008 is a *shmita* (sabbatical) year, when the Torah enjoins Jewish farmers to let their land rest. In the past, Israeli rabbis have granted kosher certificates to farmers who kept cultivating, so long as they symbolically sold their land to a non-Jew for the year. But now the Ashkenazi chief rabbinate, one of the two supreme religious authorities, is refusing.

Such disputes among rabbis, and between rabbis and the state, will grow. Over *shmita*, this is because ultra-Orthodox Jews, who care less for Zionism than for fastidious Jewish observance, have slowly come to dominate the Ashkenazi chief rabbinate.

The question of "who is a Jew"—and who can be an Israeli—is also rearing its head. In 2007 the country was outraged by young neo-Nazis, mostly ex-Soviet immigrants. That prompted calls on the religious right to tighten the "law of return", which grants citizenship to Jews and their immediate (but not necessarily Jewish) relatives.

The young generation is also showing up the rigidity of the Jewish state's laws. Some are not full citizens, despite having been born in Israel. And, since rabbis will not marry them, pressure is building for a form of civil marriage. But the rabbis will not relinquish their monopoly. A supreme court ruling that Israel must recognise same-sex marriages performed abroad provoked fury. So did another, that non-Orthodox converts to Judaism abroad are eligible for citizenship.

Such disputes could turn political. Ultra-Orthodox parties have often made up the numbers in Israel's coalitions, and Ehud Olmert might need them in 2008. That would mean buying their loyalty, and possibly causing a new secular-religious spat. ■

Gideon Lichfield: Jerusalem correspondent, *The Economist*

On and on in Iraq

Xan Smiley

The Americans won't be leaving yet

The choice in Iraq between "stay and pray" and "cut and run" will get painfully acute but neither course will be definitively taken, no matter who is elected American president in November 2008. In any event, George Bush will start to reduce the size of his forces in Iraq, while continuing to insist that the United States is determined to "stay the course" and not leave America's Iraqi allies in the lurch. By the time he leaves office in January 2009, he will have drawn his troop numbers down to 100,000 from 160,000 at the height of the military "surge" in 2007. The really hard question—whether to withdraw from Iraq at a much faster rate—will be one for his successor.

But the president-elect will not be able to cut and run in a hurry, even if he—or she—wants to. If, say, Hillary Clinton wins with a promise to "bring the boys home", she will not do so much before the end of 2009. Indeed, she may give herself enough wiggle room to keep a sizeable force there, especially if the cautious optimism of America's commander-in-the-field, General David Petraeus, is borne out.

> Irrespective of what the Americans do, several vital political questions will have to be answered by Iraqis themselves

The Kurds of northern Iraq, who have carved out a wide measure of autonomy, are one problem. Several would-be American presidents, Mrs Clinton among others, have sounded loth to let them be clobbered once again by Iraq's Arabs in the event of an American walk-out. There will be growing talk in 2008, even in Democrat circles, of keeping an American base in Kurdistan—and perhaps elsewhere in Iraq—even if most American troops are withdrawn from the chief Iraqi battlefields, where the antagonists will mainly be Iraqis fighting each other.

The Kurds will be furious at the postponement in 2007 of a promised referendum on the disputed city and province of Kirkuk. Will they accept yet another postponement in 2008? Grudgingly, perhaps. If they are wise, they will hold back from forcing the issue on Kirkuk, quietly consolidate their autonomy in the area they fully control, and perhaps, in lieu of getting Kirkuk, clinch agreements giving them more control over the management and exploration of oil.

Elsewhere in Iraq, by the middle of 2008 the surge will have run its course—for good or ill. The horrendous bloodletting in Baghdad will diminish, though it will persist at a frightening rate. Ethnic cleansing will continue too, so that formerly mixed areas where Sunnis and Shias once lived together in Baghdad and other big cities, including Mosul, Basra and Kirkuk, will become preserves of one sect or the other. Baghdad, which was around 70% Sunni Arab half a century ago, will become 70% Shia, with the Sunnis holding just a wedge in the west, plus a few beleaguered pockets elsewhere. Iraq's Christian population will be reduced to a shred of what it was before.

George Bush's legacy

The Americans' much-vaunted success in 2007 in persuading several of the Sunni sheikhs in the big tribes of Anbar province to the west of Baghdad to fight against the more extreme insurgents loyal to al-Qaeda may be sustained, though the arming of them will unnerve the Shia Arab ruling establishment in Baghdad. Some of the American-armed Sunni tribes will turn their weapons against their Shia compatriots.

Searching for answers

Irrespective of what the Americans do, several vital political questions will have to be answered by Iraqis themselves in 2008.

The first is whether Sunnis and Shias in parliament will forge an accommodation so that Iraq's coalition government is more than just a collection of competing fiefs. As the Americans draw down their troop numbers the new Iraqi political establishment may come to its senses and realise that only if power is genuinely shared is there a chance of defeating the extreme insurgents and making peace with the rest.

There was no sign of this happening in 2007; there is only a small chance that it will happen in 2008. Most Shias, mindful of their inferior status for the past half-millennium, will remain reluctant to share power, while the Sunni Arabs, refusing to accept that they comprise ▶

2008 IN BRIEF

Mozambique and Tanzania complete a **"bridge to nowhere"** over the Rovuma river, after more than 30 years on the drawing board. A ferry would have been cheaper, because there will be little traffic for the bridge.

Xan Smiley: Middle East and Africa editor, *The Economist*

2008 IN BRIEF

Anxious to be a media centre, Abu Dhabi launches an **English-language newspaper** with 200 journalists hired mainly from Europe and America.

a mere fifth of Iraqis, will seek, in vain, to resume their traditional control.

In 2008 it will become clearer whether Iraq is heading towards fragmentation, with Baghdad physically divided much as Beirut was in Lebanon's civil war between 1975 and 1990, or whether the Shias and Sunnis agree to keep the country united, albeit with a measure of devolution to the provinces. Fragmentation involving Arabs and Kurds would not be a simple three-way split; in both Sunni and Shia areas, power would splinter among competing tribes and factions.

Competition to emerge as the leading voice among the Shia Arabs will intensify, sometimes bloodily. A power struggle is almost sure to break out in 2008 between the three main groups: the Dawa party, which has provided the prime minister, Nuri al-Maliki; the Supreme Islamic Iraqi Council (SIIC), hitherto the party closest to Iran; and the group following Muqtada al-Sadr and his Mahdi Army militia, easily Iraq's biggest.

Mr Maliki will be lucky to hold on to his post. The power of Dawa and SIIC will wane, while Mr Sadr's will wax. And the influence of Grand Ayatollah Ali al-Sistani, who has been Iraq's pre-eminent clergyman and a powerful force for moderation, will probably fade too.

At the same time, no Sunni Arab interlocutor with the power to speak authoritatively for the non-al-Qaeda insurgents will emerge. But a front consisting of the four or five biggest of such groups may be formed and perhaps put out signals that it will negotiate.

One of the most critical trends in 2008 will be towards an internationalisation of peacemaking. A permanent group of regional countries will probably shape up, including, controversially, Syria and Iran, as well as Saudi Arabia, Turkey and Jordan. In this respect, the big question in 2008 will be whether Iran emerges as a stabiliser or a spoiler. It has been in two minds: it wants its fellow Shia in Iraq to entrench their power; but it also wants the Americans to be humiliated, which means wanting continuing chaos. Much therefore will depend on Iranian-American relations over Iran's suspected nuclear programme.

The United Nations' presence and involvement in Iraq will also deepen. Although the Bush administration will be reluctant to give it too much of a say, both the Americans and their Iraqi allies in Baghdad will come to realise they cannot end the conflict on their own. By the end of 2008, international peacemaking, if not yet a peace, will have begun in earnest. ■

Arab federalism, anyone?

Xan Smiley

An idea whose time is yet to come

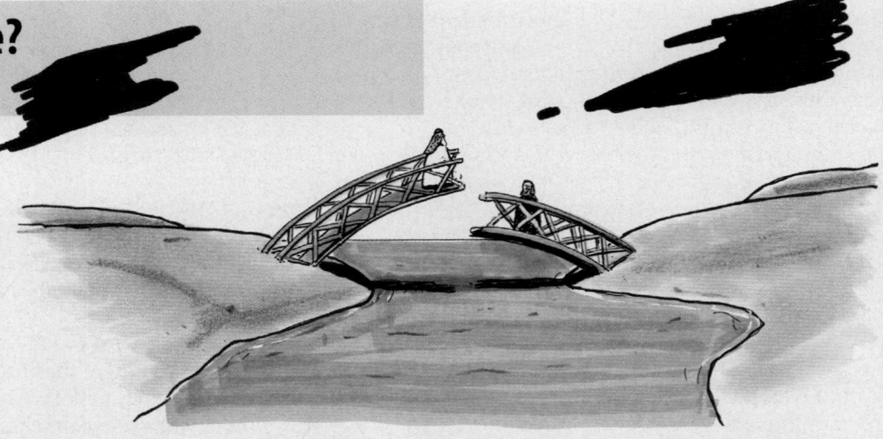

The notion of federalism is generally disliked, at least by the Arab world's predominant Sunni majority, as an old imperial device to divide and rule and undermine the *umma*, the community of Muslim nations—particularly, of late, in Iraq. Indeed, there is no proper Arabic word for it, so that, like other borrowed political terms such as *dimokratiya*, it can easily be discredited. Yet the idea, if embraced, could bring a lot more stability.

The main problem is that most Arab leaders think that decentralising power risks their losing it altogether. A number of mainly Arab countries have regions that resent domination: witness Iraqi Kurdistan, but also Saudi Arabia's Hijaz, Libya's Cyrenaica, Algeria's Berber-inhabited Kabylia, Morocco's Western Sahara (not internationally recognised as part of Morocco) and southern Sudan. Lebanon has a clutch of regions and communities that resist domination by any one particular group.

> There is no proper Arabic word for it

Some supposedly federal experiments have been tried in the Arab world. In the United Arab Emirates power is split between the seven emirates and federal institutions, but it is essentially a deal between the two richer emirates—Dubai and Abu Dhabi—to pay off the poorer five. No one challenges the right to rule of any of the seven families.

Of the other recent models, Gamal Abdul Nasser's United Arab Republic lasted only from 1958 to 1961: Nasser wanted to run Syria like a province, and failed. The two Yemens were meant to be a federal union when they came together in 1990 but the system was re-centralised after the north squashed the south in 1994.

Talk in Algeria about autonomy for the Berbers has failed to materialise in practice; it would be hard to define their territory. Morocco's Berbers are dispersed, too; Morocco also wants to settle its dispute with the Western Saharans by granting them some autonomy inside a kind of federal system, but the Sahraouis want independence.

Though Lebanon is divided into de facto feudal-cum-party cantons, its key institutions are highly centralised. A division of power at the centre is still extraordinarily hard to agree to. Hence the occasionally bloody stalemate that is likely to continue into 2008.

Sudan is a grim example of an Arab-run government, at the centre in Khartoum, deeply reluctant to embrace a federal solution for the non-Arab south and for Darfur in the west, for fear of losing power across the board.

Yet models such as mainly Muslim Malaysia, or even Spain or Germany, could suit Arab countries. One day, more Arab rulers will seriously think federal. But the example of Iraq does not inspire them. ■

Wanted: jobs for Africans

Jonathan Ledgard *MWANZA, SUKUMALAND*

Between boosterism and desperation

For Africa, 2008 will be the year of the jobless. Millions of rural poor will, as ever, go hungry and perish from curable diseases, but the focus in 2008 will be on the continent's cities and towns. The failure to create new jobs in the slums will lead to strikes, riots and a further rise in violent crime and political instability. Africa's economies will grow, many by 6% or more, but the urban underclass will grow still faster. The African Union, in its attempt to be taken more seriously on a range of political and economic issues, will launch discussions on how to increase the workforce, but little clear action will be taken.

> After a golden year in 2007 China will suffer a reverse in popularity in Africa

As a result, gangs will prosper. Kenya's Mungiki gang started decapitating its enemies in 2007. More terror is in prospect in 2008 as gangsters take a potent mix of tribal history and popular culture, drawing on American and Jamaican swagger, to recruit more disaffected young men.

Foreign investment will remain too small to have much influence on Africa's population. Most of it will continue to be extractive: oil and gas in west Africa; gems, ores and logging in central and east Africa. Some progress will be made in securing rights to Congo's trove, but not in the building of the new roads and railways needed to bring the minerals to market. Outside South Africa, Egypt and the Maghreb, manufacturing will remain limited. In several countries the dumping of cheap manufactured Chinese goods will become an issue. Indeed, after a golden year in 2007 China will suffer a reverse in popularity in Africa. Enthusiasm for turning over large parts of tropical Africa to biofuels will also falter in 2008.

Immigration policies will restrict the number of work visas available to foreigners. A similar populism, fuelled by unemployment, will also work against potentially useful measures to legalise dual-citizenship and finally capitalise on Africa's large and increasingly wealthy diaspora. At the same time, new biometric passports and more forceful policing of borders will make it much harder for undocumented Africans to get into and stay in the European Union. Record numbers of young Africans drowned or were otherwise killed in 2007 trying to escape the continent. More will die in 2008.

The city of Mwanza, population around 500,000, can serve as a benchmark for Africa's challenges and opportunities. There has been hope of remaking this capital of Tanzania's Sukumaland, on the south shore of Lake Victoria, as the new metropolis of east Africa. That will remain a dream, but tower blocks will go up in 2008 and a new lakeside park will be opened. Swanky villas will be built on the rocky points overlooking the lake, to make the most of the sunsets. The region's eerie beauty has unrealised tourism potential, but malaria, AIDS and also bilharzia mean that it will remain untapped.

This kind of disease-burden matters, as does the mud-hut poverty of Mwanza's hinterland, but more telling is the state of the local shipping. Ferries ply routes across Lake Victoria from Mwanza as far as Kenya and Uganda. The larger vessels are old and decrepit. Rusting on their moorings, they ask a question: how did they make it overland to Lake Victoria in the first place? In fact, they were built in Glasgow and Belfast, came in pieces, and were reassembled by shipbuilders during the colonial period. Those kinds of skills and capital are long gone. Newer boats are smaller and less impressive.

The fishing trade, similarly, has failed to move on. It is rudimentary and dominated by middlemen—the same middlemen who own the villas. But the modest attractions of Mwanza are such that it will suck in new poor in 2008. Mwanza's officials are caught, like Africa at large, between boosterism and desperation. The city needs to create several thousand new jobs in 2008 just to keep up with the inflow—and the chances are poor. ■

Teeming masses

Annual growth of urban populations in Africa, % 2006

Source: African Development Bank

Some Rastafarians believe that the late **Haile Selassie** of Ethiopia will rise from the dead on April 5th, after 33.3 years, the approximate age at which Jesus Christ died.

2008 IN BRIEF

Jonathan Ledgard: eastern Africa correspondent, *The Economist*

Criteria for a continent

Africa's problems stem from bad governance, argues **Mo Ibrahim** of the Mo Ibrahim Foundation. So why not reward good governance?

"Out of Africa always something new"—broad generalisations do Africa a disservice but Pliny the Elder, writing 2,000 years ago, identified a truism. Predictions for the world's second-most-populous continent should be undertaken with caution.

What, then, can we say with confidence about Africa in 2008? According to the United Nations Economic Commission for Africa, the region's economies will grow on average by over 5% in 2008. In 2008 we can also expect to see increased levels of investment on the continent. There are concerns about how and where some of these investments will be made, but better we have this debate than the old one about whether to invest at all.

These are not sudden phenomena; they are hard-won gains, showing that after years of reform—and some significant setbacks—African economies are making progress. This positive economic news marks a watershed in Africa's history and dispels the prevailing view of the continent as a region of undifferentiated hardship and despair. It is also evidence that Africa is set on a new era—one that could, if the necessary conditions are put in place, deliver lasting change in the fortunes of the continent's people.

It is a change that is much needed. Some 300m people on the continent live in poverty, with little or no access to the most basic resources. In the past quarter-century—during which 500m people managed to escape poverty worldwide—the number of poor in sub-Saharan Africa nearly doubled.

There are no simple answers to Africa's development challenges. If there were, we would have found them by now. But we can identify some fundamentals that must be put in place.

There are no simple answers to Africa's development challenges. If there were, we would have found them by now. But we can identify some fundamentals that must be put in place

It is clear to me that one issue above others will determine Africa's future: good governance. It is central to the effective administration of a state's resources, the rule of law, the creation of a functioning private sector and the development of a strong civil society.

Yet even if we agree about the primacy of good governance, the concept has seemed too opaque to be of practical use. Because we haven't had a widely held, detailed definition of what constitutes good governance, there was little by which we could judge the performance of our governments. And so, whereas the governance of a company dealing with several hundred employees and a few million dollars of investors' money is judged against comprehensive data, the governance of an entire nation is judged on relatively little.

Politics may be the art of the possible, as Otto von Bismarck remarked, but performance must be judged against objective criteria. Outlining those criteria and benchmarking performance against them is the vision of the Mo Ibrahim Foundation. With the support of the Kennedy School of Government and an advisory council of eminent African academics, the foundation has devised an index of governance, assessing all sub-Saharan African countries against 58 objective measures that together define good governance.

Vision and scrutiny

The Ibrahim Index of African Governance is shining a light on governance in Africa and, in so doing, improving its quality. Progress is being made: for the period assessed by the first Ibrahim index (2000-05), overall governance performance in sub-Saharan Africa improved. To be sure, not all countries improved. According to the Ibrahim index, governance deteriorated in just under a quarter of the region's countries.

The index will be updated yearly, providing a scorecard of national progress assessed against objective criteria, and a framework for African civil society to engage its leaders in a debate about how we are governed. This is an African initiative, occupying a space which donors, investors and governments are not able to fill. It is about Africans taking ownership, developing their own forms of accountability, and delivering change. It is about Africans setting benchmarks that the world can emulate.

In my professional life, I was involved in establishing mobile-telephone networks in Africa. Just over a decade ago, when Celtel—the company I founded—started business, there were only 2m mobile phones in Africa. Today there are nearly 200m and the continent is the fastest-growing mobile-phone market in the world. Africa has embraced mobile communications and is leapfrogging ahead, achieving technological and developmental gains that few envisaged.

For me, this speaks volumes about the potential of Africa. Improved governance is absolutely fundamental to realising that potential. And if Africa can leapfrog ahead with technology, then why not with governance? ■

Joaquim Chissano, president of Mozambique from 1986 to 2005, was awarded the first Mo Ibrahim Prize for Achievement in African Leadership in October 2007. The annual prize consists of $5m over ten years and $200,000 a year for life thereafter.

Also in this section:
Last year's predictions 102
Health is a good investment 103
The human tide 104
Cultural highlights 105
Angelina Jolie: A year for accountability 106
Hope against dope in sport 107
The year of the potato 107
Ban Ki-moon: The spirit of principled pragmatism 108
The future of futurology 110
Microtrends for 2008 111

International

The paradoxical politics of energy

Gideon Rachman

The urge to get off oil—and to find more of the stuff

Politicians worry about energy when the oil price is high. But the energy crisis of 2008 will be quite unlike the oil crises of the 1970s and 1980s for a simple reason—climate change.

Panic over global warming means that the world now faces two different sorts of energy anxiety. The first revolves around the familiar struggle for affordable fuel. The second concerns the battle to combat climate change by reducing emissions of greenhouse gases.

In theory, these two worries point in the same direction. The world's leading economies need to find new and cleaner sources of energy, allowing them to reduce their dependence on fossil fuels. In practice, things are not so simple. The problem is that new forms of clean energy are—as yet—simply not convincing enough alternatives to oil and gas. Some 97% of the American transport system is still dependent on oil. A long-term perspective demands that the world's leading economies reduce their dependence on fossil fuels. The short-term imperative is still to find more of the stuff.

As a result, in 2008 politicians will talk a great deal about the need to achieve a new international agreement on climate change. But big-country leaders will also spend a lot of time trying to secure access to the very fossil fuels that they keep saying they are trying to forswear.

At the G8 summit of leading industrialised nations, to be held in Japan in July, the Americans will insist that the next deal on climate change must include China, India and other developing nations. This is reasonable enough, given that China is surpassing the United States as the world's largest emitter of greenhouse gases. The Chinese themselves are genuinely alarmed about the implications of climate change. Any eventual deal will probably involve Americans and Europeans essentially bribing the Chinese and Indians to cut emissions—through a global system of tradable emissions permits.

But do not expect the world's leaders to move much beyond general principles in 2008. The Chinese are very nervous about agreeing to anything that might slow their economy down and create unemployment. And the Americans will need a lot of persuading that a global emissions-trading system can work. In 2008 it may fall to the European Union to make the biggest contribution to global carbon-trading. The EU has already established the world's most elaborate trading scheme. But its first phase damaged the credibility of carbon trading because it was far too lax. Phase two will kick in during 2008 and will be closely watched to see if it is any more effective.

Meanwhile, the drive to find new supplies of fossil fuels will go on. The Chinese will continue their energy-driven diplomatic offensive in Africa—pursuing more deals like their controversial oil agreement with Sudan. At home, China will keep opening new coal-fired power plants at a rate for equivalent Western-sized plants of almost one a day, to the despair of global-warming activists around the world.

In Europe, the geopolitics of energy will be dominated by the increasingly tense relationship between Russia and the EU. The Russians will maintain their

Gideon Rachman: chief foreign-affairs columnist, *Financial Times*

▶

efforts to secure long-term deals to supply energy within the EU, while buying stakes in energy companies inside the union. The governments of western and central Europe will try to reduce their dependence on Russia. But their national divisions will make this harder.

Big-country leaders will spend a lot of time trying to secure access to the very fossil fuels they are trying to forswear

In 2008, however, the EU may agree upon a common policy to limit Russian investment in EU energy assets—unless the Russians agree to open up their own energy markets further to foreign investment. The whole thrust of Russian domestic energy policy in recent years has been to lessen the involvement of foreign companies in the Russian energy sector. And, whatever the EU does, this policy is likely to continue in 2008. One deal to watch out for is the Sakhalin-1 oil and gas field, where Russia may try to put pressure on ExxonMobil, an American firm. The coming year may also see the intensification of an emerging struggle to claim sovereignty over the Arctic. The participants include Russia, Canada, America, Norway and Denmark. All of these countries are interested in previously unpromising stretches of tundra because global warming is making it easier to navigate the waters of the Arctic—and to get access to the fossil fuels beneath the ice.

The struggle for the Arctic (see the lead article in our Science section), like the new claims in Antarctica, is a perfect symbol of the paradoxical politics of energy in 2008. The world's leading industrial nations bemoan global warming and the fossil fuels that help to cause it. But they also stand ready to profit from global warming—by digging under the Poles for more fossil fuels. ■

2008 IN BRIEF

Celebrities and the idle rich compete in the **Gumball 3000** car rally. Often marked by its participants' misbehaviour, the race begins in San Francisco and ends—via North Korea—in Beijing.

Predictably right and wrong

Daniel Franklin

A look at our own track record

There is no Olympic competition for predictions, but if there were, how well might *The World in 2008* perform? In any sport, the obvious place to search for guidance on a team's chances of success is past form. So, with the benefit of hindsight, let's look at *The World in 2007*. How did we do?

In quite a few events, especially European ones, we got lucky. We called the French presidential election correctly, predicted the violent breakdown of the Spanish government's peace efforts with the Basque terrorists of ETA, flagged the likelihood of a clash between secularists and Islamists in Turkey, and sketched out how the European Union's rejected constitutional treaty would be resuscitated in a new form. In Britain, the handover from Tony Blair to Gordon Brown played out pretty much as we expected—as did Russia's use of its energy strength to throw its weight around.

It seems unfair to claim a medal for predicting the obvious, such as gridlock in the United States between the Republican White House and the newly Democratic Congress. But our economic forecast for America (no recession in 2007, despite a housing slump and general glumness) was a harder call, and proved right. So did the forecast for the global economy: slower but still rapid growth, with emerging markets leading the way. We spotted the coming backlash against private equity, as well as the pervasive presence of climate change on the global agenda.

A golden year, then? Hardly. In three entirely predictable ways, our performance fell short.

First, we were of course plain wrong about a number of things. We thought Canada would have a general election in 2007; it didn't. We reckoned the government of Japan's new prime minister, Shinzo Abe, to be "in the driving seat"; in fact, Mr Abe was driven out. We fondly imagined immigration reform might actually happen in America; yet the gridlock in Washington, DC, proved even worse than we envisaged. As usual, our sports predictions were rubbish: we expected New Zealand to win the Rugby World Cup (France knocked them out in the quarter-final), and the Cricket World Cup in the Caribbean was to be a joy (it turned out to be a fiasco).

Second, we were sometimes over-eager and jumped the starting-gun. Things that were meant to be ready in 2007—the start-up of the world's biggest particle accelerator at CERN near Geneva, the reopening of the Plaza hotel in New York, the disbanding of the Netherlands Antilles—will in fact happen in 2008.

Third, and most important, some of the main events of 2007 turned out (as they do every year) to be ones that were completely off our radar screen. We didn't mention monks in Myanmar. The word "subprime" was not in our vocabulary. We were silent about collapsed bridges in Minneapolis, forest fires in Greece and the recall of toys made in China. Closer to home, we did not forecast that there would be miserable floods in Britain, or a run on a bank—let alone that Mr Brown would have Lady Thatcher round for tea at Downing Street.

All these are healthy reminders of what to expect of our latest batch of predictions for the coming Olympic year. We can hope to impress in some events. In others, we'll no doubt disappoint. And a few we'll miss out altogether. That's the nature—but also the fun—of these forecasting games. ■

Daniel Franklin: editor, *The World in 2008*

Stopping the plagues

Michel Kazatchkine

Investing in health can create stronger economies

At the beginning of this decade a revolution was set in motion. The world began to see that health was essential to achieving development, rather than just something countries could award themselves once they had dragged themselves out of poverty. Leaders began devoting attention and resources to fighting the diseases that take the greatest toll on the poor: AIDS, tuberculosis, malaria and vaccine-preventable diseases. Less than ten years later, the investments are showing results.

Major global health financiers, such as the Global Fund to Fight AIDS, Tuberculosis and Malaria and the Global Alliance for Vaccines and Immunisation, are showing concrete returns on their investments. In less than four years, financing through the Global Fund alone has resulted in more than 1.1m people receiving treatment for AIDS. Now, overall, more than 2m people receive AIDS treatment—a tenfold increase in four years. Tuberculosis treatment has been brought to nearly 3m people. And more than 30m insecticide-treated bed nets have been distributed to protect families from malaria. The number of people saved from early death through these interventions is already 2m, and this increases by 100,000 every month. Child mortality has dropped by as much as 90% in endemic areas that have taken effective malaria control to scale, such as in southern Mozambique.

The number of people saved from early death increases by 100,000 every month

Those who have regained their health are able to care for their children, return to work and lead meaningful, productive lives. Eventually, societies hobbled by severe declines in human capital due to illness and death will be able to translate these gains into economic growth. A study by Yale University's Economic Growth Centre showed a 20% increase in labour-force participation and a 35% increase in hours worked among AIDS patients in western Kenya within six months of starting treatment with antiretroviral drugs.

Investment in disease prevention and treatment also enables countries to begin thinking about putting in place the building blocks of sustainable social protection, such as health insurance. Rwanda provides an inspirational example in the form of community-based health-insurance schemes that use aid as seed money to pay health-insurance premiums for the poor.

Remedy for some
Projected coverage of antiretroviral treatment* 2008, %

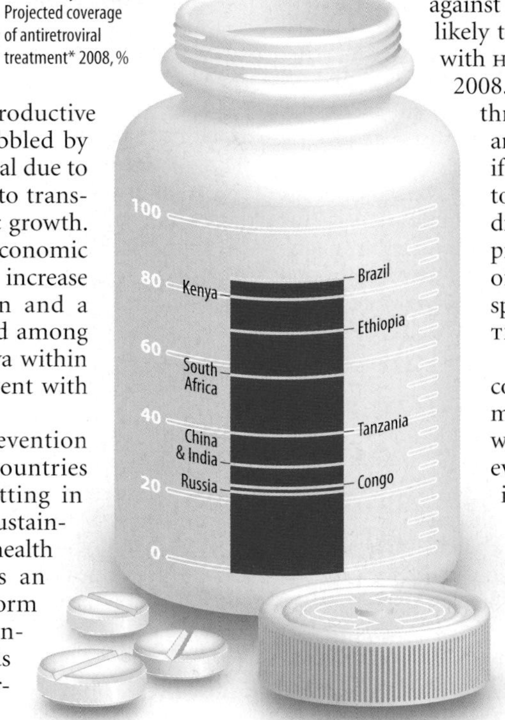

Source: UNAIDS

*At 2005-06 rate of increase

Countries are increasingly being encouraged to convert some of their national debt into funding for programmes that provide health services. This involves a creditor cancelling a portion of a country's debt on the condition that the beneficiary invests some of the savings in health. In 2007 Germany made the first offer to forgo repayment of €50m ($70m) on the condition that Indonesia invests the equivalent of €25m in health. Kenya, Pakistan and Peru are expected to follow with similar agreements.

Improving maternal and child health and gaining control over AIDS, TB and malaria are essential to reaching the Millennium Development Goals which the United Nations agreed to as part of a push to halve the number of people living in poverty by 2015. In order to do so, two things must happen. First, the world must continue to increase its investments in health: $20 billion-$30 billion a year would do the trick, less than 5% of the growth in global wealth that is now being generated annually. Second, the numerous streams of resources available need to be channelled more effectively—for example, in support of national health plans developed by countries themselves, not driven by multiple initiatives and donor priorities.

Encouragingly, the funds transferred to countries by the Global Fund are projected to top $2 billion for the first time in 2008, helping to accelerate the fight against the three diseases. For TB, we expect an increase in the number of countries reaching their case-detection and treatment targets. Wider access to the more effective artemisinin-based combination therapies, along with acceptance of the need for large-scale distribution of insecticide-treated bed nets, will offer real hope that major gains can be made in the fight against malaria. The developing world is likely to reach the target of 3m people with HIV on antiretroviral treatment in 2008. However, this milestone comes three years later than was hoped, and progress remains far too slow if the G8 goal of universal access is to be achieved by 2010. There is discouragingly little sign of major progress in reducing the number of new HIV infections, and the spread of drug-resistant strains of TB remains a serious concern.

AIDS, tuberculosis and malaria continue to take a terrible toll on millions of lives in the developing world. Certainly, we must make every effort to build general health infrastructure and capacity in poor countries over the long term. But the opportunities for economic and social advancement through immediate and aggressive action are also enormous. Tackling these major killers remains the most pressing public-health challenge of our time. ■

2008 IN BRIEF

Thanks to the UN General Assembly, 2008 is the **International Year of Planet Earth**. The aim is to raise $20m to educate the world about earth sciences and their impact on society.

Michel Kazatchkine: executive director, Global Fund to Fight AIDS, TB and Malaria

A world in flux

Adam Roberts

As with goods and capital, labour is moving quicker

People move country for many reasons. Refugees become job-seekers; pensioners retire abroad; climate change is beginning to dislodge large numbers of those vulnerable to rising seas and worsening droughts. The reasons may be varied but the result, in 2008, will be simple: plenty of people on the move. Estimates of the number of migrants (ie, people living in a foreign country) may pass 200m, 3% of the world's population.

Just as capital and goods are moving more freely, labour seems to be flowing more quickly too. As rich-country natives grey, migrants—especially those with skills—will be in ever greater demand. Some industries in the West, notably construction, elderly care and agriculture, would grind to a halt without foreign hands.

The human tide will ebb and flow. As housing booms end in countries which have seen lots of migrants—Ireland, Britain, Spain, Greece—young east Europeans may turn elsewhere. Germany faces a severe shortage of skilled hands, and may see bigger flows. More young Poles and Hungarians in the West will be tempted by rising wages back home.

The pitiful sight of Africans bobbing in the Mediterranean may grow less common. Despite some awful cases, fewer migrants reportedly made the hazardous sea trip in 2007 than in the year before. European co-operation to deter them will get a bit more effective as patrol boats, helicopters and spotter planes are deployed. At the same time the Schengen area—which allows passport-free movement of people between member countries—will be extended eastwards within the European Union. Barriers at land and sea borders are to be lifted by January 1st, and at airports by April. Look out, too, for more use of technology to monitor migrants: the EU wants to expand a centralised system for storing and sharing fingerprints that currently covers asylum-seekers. In more enthusiastic places, like Britain, the collection of fingerprints from visa applicants and passport holders will become the norm.

Putting up more fences—literally, on the American border with Mexico—will not stop illegal migration, at least not while rich countries demand cheap and flexible labour without offering legal entry routes. The trouble is politics. France's president, Nicolas Sarkozy, won a handsome electoral victory in 2007 partly by talking tough about foreigners. Mr Sarkozy will probably make integration of migrants a theme of the French presidency of the EU in the second half of 2008. He wants more integration tests, language courses and tougher rules for the reunification of families. In Europe (as in America) there is growing unease about dual citizenship.

At the same time, however, Europe will debate how to attract more skilled foreign workers from the rest of the world. There will be a push to make it easier for the highest-skilled migrants to move easily within the EU, to let their families accompany them and to let spouses work. "Points systems" (when young and well-educated migrants are ushered in quickly to rich countries) will get more popular. Britain will introduce such a points-based approach. A wider gap will open between the welcome for skilled and unskilled foreigners in Europe.

In America public hostility towards 12m illegal foreign residents killed George Bush's immigration-reform efforts in 2007—the idea was to tighten borders while offering a route for the undocumented to become legal. So expect more crackdowns on American employers who use undocumented labour in 2008, in an effort to stop the exploitation of alien workers and to persuade the public that immigration can be controlled. That might make it possible to reconsider reforms in a few years' time. In the 2008 elections, however, tough talk on migration will win votes.

Squaring the circle

The Global Forum on Migration and Development meets in the Philippines in 2008 to ruminate on how to use remittances to cut poverty. Another theme which will get international attention is the notion of temporary workers' schemes—rebranded as "circular migration". The idea may be easier to sell to voters in rich countries, as the circular bit implies the workers go home when they are no longer needed. In practice, forcing people to leave is never easy.

Another trend to watch is emigration from rich countries. Booming Asia is already drawing in highly skilled Westerners. Many skilled migrants will re-emigrate. It is becoming more normal for the well-educated and wealthy to spend a large part of the year in someone else's country. Around 5m Britons, out of 60m, now live abroad (Australia and Spain get many of them) and it is not just the wrinkly who go. The market for talented people is increasingly fierce—and global. ■

It is becoming more normal for the well-educated and wealthy to spend at least a large part of the year in someone else's country

2008 IN BRIEF

Travellers increasingly stay in touch through the **Cubic cellphone**, which uses the internet to provide cheap international calls—and with no monthly fee.

Adam Roberts: news editor, Economist.com

Artistic fireworks

Steve King

A preview of the year's cultural highlights

Pigs will fly at New York's Guggenheim Museum in 2008. Tigers and wolves too. And fleets of cars, levitating 20 feet above the gallery floor, radiating shafts of light as if they had been frozen in mid-explosion. But these strange apparitions will be nothing to worry about: just some of the works by Cai Guo-Qiang, a remarkable Chinese artist, on display for his mid-career retrospective. It is sure to be one of the outstanding exhibitions of 2008.

For the past 20 years or so Mr Cai (pronounced "tsigh") has been dazzling audiences with his spectacular installations and happenings—often dazzling them quite literally, through his use of pyrotechnics. He is best known for his "Projects for Extraterrestrials": outdoor pieces that use sequences of explosions to create short-lived symbolic patterns. One of his biggest firework displays, detonated above Central Park in 2003, produced a 1,000-foot (305-metre) halo over the reservoir.

Not all of his works are on such a large scale. He is also known for his gunpowder drawings, in which he arranges and ignites gunpowder on paper or canvas, controlling the burn patterns with carefully placed stones and pieces of board. Gunpowder provides a strong link to ancient Chinese tradition, which informs much of Mr Cai's work.

"Cai Guo-Qiang: I Want To Believe" opens on February 22nd at the Guggenheim in New York, then travels to the National Museum of China in Beijing in August, possibly to Japan, and finally on to the Guggenheim Bilbao in 2009. A further bonus for Mr Cai's admirers: as he is the man behind the special effects for the 2008 Beijing Olympics, you can be sure that the opening and closing ceremonies will be stunning.

Do not expect fireworks to mark the quatercentenary of John Milton's birth. Milton is, by general consent, one of the greatest poets to have written in any language at any time. But he is not the kind to inspire wild celebrations. The idea of throwing a party to celebrate his birthday—400th or otherwise—seems wincingly inappropriate, like taking your grandmother to a pole-dancing club.

Nevertheless, some will try. Christ's College, Cambridge, where Milton was a student in the 1620s, will lead the charge. Quentin Skinner, a distinguished Renaissance scholar, is set to kick things off with a lecture on "John Milton as a Theorist of Liberty" (January 30th). The college's other celebration plans remain hazy. It is probably safe to say that largish quantities of sherry will be involved, as well as a good deal of recondite one-upmanship and perhaps a bitter row or two. Meanwhile, the honour of publishing a massive new 12-volume edition of Milton's complete works has gone to the Other Place. The first volumes will roll off the Oxford University Press in 2008, with the remainder to follow over the next two years.

Hundreds of boffins from all round the world will attend the Ninth International Milton Symposium, a five-day bunfight held under the auspices of the Institute of English Studies at the University of London (July 7th–11th). The organisers promise, among other things, papers on heresy and radicalism, so things could get pretty feisty. Across the pond, the New York Public Library mounts an exhibition entitled "John Milton at 400: A Life Beyond Life" (February 29th–June 14th). The show will chart the ways in which, over the centuries, "readers have brought their own concerns, values and biases to his poetry."

> Hollywood plans to turn "Paradise Lost" into a film

Not to be left out, Hollywood plans to turn "Paradise Lost" into a film. "This could be like 'The Lord of the Rings' or bigger," the prospective producer, Vincent Newman, has been quoted as saying.

One cultural paradise will be regained in 2008: the splendid Teatro Colón in Buenos Aires, one of the world's great opera houses, reopens after extensive renovation. The occasion is supposed to coincide with the theatre's 100th anniversary—though it has an interesting history of deadline-breaking. It was originally supposed to open in 1892 but did not do so until 1908, almost 20 years after the cornerstone was laid. From the start it was beset by grim mishaps of a spookily operatic nature. The architect, the musically named Francesco Tamburini, dropped dead a couple of years after construction began. Then his successor, Vittorio Meano, was murdered when a love triangle went sour. And then one of the financiers—yet another Italian, Angelo Ferrari—was bumped off. *O mio bambino caro!*

At last the theatre opened, with a performance of Verdi's "Aida". It went on to become one of the world's top opera venues, graced by the likes of Arturo Toscanini, Enrico Caruso, Maria Callas and Astor Piazzolla, an Argentine tango god. El Colón closed for a $25m facelift in 2006. Its reopening—assuming there are no tragic delays—will be a high note of 2008. ■

2008 IN BRIEF

The **Millennium Theatre,** America's biggest, opens in Branson, Missouri, with "Noah—The Musical", featuring 75 live animals, 75 robotic animals and more than 40 humans.

Steve King: works for *Vanity Fair*

A year for accountability

Angelina Jolie, goodwill ambassador to the UNHCR, hopes for progress in bringing war criminals to justice

On a recent mission for the United Nations High Commissioner for Refugees, I had the opportunity to visit a refugee camp in Chad just across the border with Sudan. Sitting with a group of refugees, I asked them what they needed. These were people who had seen family members killed, neighbours raped, their villages burned and looted, their entire communities driven from their land. So it was no surprise when people began listing the things that could improve their lives just a little bit. Better tents, said one; better access to medical facilities, said another. But then a teenage boy raised his hand and said, with powerful simplicity, "*Nous voulons un procès.*" We want a trial.

A trial might seem a distant and abstract notion to a young man for whom the inside of a courtroom is worlds away from the inside of a refugee camp. But his statement showed a recognition of something elemental: that accountability is perhaps the only force powerful enough to break the cycle of violence and retribution that marks so many conflicts.

I believe 2008 can be the year in which we begin seeking true accountability and demanding justice for the victims in Darfur and elsewhere. Through accountability we can begin the process of righting past wrongs, and even change the behaviour of some of the world's worst criminals.

The international tribunals for the former Yugoslavia and for Rwanda have shown the way in convicting heads of state and generals for genocide and crimes against humanity. The UN-backed special court for Sierra Leone has already sentenced three former leaders of a pro-government militia to jail for war crimes committed during the country's civil war in the 1990s.

In Cambodia, the joint UN-Cambodian court to try top former Khmer Rouge leaders with war crimes and crimes against humanity has begun calling witnesses. It has taken a long time to get even this far, but a trial is likely in 2008. In The Hague, the International Criminal Court (ICC) has begun trials of two of the Congolese leaders charged with fomenting killings and rapes amid the violence that has raged there for over a decade.

Make no mistake, the existence of these trials alone changes behaviour. Seeing the indictment of Thomas Lubanga and the detention of Germain Katanga by the ICC brought to mind a trip I had taken to Congo five years ago. In the Ituri region, where Mr Katanga's reign of terror had been most intense, our group attended a meeting of rebel leaders. They had gathered in a field to discuss the prospects for a peace agreement—which were not looking very good. The conversation turned hostile and the situation grew extremely tense. At that point, one of my colleagues asked for the name of one of the rebels, announcing, perhaps a bit recklessly, that he was going to pass it along to the ICC.

Make no mistake, the existence of these trials alone changes behaviour

It was remarkable: this rebel leader's whole posture changed from aggression to conciliation. The ICC had been around for only five months. It had tried no one. Yet its very existence was enough to intimidate a man who had been terrorising the population for years.

Ending the cycle of violence

This is not an isolated example. Accountability has the potential to change behaviour, to check aggression by those who are used to acting with impunity. Luis Moreno-Ocampo, the prosecutor of the ICC, has said that even genocide is not a crime of passion; it is a calculated decision. He is right. Common sense tells us that when risks are weighed, decisions are made differently. When crimes against humanity are punished consistently and severely, the killers' calculus will change.

My hope is that these examples of justice in the name of accountability will be just a few of the many to come. I hope that the Sudanese government will hand over the government minister and the *janjaweed* militia leader who have been indicted for war crimes by the ICC, and that the teenager I met in Chad will get to see the trial he seeks. I hope that those responsible for the atrocities in Darfur will be held to account, not only for that young man's sake, but for the world's.

Only through justice will we achieve peace. And only when there is peace will the world's nearly 39m displaced persons and refugees be able to return home.

The strong preying upon the weak and the weak, upon achieving strength, extracting retribution: this is the nature of so many of the world's conflicts. The role of aggressor and victim may alternate over time, the tools of destruction may become more sophisticated, but little else changes.

Despite the horror I have seen in my travels, the hopeful lesson I take is that we can begin to put an end to the cycle of violence and retribution that gives rise to war criminals and sets forth floods of refugees. Let 2008 be the year in which we see the principle of accountability put into action. ■

Hope against dope

Barney Southin

In an Olympic year, sport's war on drugs will intensify

Two bruising battles in sport's war on drugs will be fought in the summer of 2008. The first will begin in the port of Brest, on France's north-west coast, on July 5th. From here 200 of the world's top cyclists will set off on the 95th edition of the Tour de France. Doping scandals have ruined the previous two tours and left the sport's credibility in tatters. A drug-free race in 2008 is crucial to restoring cycling's respectability. Then, on August 8th, about 11,500 athletes from around the world will gather in Beijing for the Olympic games. More athletes were disqualified from the 2004 Olympics in Athens than from any games since drug-testing was introduced in 1968. The progress of anti-doping initiatives launched in the wake of the Athens games will be judged by what happens in Beijing.

The temptation to cheat will be at least as great as ever. But the anti-dopers, led by the World Anti-Doping Agency (WADA), will also be more zealous. France's government has vowed the 2008 tour will be "clean and renovated", with tougher sanctions for doping and more aggressive testing. In Beijing athletes will face more, and better targeted, tests than at any previous games.

Some educated guesses can be made as to the identity of those caught cheating in 2008. At least one will be a weightlifter: the sport has accounted for 37 of the 85 athletes expelled from the summer games since drug-testing's introduction. On past form track athletes, baseball players, boxers—and, of course, cyclists—will also fall foul of the testers. Eastern Europe, with its history of state-sponsored doping and relatively few anti-doping initiatives, will provide more than its share. And what of America? Having skewered Marion Jones, a star athlete, federal prosecutors are expected to go after other big fish.

Pumped up

Olympic drug testing

		Athletes tested	Positive tests
1968	Mexico City	667	1
1972	Munich	2,079	7
1976	Montreal	786	11
1980	Moscow	645	0
1984	Los Angeles	1,507	12
1988	Seoul	1,598	10
1992	Barcelona	1,848	5
1996	Atlanta	1,923	2
2000	Sydney	2,758	11
2004	Athens	3,667	26†
2008	Beijing	4,500*	?

* Estimate † Some cases still to be concluded
Source: House of Commons

In the short term the main problem for anti-doping efforts is unknown steroids—such as tetrahydrogestrinone (THG), for which no test existed before its discovery—and, in endurance sport, blood-doping. But genetic doping looms as a future threat. Will 2008 see the first instance? WADA's hard-boiled chief, Dick Pound, has described this prospect as "disturbing but not out of the realm of possibility". Few doubt that some are willing to try. Geneticists have reported approaches from athletes offering to be their guinea pigs, and recent doping scandals have highlighted the existence of "rogue" laboratories willing to flout the rules. Yet gene therapy remains immature and highly risky.

Gene dopers may not be detected until many years after the event—if at all. WADA, which outlawed the practice in 2003, is funding research into detecting its potential side-effects. But a reliable test will not be ready in time for the Tour de France or the Beijing Olympics. So, long after the crowds have left, sport's war on drugs will rumble on. ■

Barney Southin: managing editor, Economist.com

The year of the spud

Food for thought

Pity the potato. Dan Quayle mashed up its spelling. The Atkins diet trashed it. Generations of children have laughed at it as Mr Potato Head. But in 2008 it will be top of the crops. The United Nations has declared this the International Year of the Potato, to increase awareness (an official aim is to achieve an "enhanced profile of the potato"). The idea was suggested by Peru, the home of the potato and of the International Potato Centre, a locus of cutting-edge potato research.

Brought to Europe by the Spanish, potatoes were first eaten reluctantly—Europeans had no idea which parts of the plant were poisonous. But over time they became a dietary staple (tragically so in Ireland, where the failed potato crop between 1845 and 1849 dramatically reduced the population through starvation, disease and mass emigration). Now Europeans each consume about 93kg a year. Production, like consumption, has gone global: China and India harvest almost a third of today's supply.

Versatility is the secret of the spud's success. It comes in 7,500 varieties (Peruvians especially prize the yellow potato). It keeps company with burgers and bangers around the world. It also hobnobs with food aristocracy—for example as the froth on top of a Spanish omelette served in a martini glass at Spain's ultra-sophisticated El Bulli restaurant. In 2008 it will be frothed, fried and feted too. ■

Five potato, six potato, seven potato, more

Consumption, grams per person per day, 2005

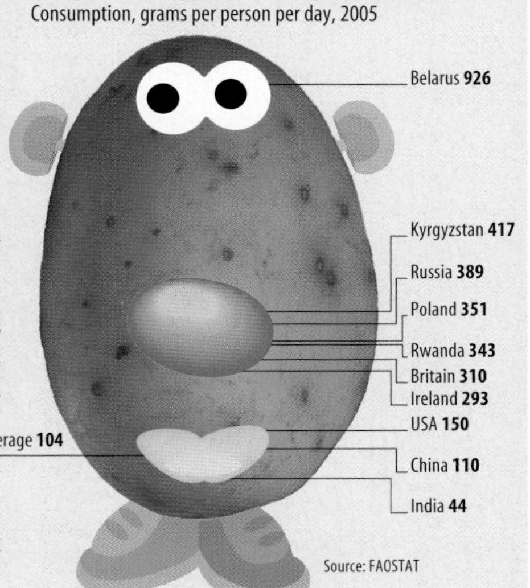

Source: FAOSTAT

The spirit of principled pragmatism

Ban Ki-moon, secretary-general of the United Nations, suggests three priorities for the world in 2008

If I were to sum up my view of the United Nations and its work today, it would be a spirit of principled pragmatism. By virtue of its charter and its calling, the UN must be a voice of moral conscience in the world. Part of that moral duty is to make good on the hopes and expectations vested in us—to deliver results, not mere promises.

The coming year will bring extraordinary challenges. They range from the crisis in Darfur to Somalia, Iraq and the Middle East. We must act on climate change, and we must find ways to make development work in Africa. Too often, the UN has tackled such challenges rhetorically, contributing to its reputation as a talking-shop. For that to change, the UN must rediscover the pragmatism of its principles. Solutions we offer must be real solutions, not band-aids. Complex problems must be dealt with comprehensively, in their full economic, social and political dimension.

A global agenda

I see three main priorities for 2008. Each must be the work of every nation, for each embodies a fundamental principle of justice and human rights—as befits the year marking the 60th anniversary of the Universal Declaration of Human Rights. Begin with Darfur—a case study in complexity. The UN will soon deploy 26,000 peacekeepers in one of the largest and logistically most difficult assignments in its history. That it will be undertaken in partnership with the African Union is a precedent in itself. Yet this mission can succeed only if there is a peace to keep.

In the case of Darfur, principled pragmatism means painstaking hard work for a real political settlement. Negotiations began in Libya in 2007. They will succeed or fail depending on whether we get the parties to the conflict around a table and persuade them to agree: the government of Sudan, rebel movements and leaders of neighbouring countries. We must also remember that Darfur is an environmental and development crisis, arising at least in part from desertification, ecological degradation and a scarcity of resources, foremost among them water. Any solution must take this economic dimension into account: water, agriculture, transport, jobs, social services—all must be addressed if 2.5m displaced people are to return home and resume their daily lives. Dealing with such complexity is the only way to a solution that endures.

Too often, the UN has tackled such challenges rhetorically, contributing to its reputation as a talking-shop

As in Darfur, so elsewhere. If we seek, genuinely, to create a more just world, then it is axiomatic: development cannot take a back seat to issues of peace and security. Hence the second priority for 2008. We are now at the mid-point of a multinational effort to aid the poorest of the world's poor, set forth in the UN Millennium Development Goals. Here, principled pragmatism means sweating the details: working hard to deliver what has been promised instead of offering more high-minded words about what ought to be done.

We have had successes. Around the world, economic growth is lifting unprecedented numbers of people out of poverty. Yet this rising tide of globalisation has not raised all boats. We see this most acutely in Africa, home to most of what one World Bank economist calls "the bottom billion" of the world's poor. It is intolerable that HIV/AIDS continues as a modern-day scourge; and that 10m children die each year before their fifth birthday, mostly from preventable diseases such as malaria. It is a moral scar on our conscience.

As I see it, 2008 must be a year of fresh thinking. This is not to say we will do things that these countries should, and can, do for themselves. The "Asian miracle" has shown that successful development owes much to smart choices and rigorous execution. But we can do better. Developed nations must make good on promises of aid, debt relief and market access. Open, fair and non-discriminatory trading and financial systems are critical to the future of every developing country. This should be the main theme of the year's Doha negotiations. Principled pragmatism means that business-as-usual doesn't cut it any more.

Lastly, global warming—the defining issue of our era, as the Nobel prize committee has recognised. Here, principled pragmatism means not setting out a vision for a perfect regime to combat it. Rather, it means getting everyone around the negotiating table in Bali in December 2007, so that countries with different interests can hammer out an agreement all can embrace. Any such deal must be built on a foundation of justice. We are all aware of the terrible irony of climate change: developing countries have contributed least to the problem, but bear the brunt of the consequences. There can be no solutions that ignore this reality—just as there can be none that denies poor nations their chance to develop, to share in global prosperity.

Peace and security, the UN charter noted long ago, ultimately depend on "the social and economic advancement of people". This is the spirit of principled pragmatism. ■

The future of futurology

Robert Cottrell *NEW YORK*

Think small, think short—and listen

So there you are on the moon, reading *The World in 2008* on disposable digital paper and waiting for the videophone to ring. But no rush, because you're going to live for ever—and if you don't, there's a backed-up copy of your brain for downloading to your clone.

Yes? No? Well, that's how the 21st century looked to some futurologists 40 or 50 years ago, and they're having a hard time living it down now. You can still get away (as we do) with predicting trends in the world next year, but push the timeline out much further, and you might as well wear a T-shirt saying "crackpot". Besides, since the West began obsessing a generation ago about accelerating social and technological change, people in government and industry can spend weeks each year in retreats brainstorming and scenario-building about the future of their company or their industry or their world. The only thing special about a futurologist is that he or she has no other job to do.

Uncertainty looks smarter than ever before

Small wonder that futurology as we knew it 30 or 40 years ago—the heyday of Alvin Toffler's "Future Shock", the most popular work of prophecy since Nostradamus—is all but dead. The word "futurologist" has more or less disappeared from the business and academic world, and with it the implication that there might be some established discipline called "futurology". Futurologists prefer to call themselves "futurists", and they have stopped claiming to predict what "will" happen. They say that they "tell stories" about what might happen. There are plenty of them about, but they have stopped being famous. You have probably never heard of them unless you are in their world, or in the business of booking speakers for corporate dinners and retreats.

We can see now that the golden age of blockbuster futurology in the 1960s and 1970s was caused, not by the onset of profound technological and social change (as its champions claimed), but by the absence of it. The great determining technologies—electricity, the telephone, the internal combustion engine, even manned flight—were the products of a previous century, and their applications were well understood. The geopolitical fundamentals were stable, too, thanks to the cold war. Futurologists extrapolated the most obvious possibilities, with computers and nuclear weapons as their wild cards. The big difference today is that we assume our determining forces to be ones that 99% of us do not understand at all: genetic engineering, nanotechnology, climate change, clashing cultures and seemingly limitless computing power. When the popular sense of direction is baffled, there is no conventional wisdom for futurologists to appropriate or contradict.

Popcorn and prediction markets

There are still some hold-outs prophesying at the planetary level: James Canton, for example, author of "Extreme Future". But the best advice for aspirant futurists these days is: think small. The best what-lies-ahead book of 1982 was "Megatrends", by John Naisbitt, which prophesied the future of humanity. A quarter-century later, its counterpart for 2007 was "Microtrends", by Mark Penn, a public-relations man who doubles as chief strategy adviser to Hillary Clinton's 2008 presidential campaign. "Microtrends" looks at the prospects for niche social groups such as left-handers and vegan children. The logical next step would be a book called "Nanotrends", save that the title already belongs to a journal of nano-engineering.

The next rule is: think short-term. An American practitioner, Faith Popcorn, showed the way with "The Popcorn Report" in 1991, applying her foresight to consumer trends instead of rocket science. The Popcornised end of the industry thrives as an adjunct of the marketing business, a research arm for its continuous innovation in consumer goods. One firm, Trendwatching of Amsterdam, predicts in its *Trend Report* for 2008 a list of social fads and niche markets including "eco-embedded brands" (so green they don't even need to emphasise it) and "the next small thing" ("What happens when consumers want to be anything but the Joneses?").

A third piece of advice: say you don't know. Uncertainty looks smarter than ever before. Even politicians are seeing the use of it: governments that signed the Kyoto protocol on climate change said, in effect: "We don't know for sure, but best to be on the safe side"—and they have come to look a lot smarter than countries such as America and Australia which claimed to understand climate change well enough to see no need for action.

The last great redoubt of the know-alls has been the financial markets, hedge funds claiming to have winning strategies for beating the average. But after the market panic of 2007 more humility is to be expected there too.

A fourth piece of advice for the budding futurist: get embedded in a particular industry, preferably something to do with computing or national security or global warming. All are fast-growing industries fascinated by uncertainty and with little

use for generalists. Global warming, in particular, is making general-purpose futurology all but futile. When the best scientists in the field say openly that they can only guess at the long-term effects, how can a futurologist do better? "I cannot stop my life to spend the next two or ten years to become an expert on the environment," complains Mr Naisbitt in his latest book, "Mindset" (although the rewards for Al Gore, who did just that, have been high).

A fifth piece of advice: talk less, listen more. Thanks to the internet, every intelligent person can amass the sort of information that used to need travel, networking, research assistants, access to power. It is no coincidence that the old standard work on herd instinct, Charles Mackay's "Extraordinary Popular Delusions and the Madness of Crowds", has been displaced by James Surowiecki's "The Wisdom of Crowds".

The most heeded futurists these days are not individuals, but prediction markets, where the informed guesswork of many is consolidated into hard probability. Will Osama bin Laden be caught in 2008? Only a 15% chance, said Newsfutures in mid-October 2007. Would Iran have nuclear weapons by January 1st 2008? Only a 6.6% chance, said Inkling Markets. Will George Bush pardon Lewis "Scooter" Libby? A better-than-40% chance, said Intrade. There may even be a prediction market somewhere taking bets on immortality. But beware: long- and short-sellers alike will find it hard to collect. ■

Robert Cottrell: deputy editor, Economist.com

Six of the best

Our selection of trend-spotters' tips for 2008

Sleep is the new sex, reckons Marian Salzman, a New York advertising executive and author of "Next Now". In hectic lives, sleep is at a premium. And sleep sells, whether it's flat beds on airlines, sleep consultancy, or a nap at MetroNaps in the Empire State Building. In America, growing numbers of couples are installing "sleep chambers" to give them a sleep-alone option as well as a sleep-together option. Why suffer from a partner's snoring? People are "finding it harder to do the sharing thing," says Ms Salzman.

Person-to-person lending will flourish in 2008, predicts Jeremy Gutsche, the Toronto-based head of TrendHunter.com. Borrowers and lenders come together directly on the web and cut out the banks. Some of these lending operations use an auction like eBay in which the lender willing to provide the lowest interest rate gets the borrower's loan; others (like CircleLending, an American firm) are for people who already know one another but who want someone to help formalise the loan arrangement. "Peer-to-peer" lending is working its way into the charitable sector, too: Kiva.org puts potential "social investors" in touch with small businesses in the developing world, which promise to send e-mail updates on how the business is developing.

N11 is Goldman Sachs's shorthand for the "next 11" countries snapping at the heels of the BRIC countries (Brazil, Russia, India and China) as investment opportunities. They are Bangladesh, Egypt, Indonesia, Iran, South Korea, Mexico, Nigeria, Pakistan, the Philippines, Turkey and Vietnam. In 2008, watch especially for booming Vietnam.

Vicarious consumption, a term coined a century ago by an economist, Thorstein Veblen, to describe the thrill rich people get when they buy their butler a lovely new uniform, is making a comeback in a new form, according to Amsterdam-based Trendwatching. It involves services for telling consumers "exactly what other consumers are enjoying and valuing most"—websites such as iliketotallyloveit.com and ballofdirt.com are part of the trend.

Newly released ex-cons—one of Mark Penn's many "microtrends"—will continue to flood out of America's jails, needing training and jobs. In the 1980s and 1990s, America's prison population quintupled. Now, their time served, prisoners are being released in record numbers. This is a microtrend, argues Mr Penn, that "government and business need to get going on right away". And if the credit crunch of 2007 continues to bite, another of Mr Penn's microtrends will become all too pertinent in 2008: ***bourgeois and bankrupt***. ■

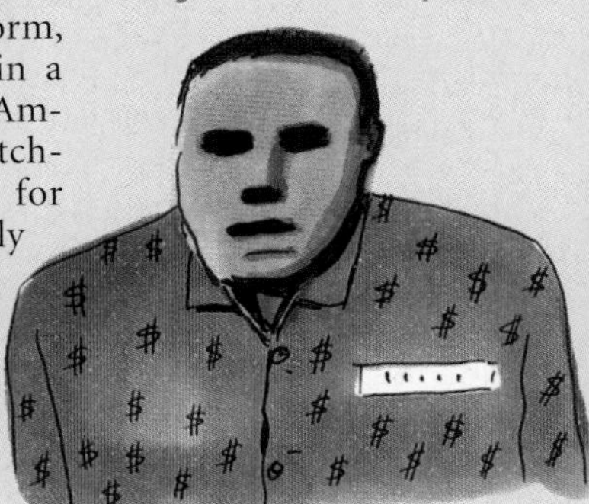

The world in figures: Countries

Europe
Austria 113
Belgium 113
Bulgaria 113
Croatia 113
Czech Republic 113
Denmark 114
Estonia 114
Finland 114
France 114
Germany 114
Greece 114
Hungary 114
Ireland 114
Italy 114
Latvia 115
Lithuania 115
Netherlands 115
Norway 115
Poland 115
Portugal 115
Romania 115
Russia 115
Slovakia 115
Slovenia 115
Spain 116
Sweden 116
Switzerland 116
Turkey 116
Ukraine 116
United Kingdom 116

Asia
Australia 116
China 116
Hong Kong 116
India 116
Indonesia 117
Japan 117
Kazakhstan 117
Malaysia 117
New Zealand 117
Pakistan 117
Philippines 117
Singapore 117
South Korea 118
Sri Lanka 118
Taiwan 118
Thailand 118
Uzbekistan 118
Vietnam 118

North America
Canada 118
Mexico 118
United States 118

South America
Argentina 119
Bolivia 119
Brazil 119
Chile 119
Colombia 119
Cuba 119
Ecuador 119
Paraguay 119
Peru 119
Uruguay 119
Venezuela 119

Middle East and Africa
Algeria 120
Angola 120
Cameroon 120
Egypt 120
Ethiopia 120
Iran 120
Iraq 120
Israel 120
Jordan 120
Kenya 122
Lebanon 122
Morocco 122
Nigeria 122
Saudi Arabia 122
South Africa 122
Tanzania 122
Uganda 122
Zimbabwe 122

TOP GROWERS

Three African countries figure in our list of 2008's most buoyant economies, including Angola at number one. But these countries have scaled the heights for two unsettling reasons: sky-high oil prices, which will not be around for ever, and a low starting-point, which suggests they have struggled of late and may not sustain the turnaround. Other top performers have sounder stories to tell. Panama's farmers, financiers and builders are all thriving, and the canal is a reliable money-spinner. Foreign investors will pour billions of dollars into Vietnam, attracted by textiles and tourism.

And then there is China, by far the heaviest hitter in this league of honour. China will inject more wealth into the world economy in 2008 than any other country (as much as the United States, India and Japan combined). That's one big reason for optimism about global prospects in a year likely to be overshadowed by financial uncertainty.

Rank	Country	GDP growth, %
1	Angola	21.1
2	Azerbaijan	17.4
3	Equatorial Guinea	11.1
4	China	10.1
5	Qatar	9.5
6	Kazakhstan	9.2
7	United Arab Emirates	8.6
8	Georgia	8.5
8	Panama	8.5
10	Vietnam	8.1
11	Armenia	8.0
12	São Tomé and Principe	8.0

2008 forecasts unless otherwise indicated.
Inflation: year-on-year annual average.
Dollar GDPs calculated using 2008 forecasts for dollar exchange rates (GDP at PPP, or purchasing-power parity, shown in brackets).
Source: **Economist Intelligence Unit**
london@eiu.com

Wider still and wider
Eastern Europe: current-account balance 2008, % of GDP

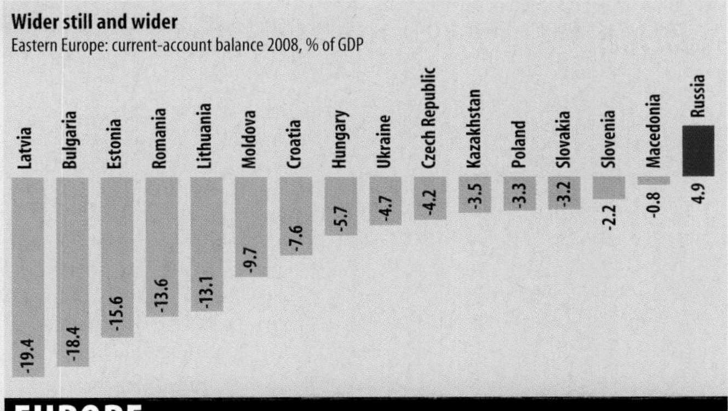

EUROPE

Main event: A new tsar takes the throne in Russia? **Euro-zone growth:** 2.0%
EU-27 growth: 2.1% **Eastern and Central Europe:** 4.7% **Russia and CIS:** 6.6%

AUSTRIA

GDP growth:	[illegible]%
GDP:	$390bn (PPP: $3[illegible]n)
Inflation:	[illegible]%
Population:	[illegible]m
GDP per head:	$46,600 (PPP: $40,120)

The Social Democratic Party (SPÖ) and the Austrian People's Party (ÖVP) will continue their uneasy coalition, if only because the rewards of co-operation outweigh the challenge of regaining public confidence ahead of early elections. The SPÖ and the chancellor, Alfred Gusenbauer, will press for the introduction of a minimum wage, but the centre-right ÖVP has its own agenda. The economy will hum along at 2.8%, tidy enough by west European standards.

BELGIUM

GDP growth:	2.5%
GDP:	$465bn (PPP: $394bn)
Inflation:	1.5%
Population:	10.4m
GDP per head:	$44,730 (PPP: $37,890)

Coalition negotiations are likely to usher in a centre-right government of Flemish- and French-speaking Christian Democrat and liberal parties, with the Socialists retiring to the opposition benches. The Flemings, representing 60% of the population, will press for greater regional autonomy, but will face stiff resistance from their Wallonia- and Brussels-based Francophone partners. The economy will tick along, with growth matching 2007's 2.5%.

To watch: Weird and wonderful. Belgians will burnish their zany reputation with the Scarecrow Festival (Brussels, April); Gold Stilt Contest (Namur, September); and the Waiter Race (Brussels, September).

BULGARIA

GDP growth:	5.8%
GDP:	$42bn (PPP: $91bn)
Inflation:	3.3%
Population:	7.5m
GDP per head:	$5,640 (PPP: $12,140)

Strains are increasing between the leading partners in the government coalition, the Bulgarian Socialist Party and the National Movement for Stability and Progress (NMSP). The NMSP leader, the former king Simeon Saxe-Coburg, is increasingly alienated from his party over his support for the government. Boiko Borisov, mayor of Sofia and leader of Citizens for European Development of Bulgaria, a rival party, could be the beneficiary if NMSP defections trigger early elections. The current-account gap will narrow slightly, but at a staggering 18.4% of GDP it will remain a big concern.

CROATIA

GDP growth:	5.4%
GDP:	$56bn (PPP: $69bn)
Inflation:	2.5%
Population:	4.6m
GDP per head:	$12,220 (PPP: $15,120)

Minor parties will hold the balance of power after the November 2007 elections as they are courted by the centre-left opposition Social Democratic Party and the centre-right Croatian Democratic Union. Kingmaker-in-chief will be the newly allied Croatian Social Liberal Party and Croatian Peasants Party, which could swing negotiations—though in which direction is unclear. EU membership could happen as early as 2009. Economic growth will be a comfortable 5.4%.

CZECH REPUBLIC

GDP growth:	4.2%
GDP:	$177bn (PPP: $245bn)
Inflation:	3.6%
Population:	10.2m
GDP per head:	$17,280 (PPP: $23,970)

Having failed twice in 2007 to push through no-confidence votes against the government, the opposition Czech Social Democratic Party (CSSD) will hope for third time lucky in 2008. The prime minister, Mirek Topolanek, will try to fend off the CSSD while preserving unity in his three-party coalition government. The task will be complicated by squabbling within Mr Topolanek's own Civic Democratic Party over fiscal reforms; this will determine the size of the budget deficit in 2008, and the timetable for euro adoption, with a target date of 2012.

To watch: Missile offence. The strength of public opposition to plans for a US anti-missile base on Czech territory will be tested when parliament votes on the issue early in the year.

DENMARK

GDP growth:	1.5%
GDP:	$332bn (PPP: $214bn)
Inflation:	1.9%
Population:	5.5m
GDP per head:	$60,800 (PPP: $39,260)

The rise of the newly formed centrist party, New Alliance, offers the minority centre-right coalition government a stable partner, and increases the likelihood that the prime minister, Anders Fogh Rasmussen, will call snap elections before the January 2009 deadline. He would probably be rewarded with another term, with the main opposition Social Democratic Party struggling to regain popularity.

To watch: Hello, neighbour. Denmark badly needs skilled foreign workers, and will change laws to make them welcome.

ESTONIA

GDP growth:	5.8%
GDP:	$23bn (PPP: $32bn)
Inflation:	6.8%
Population:	1.3m
GDP per head:	$17,270 (PPP: $23,560)

Internal strains will hamstring the coalition government, a jumble of conservatives, liberal reformers and centre-left social democrats. A superheating economy will slow to a relatively sedate 5.8%. The current-account deficit, at nearly 16% of GDP, is a worry. Stubborn inflation will delay adoption of the euro to beyond 2010.

FINLAND

GDP growth:	2.7%
GDP:	$253bn (PPP: $192bn)
Inflation:	2.2%
Population:	5.2m
GDP per head:	$48,140 (PPP: $36,520)

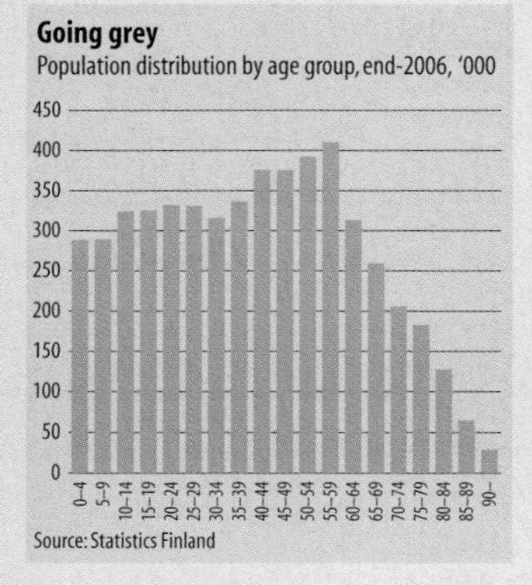

Going grey
Population distribution by age group, end-2006, '000
Source: Statistics Finland

A stable four-party centre-right coalition government, under the second-term prime minister, Matti Vanhanen, will encourage entrepreneurship and energy reforms, while rejigging the administrative structure of the municipalities. The addition of the Conservatives to the coalition suggests a more active foreign policy, including stronger ties with America, but also a mediating role in the EU's strained relations with Russia.

To watch: Blade runners. Join the 10,000-odd participants in February's Ice Marathon in the northern town of Kuipio. Don't forget your skates.

FRANCE

GDP growth:	2.2%
GDP:	$2.68trn (PPP: $2.17trn)
Inflation:	1.9%
Population:	61.4m
GDP per head:	$43,640 (PPP: $35,430)

Budget gap
Fiscal deficit as % of GDP

1
0
-1
-2
-3
-4
-5
Germany
France
2001 2002 2003 2004 2005 2006 2007 2008

France's Margaret Thatcher? Perhaps not, but the first full year of Nicolas Sarkozy's presidency will nevertheless focus on a tussle over employment between a reforming government and entrenched unions, whose taste for protest has scuppered most past efforts at reform. Mr Sarkozy will avoid open confrontation, and therefore won't deliver the break with the past he promised during his campaign. Instead of abolishing the 35-hour work week, he may use tax incentives to ease its impact.

To watch: Fiscal delinquent. France will buck the EU trend towards slimmer budget deficits by offering tax cuts without curbing spending. The fiscal spark will boost the economy, driving growth to 2.2% from 1.8% in 2007.

GERMANY

GDP growth:	2.5%
GDP:	$3.43trn (PPP: $2.84bn)
Inflation:	1.6%
Population:	82.7m
GDP per head:	$41,400 (PPP: $34,270)

The future of the grand-coalition government, led by the chancellor, Angela Merkel, may hinge on the performance of its junior partner, the Social Democratic Party (SPD), in state elections early in the year, particularly in Lower Saxony and Hesse. Divisions between centrists and left-wingers could erupt if the party does badly, strengthening those who want to break with Ms Merkel's Christian Democratic Union and its partner, the Christian Social Union. If the "splittists" prevail, the SPD is likely to be punished in the subsequent election.

High-quality German machinery will be in demand by big emerging-market economies and oil-producing countries.

To watch: Business boost. The tax rate on corporations will be cut from 39% to 30%, giving companies more money to invest in a reviving economy.

GREECE

GDP growth:	3.2%
GDP:	$372bn (PPP: $386bn)
Inflation:	2.5%
Population:	11.0m
GDP per head:	$33,850 (PPP: $35,150)

The centre-right New Democracy government under Costas Karamanlis begins its second term, following its victory over the Panhellenic Socialist Movement (Pasok) in September 2007 elections. The government must operate with a reduced majority, and contend with a popular ultra-nationalist party in parliament, the Popular Orthodox Rally, that is quickly gaining support.

Having quelled protests from students and teachers against its education reforms, the re-elected government will open a new front against another formidable group: civil servants. Increasingly indebted consumers will spend less, slowing economic growth.

HUNGARY

GDP growth:	3.0%
GDP:	$138bn (PPP: $202bn)
Inflation:	4.1%
Population:	9.9m
GDP per head:	$13,860 (PPP: $20,370)

Two years after admitting he lied to voters, Ferenc Gyurcsany's government is still struggling to stay afloat. The yawning budget deficit, the main reason for the economic mess at the heart of Mr Gyurcsany's deception, will narrow, but not to the target of 4.3% of GDP—particularly if an opposition referendum succeeds in stopping some of the government's austerity measures.

Less belt-tightening will boost the economy, as will increasing integration into west European production and supply chains.

To watch: Leadership challenge. Mr Gyurcsany's budget-cutting isn't popular with his Socialist Party's ideological base, and the party may try to replace him if support dwindles further. This would spell the end of austerity and, in effect, open campaigning for the 2010 election.

IRELAND

GDP growth:	3.4%
GDP:	$270bn (PPP: $195bn)
Inflation:	3.0%
Population:	4.3m
GDP per head:	$62,450 (PPP: $45,110)

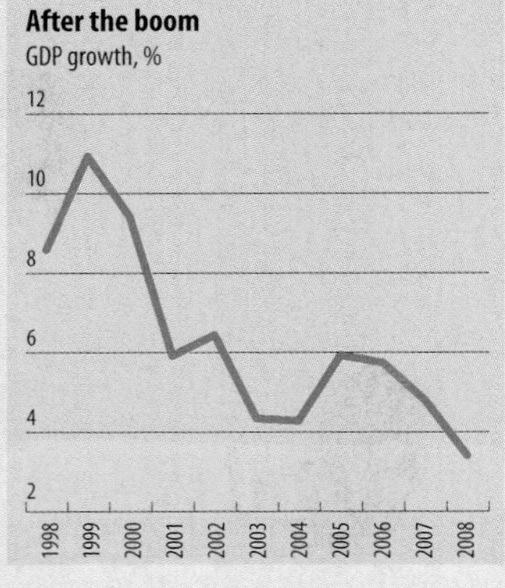

With the Green Party now in the coalition government, policy will shift slightly towards environmental issues, though the government's overall focus—keeping businesses competitive—won't change. Economic management will be more complicated than during the boom years; spending cuts, for example, may now be required, creating stresses within the government. Economic growth will slow to 3.4% from almost 6% in 2005-06. A referendum, expected in May, will approve the new EU treaty.

To watch: Taoiseach on trial. The taoiseach (prime minister), Bertie Ahern, is facing questioning from a judicial inquiry into alleged financial irregularities during his years as finance minister. Should he be seriously tainted, his coalition partners may leave government, bringing early elections.

ITALY

GDP growth:	1.6%
GDP:	$2.22trn (PPP: $1.88trn)
Inflation:	1.9%
Population:	58.1m
GDP per head:	$38,190 (PPP: $32,390)

The Unione coalition government, led by the prime minister, Romano Prodi, is odds-on to stay in office in 2008, though all bets are off thereafter. Should the coalition collapse over any of the many issues that divide its ideologically diverse members, Silvio Berlusconi, a former prime minister, and his Casa delle Libertá alliance would probably return to power. But without a change to the electoral rules he himself introduced, a new Berlusconi regime would be no more effective than the last.

Economic growth will slow and the government will miss its budget goal, but won't breach the EU's 3%-of-GDP ceiling.

LATVIA

GDP growth:	7.5%
GDP:	$30bn (PPP: $43bn)
Inflation:	6.2%
Population:	2.3m
GDP per head:	$13,270 (PPP: $18,980)

The four-party centre-right coalition government will be lucky to complete the year intact, despite its comfortable legislative majority. Revelations from the trial of Aivars Lembergs, the former mayor of Ventspils, have tainted one of the government's constituent parties. Should the coalition collapse, none of the likely successors would be very durable. Economic growth will slow but remain impressive at 7.5%.

LITHUANIA

GDP growth:	6.9%
GDP:	$41bn (PPP: $66bn)
Inflation:	4.4%
Population:	3.4m
GDP per head:	$12,240 (PPP: $19,730)

Elections are due in October, but the four-party minority government led by Gediminas Kirkilas of the Social Democratic Party (LSP) is unlikely to last that long. Strains between the centre-left LSP and the opposition centre-right Homeland Union, which has been voting with the government, are becoming unmanageable.

NETHERLANDS

GDP growth:	2.3%
GDP:	$820bn (PPP: $687bn)
Inflation:	1.9%
Population:	16.6m
GDP per head:	$49,550 (PPP: $41,490)

The ruling coalition of the Christian Democratic Appeal, the Labour Party and a small Protestant religious party, the ChristenUnie, plans a modest increase in government spending. Health care, education, environmental protection and urban renewal are the likely beneficiaries. The budget balance therefore will move back into the red.

To watch: *Nee* again. If the government puts new EU treaty proposals to a referendum, Dutch voters could reprise their 2005 "no" vote, which helped to kill the idea of a full EU constitution.

NORWAY

GDP growth:	2.6%
GDP:	$426bn (PPP: $278bn)
Inflation:	2.2%
Population:	4.7m
GDP per head:	$90,180 (PPP: $58,850)

A good performance in local elections in late 2007 will assure the three-party "red-green" coalition smooth passage through 2008. High oil prices are bringing in plenty of cash, and the current account will close the year with a buoyant surplus equal to 15% of GDP. Taxes rose in 2007, and the money will be spent this year on local government and transport initiatives, as well as the staples of health and education.

To watch: All you need is herring. The port city of Stavanger will share European Capital of Culture honours with Liverpool, home of the Beatles.

POLAND

GDP growth:	5.1%
GDP:	$453bn (PPP: $640bn)
Inflation:	3.0%
Population:	38.1m
GDP per head:	$11,880 (PPP: $16,810)

Donald's Tusk's liberal-conservative Civic Platform (PO) defeated Jaroslaw Kaczynski's ruling Law and Justice party (PiS) by an unexpectedly large margin in Poland's 2007 parliamentary election. But a PO-led coalition, which will be needed to secure a parliamentary majority, could be fractious, and will find it difficult to overcome presidential vetoes from Lech Kaczynski, a former leader of the PiS. Thus the PO will find it hard to push economic reforms through parliament. A PO-led government will move ahead in areas which do not require new legislation, such as privatisation. Economic growth will slow, but remain at a comfortable 5.1%.

To watch: Joyous sounds. The International Choirs' Festival, Mundus Cantat, will bring amateur voices to the seaside town of Sopot in May.

PORTUGAL

GDP growth:	2.1%
GDP:	$231bn (PPP: $240bn)
Inflation:	2.0%
Population:	10.6m
GDP per head:	$21,710 (PPP: $22,550)

On target
GDP and budget performance

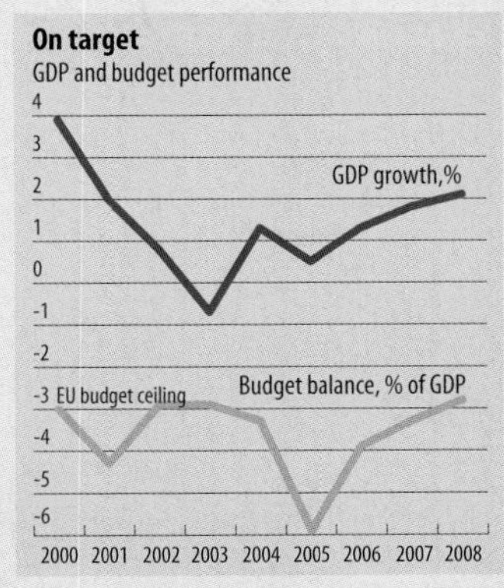

One of the EU's budget-busters in recent years, Portugal has been given until 2008 to get its house in order. Belt-tightening is likely to deliver a fiscal gap within acceptable euro-zone limits, but this may be temporary. Austerity has been largely at the cost of public servants, whose powerful unions have put up a strong fight. With elections due in 2009, commitment to the fiscal cause may slip. Economic growth will tick higher as businesses start spending again.

To watch: Hang ten. The World Surfing Games will be held here in October.

2008 IN PERSON

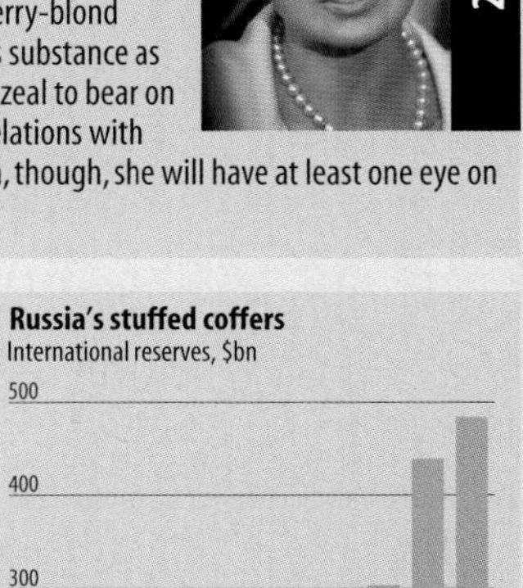

Yulia Tymoshenko, who played a leading role in Ukraine's "orange revolution", was later sidelined, but 2008 will see her back with a bang. A big performance in the September 2007 legislative election guaranteed her renewed prominence—though whether as the leader of the government or a thorn in its side was dependent on post-election talks. Ms Tymoshenko's strawberry-blond braids have become a trademark, but she has substance as well as style. She will bring her campaigning zeal to bear on corruption, Ukraine's vital gas industry and relations with Russia. Whether in government or opposition, though, she will have at least one eye on the presidential race expected in 2009.

ROMANIA

GDP growth:	5.5%
GDP:	$185bn (PPP: $249bn)
Inflation:	4.3%
Population:	21.6m
GDP per head:	$8,550 (PPP: $11,490)

With the goal of joining the EU achieved, the country's political forces have little to bind them. Elections, first for the European Parliament in late 2007, then for local government in the first half of 2008 and, finally, in November for the national parliament, will matter. The results will reflect the decline in support for the National Liberal Party (NLP), which heads the minority government, and the rise of the Democratic Party, the NLP's former partner, now in opposition.

To watch: Deficit dangers. The current-account gap will exceed 13% of GDP and, with privatisation receipts tailing off, will cause much worry. The budget deficit will also raise eyebrows.

RUSSIA

GDP growth:	6.3%
GDP:	$1.42trn (PPP: $2.08trn)
Inflation:	7.8%
Population:	141.8m
GDP per head:	$10,010 (PPP: $14,650)

Russia's democratic traditions are not deep, and Vladimir Putin is at the height of his powers, so the president—whose second and last term ends in 2008—may find a way to keep control. Whether the popular Mr Putin remains president, becomes prime minister or merely fights his successor for influence from the outside, Russian politics will be unsettled. Centralised rule, sustained economic growth and the satisfying spectacle of rising Russian influence abroad will keep the growing middle class content for now, as democracy evaporates.

Another year of high oil prices will keep the economy churning, but weak investment will restrain energy output.

Russia's stuffed coffers
International reserves, $bn

500
400
300
200
100
1998 1999 2000 2001 2002 2003 2004 2005 2006 2007 2008

SLOVAKIA

GDP growth:	6.0%
GDP:	$80bn (PPP: $117bn)
Inflation:	2.5%
Population:	5.5m
GDP per head:	$14,600 (PPP: $21,380)

The goal of adopting the euro by 2009 will make for responsible economic policy, although lax budget controls and a volatile currency could force a delay. The leaders of the three coalition parties, the centre-left prime minister, Robert Fico, populist Vladimir Meciar and the far-right Jan Slota, are united in their mutual dislike, but will co-operate in the interests of staying in power. Growth will slow but will still put much of Europe in the shade at 6%.

SLOVENIA

GDP growth:	4.6%
GDP:	$48bn (PPP: $58bn)
Inflation:	2.7%
Population:	2.0m
GDP per head:	$23,850 (PPP: $28,870)

The outlook is bright for the prime minister, Janez Jansa, and his Slovenian Democratic Party as the country prepares for elections late in the year. Adoption of the euro has been well received, and the government has a further opportunity to flaunt its credentials when Slovenia takes on the six-month rolling presidency of the EU in the first half of 2008.

A housing-fuelled investment boom that drove the economy in 2006-07 will begin to fade.

SPAIN

GDP growth:	2.6%
GDP:	$1.53trn (PPP: $1.45trn)
Inflation:	2.4%
Population:	45.7m
GDP per head:	$33,530 (PPP: $31,650)

Oddly, groups whose express ambition is autonomy from Spain could decide who governs after the March election. The failure of the Spanish Socialist Workers Party to sustain peace talks with the Basque separatists means a resumption of major attacks is likely. After the balloting, the centre-right Catalan nationalist party, Convergence and Union, will hold the balance of power. The Socialists are narrow favourites to win another term. The economy will slow as consumers pull back and the housing market fades.

SWEDEN

GDP growth:	3.4%
GDP:	$464bn (PPP: $336bn)
Inflation:	2.1%
Population:	9.2m
GDP per head:	$50,310 (PPP: $36,420)

Shrinking government
Budget expenditure, % of GDP

Sweden

1992 1994 1996 1998 2000 2002 2004 2006 2008

The four-party centre-right Alliance for Sweden government will press on with market-friendly reforms, steering the country further from the statist legacy of the long-dominant Social Democratic Party. Privatisation, market liberalisation, an attack on welfare dependency and the promotion of entrepreneurial activity will dominate the government agenda.

SWITZERLAND

GDP growth:	2.4%
GDP:	$424bn (PPP: $306bn)
Inflation:	1.2%
Population:	7.6m
GDP per head:	$55,780 (PPP: $40,260)

The ultra-conservative Swiss People's Party (SVP) strengthened its dominant position in government following a hard-fought election in late 2007. The big losers were the left-of-centre Social Democrats. While the SVP's gains have added an adversarial tone to the four-party, consensus-based coalition that has long ruled Switzerland, it will remain intact.

To watch: Blogocracy. Campaigners for the 2007 election used the web extensively. Expect Swiss "people power" to move increasingly online in response.

TURKEY

GDP growth:	5.3%
GDP:	$508bn (PPP: $791bn)
Inflation:	6.1%
Population:	76.2m
GDP per head:	$6,670 (PPP: $10,380)

The prime minister, Recep Tayyip Erdogan, and his second-term Justice and Development party government will use a stronger electoral mandate to lock in economic gains and attract fresh foreign investment. It will also advance liberal reforms, including freedom of expression, while the secularist opposition and its military allies still fret over the party's mildly Islamist background. Eventual EU membership will continue to guide economic policymaking, but remains a distant prospect.

UKRAINE

GDP growth:	6.2%
GDP:	$152bn (PPP: $431bn)
Inflation:	9.0%
Population:	46.0m
GDP per head:	$3,307 (PPP: $9,370)

Ukraine remains evenly divided between east and west: since the orange revolution, both sides have held power, and neither has achieved much in the face of opposition from the other. The leading figures—Viktor Yanukovych of the Party of Regions, Viktor Yushchenko of Our Ukraine and Yulia Tymoshenko of her eponymous block (see In Person on previous page)—will jockey for control in 2008. The presidency beckons in 2009.

UNITED KINGDOM

GDP growth:	2.2%
GDP:	$2.84trn (PPP: $2.33trn)
Inflation:	1.9%
Population:	60.7m
GDP per head:	$46,740 (PPP: $38,340)

Gordon Brown's honeymoon as prime minister is over, following a botched plan to call an early election in October 2007. With no ballot likely in 2008, Mr Brown will be open to charges he has no mandate to govern. But he remains a formidable figure who still attracts people's confidence. The opposition Conservatives, behind a centrist leader, David Cameron, will be a credible force in 2008, but will struggle to bury their ideological differences.

To watch: Continental drift. Mr Brown's pro-American sympathies will be tempered by the political cost of pursuing Mr Blair's engagement in Iraq, and tensions could emerge with America as Britain redefines its military priorities.

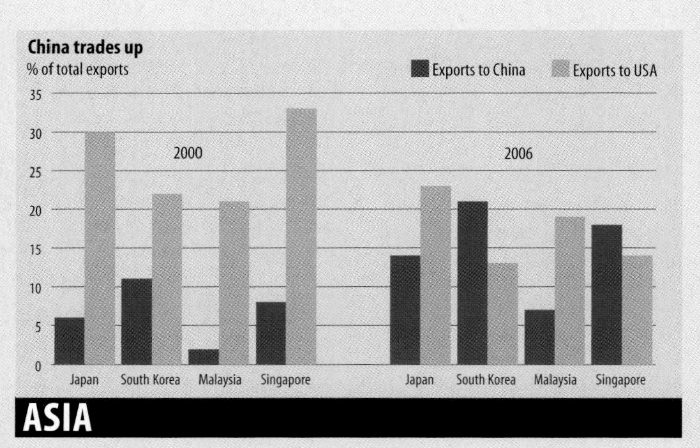

ASIA

Main event: China's coming-out party at the 29th Olympiad

Asia and Australasia growth (excl Japan): 6.6% **ASEAN growth**: 5.1%

AUSTRALIA

GDP growth:	3.0%
GDP:	$874bn (PPP: $805bn)
Inflation:	2.9%
Population:	20.6m
GDP per head:	$42,420 (PPP: $39,060)

A combination of voter fatigue and self-inflicted injury means the 11-year-old government of John Howard and his Liberal-National coalition may well expire when elections are held at the end of 2007. If the opposition Labor party, led by Kevin Rudd, takes power, it is likely to row back on some of Mr Howard's market-oriented reforms, including a 2006 law that limited collective-bargaining rights. Economic growth will slow as companies spend less.

CHINA

GDP growth:	10.1%
GDP:	$3.94trn (PPP: $12.91trn)
Inflation:	3.0%
Population:	1.33bn
GDP per head:	$2,960 (PPP: $9,700)

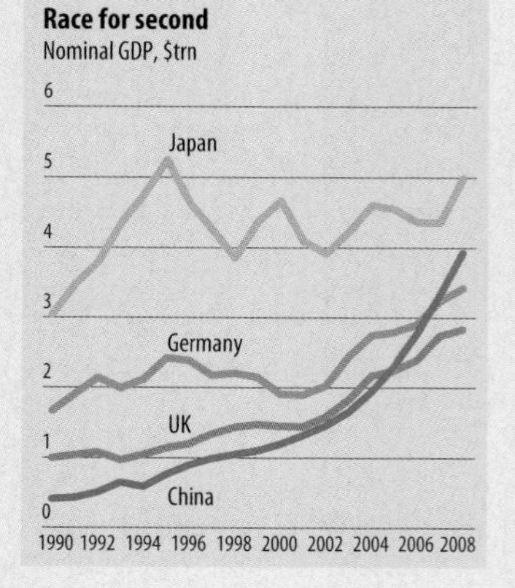

The greatest show on earth comes to the planet's most populous country. China's Communist leaders see the Olympic games as the ideal opportunity to polish an international image tarnished by autocracy, low regard for human rights, eye-watering pollution and uncertainty over how to wield its growing influence.

At home, the government will continue to wrestle down an economy threatening to break its own speed limit, but will be helped by a slowdown in global demand for its exports.

HONG KONG

GDP growth:	5.2%
GDP:	$219bn (PPP: $306bn)
Inflation:	3.6%
Population:	7.0m
GDP per head:	$31,150 (PPP: $43,560)

Calls for the early introduction of universal suffrage will intensify ahead of elections for the territory's legislative body, but mainland ears will be firmly plugged. Economic policy will focus on harnessing China's spectacular rise, largely through closer economic ties. Calls will grow for a minimum wage or redistributive taxes to cushion growing inequality, but the government will turn a deaf ear of its own. Economic growth will continue to slow, but only to a fairly comfortable 5.2%.

INDIA

GDP growth:	7.9%
GDP:	$1.33trn (PPP: $5.31trn)
Inflation:	5.2%
Population:	1.13bn
GDP per head:	$1,180 (PPP: $4,720)

An early parliamentary election is on the cards after the Congress-led United Progressive Alliance (UPA) coalition government fell out with its Communist allies over the nuclear deal with the US (which the Communists consider a betrayal of India's non-aligned status). February is the likely date, though the task of marshalling more than half-a-billion voters may take longer. The UPA is unlikely to be toppled as the biggest block, but neither will it achieve majority

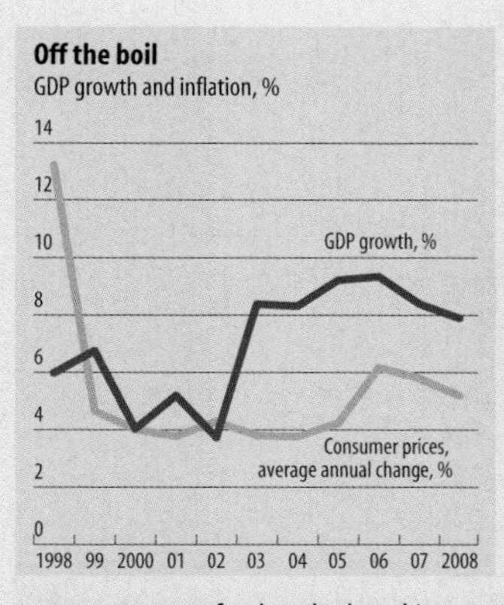

status, so expect further deal-making and political instability.

To watch: Temperature check. Economic growth will slow to 7.9%, and wholesale inflation (which the central bank targets) will fall to 5.2%, so fears of overheating should subside.

INDONESIA

GDP growth:	6.4%
GDP:	$462bn (PPP: $1.10trn)
Inflation:	5.8%
Population:	237.5m
GDP per head:	$1,950 (PPP: $4,680)

President Susilo Bambang Yudhoyono will be watching for fading loyalty from Golkar, the party whose support has given him a legislative majority, as it prepares for presidential and parliamentary elections in 2009. Golkar is looking to the opposition Indonesian Democratic Party-Struggle; if they co-operated, they could win big in the parliamentary vote, but probably could not stop Mr Yudhoyono's re-election as president. The government will struggle to restore investors' confidence.

To watch: Trade tie-up. A free-trade agreement with Japan, Indonesia's first, comes into force at the start of the year.

JAPAN

GDP growth:	1.9%
GDP:	$4.96trn (PPP: $4.48trn)
Inflation:	0.5%
Population:	127.5m
GDP per head:	$38,930 (PPP: $35,170)

The prime minister, Yasuo Fukuda, will focus on cleaning up after the disastrous tenure of his predecessor, Shinzo Abe. His main task is to rebuild public faith in the long-ruling Liberal Democratic Party. The disclosure of massive pensions mismanagement will still reverberate, and his competence will be on trial from the start. The temptation will be strong to rebuild rural support by spending lots of government cash, threatening the budget-deficit reduction target. Still, if the world stays healthy enough to buy Japan's exports, the economy should grow by a respectable 1.9%.

To watch: Brick economies. Future management consultants will be competing at the Open Asia Championship of the First Lego League, to be held in Tokyo in April.

KAZAKHSTAN

GDP growth:	9.2%
GDP:	$116bn (PPP: $183bn)
Inflation:	8.7%
Population:	15.6m
GDP per head:	$7,450 (PPP: $11,760)

Nursultan Nazarbayev has transferred some of his presidential powers to the legislature, but this is dominated by loyalists, so he faces no threat. With presidential term limits lifted and plans for a dynastic succession on hold, Mr Nazarbayev seems to be settling in for the long term. Disaffection among a growing entrepreneurial class is on the rise, but is unlikely to threaten the incumbent.

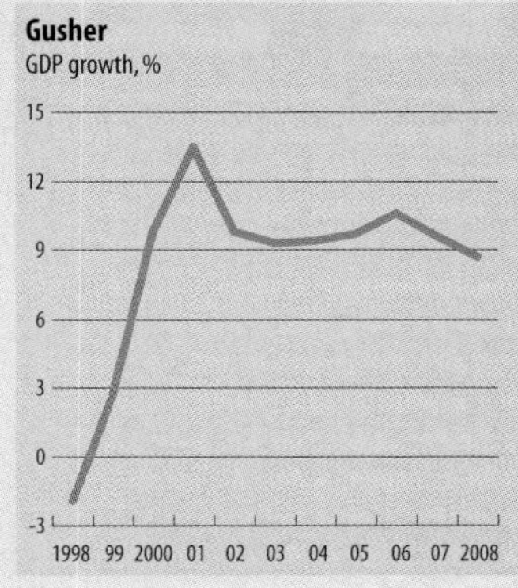

To watch: Turn at the top. Kazakhstan is a potential alternative to Russia as an energy supplier to the West, and could be encouraged by confirmation that it will chair the Organisation for Security and Co-operation in Europe in 2009.

MALAYSIA

GDP growth:	5.8%
GDP:	$209bn (PPP: $358bn)
Inflation:	2.6%
Population:	27.7m
GDP per head:	$7,550 (PPP: $12,960)

A string of government successes and a divided opposition suggest the general election due in 2009 will be brought forward. The ruling Barisan Nasional front and the prime minister, Abdullah Badawi, will hold on to power; ideological differences, particularly around the role of Islam in politics, will prevent the opposition figurehead, Anwar Ibrahim, from re-forming the once-successful Barisan Alternatif Front.

To watch: Affirmative action. The policy of favouring the less well-off Malay population in government tenders will come under pressure as America seeks fair access in a free-trade agreement.

NEW ZEALAND

GDP growth:	3.0%
GDP:	$124bn (PPP: $126bn)
Inflation:	2.2%
Population:	4.2m
GDP per head:	$29,240 (PPP: $29,650)

The coalition government headed by the Labour Party faces flagging public support as high interest rates and stingy tax relief erode spending power. John Key, leader of the opposition National Party, has made hay by attacking this record, and by pointing to the government's poor performance on social welfare. But economic growth will hold firm, at 3%, supporting the government's credibility and ensuring it remains in power—at least until the election due by November.

PAKISTAN

GDP growth:	5.9%
GDP:	$157bn (PPP: $492bn)
Inflation:	6.3%
Population:	167.2m
GDP per head:	$940 (PPP: $2,940)

President Pervez Musharraf will continue to speak of restoring democracy following the suspension of civil rights in late-2007, but few at home or abroad will take him at his word. Instead, General Musharraf's authority will depend on the support of the army, and on the apparent inability of the political opposition to unite (though the judiciary, something of a proxy opposition, may prove a more effective foil). America will scold, but will carry on backing a key ally in the "war on terror".

PHILIPPINES

GDP growth:	5.6%
GDP:	$151bn (PPP: $521bn)
Inflation:	3.4%
Population:	92.7m
GDP per head:	$1,640 (PPP: $5,620)

A strong showing in the 2007 mid-terms removes the threat of impeachment from the president, Gloria Macapagal Arroyo. But unrest among lower-ranking soldiers and the constant threat of a "people power" rebellion mean she will

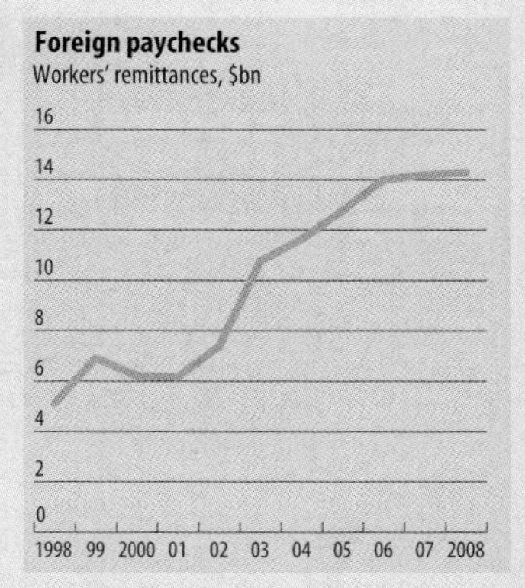

not be altogether secure. The lack of an upper-house majority will slow the pace of economic reform. Strong consumer spending will keep the economy humming, with growth likely to hit 5.6%. Remittances by expatriate Filipinos will relieve pressure on the currrent account.

To watch: Southern discomfort. Anti-terror legislation introduced in 2007 will fail to quell insurgencies based in the lawless southern islands, and these could make their presence felt in the capital, Manila.

SINGAPORE

GDP growth:	5.1%
GDP:	$162bn (PPP: $198bn)
Inflation:	1.0%
Population:	4.6m
GDP per head:	$35,640 (PPP: $43,420)

The ruling People's Action Party will continue to provide Singaporeans with rapid economic growth in exchange for tolerating its stifling grip on power. But its capacity to deliver is being eroded, and the party will be tested: it must address increasing regional competition, an ageing population and the need to restructure the manufacturing base. That said, the economy will have another respectable year, thanks to healthy demand for electronics and pharmaceuticals.

To watch: Trade links. A free-trade deal with China, likely to be completed in 2008, is an important part of the government's plan to ride the globalisation wave.

2008 IN PERSON

Li Keqiang, party secretary of Liaoning province, is in contention for China's top job. Mr Li was one of two additions (with Xi Jinping from Shanghai) to the nine-member standing committee of the politburo at the Communist Party's People's Congress in late 2007. They will have a bit of a wait, though; the term of Hu Jintao, the current president, runs until 2012. But grooming Chinese leaders is a lengthy process, and it will be important to get a good start. Mr Li will, for example, want to gloss over his association with a blood-transfusion scandal in Henan that raised the province's AIDS death rate. More recently, Mr Li has pioneered reforms linked to Mr Hu's "harmonious society" policy. If Mr Li is the future, he is reminiscent of the present leadership: competent rather than charismatic. He will represent continuity rather than a break with the past.

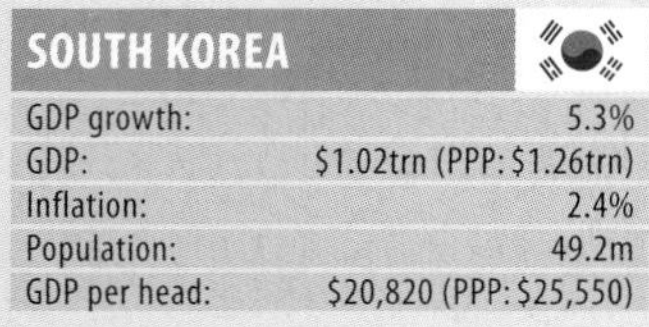

SOUTH KOREA

GDP growth:	5.3%
GDP:	$1.02trn (PPP: $1.26trn)
Inflation:	2.4%
Population:	49.2m
GDP per head:	$20,820 (PPP: $25,550)

The year will probably open with the inauguration as president of Lee Myung-bak, who collected rubbish in the streets of Seoul as a child before growing up to become mayor. His conservative Grand National Party government would concentrate on boosting economic growth, setting aside the previous government's redistributive agenda. Nationalism would be undimmed under Mr Lee, who would nevertheless aim to reinforce relations with America.

To watch: Philosophy. The World Congress of Philosophy will meet in Seoul in July "to call attention to the importance of philosophical reflection on philosophy".

SRI LANKA

GDP growth:	6.1%
GDP:	$35bn (PPP: $100bn)
Inflation:	8.2%
Population:	19.4m
GDP per head:	$1,790 (PPP: $5,190)

The ceasefire between the government and the Tamil Tigers will be buried in 2008, putting hostilities back on an official footing. The president, Mahinda Rajapakse, may end the political alliance with his coalition partner, the Janatha Vimukthi Peramuna party. But he has enough support elsewhere to control parliament. Improved political stability will boost investment.

TAIWAN

GDP growth:	4.6%
GDP:	$409bn (PPP: $827bn)
Inflation:	1.4%
Population:	22.8m
GDP per head:	$17,950 (PPP: $36,330)

Relations with China will be watched closely as Taiwan elects a new legislature (January) and president (March). But with candidates downplaying separatist rhetoric, campaigning will focus on corruption and political reform. The outcome of the legislative vote will influence the presidential race but the opposition Kuomintang is well placed to dominate both. A KMT-led government would focus on raising economic growth rates towards the Asian average.

To watch: Strait talking. Direct flights between Taiwan and the mainland may begin in 2008.

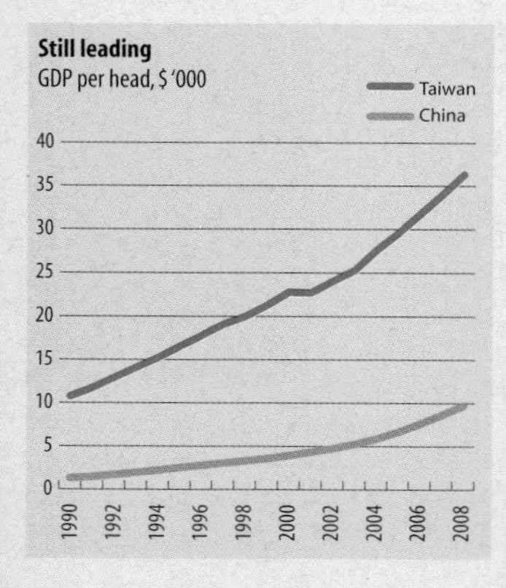

Still leading
GDP per head, $ '000

THAILAND

GDP growth:	5.0%
GDP:	$263bn (PPP: $697bn)
Inflation:	2.1%
Population:	67.0m
GDP per head:	$3,930 (PPP: $10,400)

Voters may have thought that by supporting a new constitution in late 2007 they were saying "Thank you and goodbye" to the generals who ousted Thaksin Shinawatra's government a year earlier. But if, as seems likely, candidates from Mr Shinawatra's disbanded Thai Rak Thai party do well in the election scheduled for the end of 2007, the old rifts could re-open, and the model of a military-backed civilian government could return to fashion before the end of 2008.

UZBEKISTAN

GDP growth:	7.3%
GDP:	$23bn (PPP: $74bn)
Inflation:	14.5%
Population:	27.1m
GDP per head:	$847(PPP: $2,720)

Re-election for the president, Islam Karimov, in late 2007 will keep Uzbek politics in the freezer. Western investors will be put off by gaps in the legal system and human-rights concerns. Russian and Chinese investors, frequently less squeamish, will help drive the economy to 7.3% growth.

To watch: Northern exposure. Russia will continue a charm offensive designed to recover influence in Central Asia and the oil-rich Caspian basin.

VIETNAM

GDP growth:	8.1%
GDP:	$83bn (PPP: $347bn)
Inflation:	7.3%
Population:	87.0m
GDP per head:	$953 (PPP: $3,990)

The country's Communist leaders will continue to tackle official corruption, seen as the greatest threat to the party's legitimacy. To improve government, the ruling triumvirate, headed by the party secretary, Nong Duc Manh, will grant greater oversight to the directly elected National Assembly, but political reform will stop there. The economy will continue to boom, growing by 8.1%.

To watch: Tax competition. The corporate tax rate will probably be cut to 25% from 28% to compete with the neighbours.

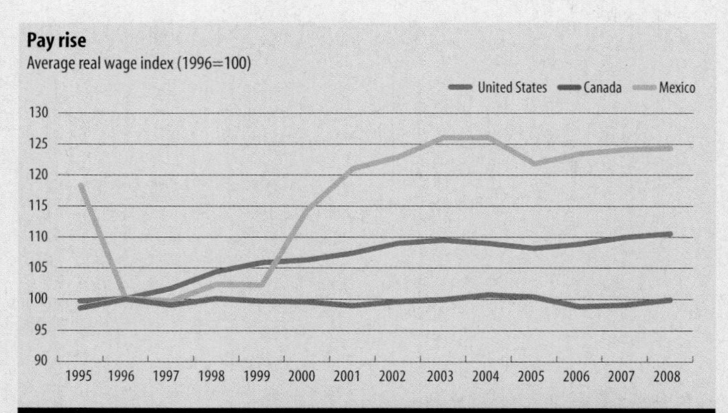

Pay rise
Average real wage index (1996=100)

NORTH AMERICA

Main event: Presidential election in the USA **North American (NAFTA) growth**: 2.2%

CANADA

GDP growth:	2.2%
GDP:	$1.30trn (PPP: $1.22trn)
Inflation:	2.0%
Population:	33.2m
GDP per head:	$40,010 (PPP: $38,500)

The minority Conservative government headed by the prime minister, Stephen Harper, may seek an overall majority in early elections, but another term as a minority is the most likely outcome. The government is under pressure over environmental policy, the revenue share-out with the provinces and the presence of Canadian troops in Afghanistan, but a divided opposition has been unable fully to exploit public discontent. The economy is expected to grow by 2.2%, but this assumes the United States shakes off its subprime mortgage woes and avoids a recession.

To watch: Advance viewing. The Extra-Sensory Perception Psychic Expo will be held at Toronto's International Centre in March.

MEXICO

GDP growth:	3.1%
GDP:	$900bn (PPP: $1.29bn)
Inflation:	3.8%
Population:	110.0m
GDP per head:	$8,200 (PPP: $11,840)

This is an important year for the president, Felipe Calderón, who must persuade the opposition Partido Revolucionario Institucional (PRI) to support his minority Partido de Acción Nacional government in pushing key reforms through congress. Smooth progress on pensions in 2007 raised hopes, but last-minute wrangling nearly scuppered even more important fiscal reforms. Time for co-operation is running out; PRI magnanimity will decline as the political focus turns to congressional mid-term elections in 2009.

To watch: Cartel wars. Mr Calderón won applause when he despatched soldiers to fight drug cartels along the American border, but the hardline approach threatens to descend into a messy stand-off, undermining support for the strategy and the government.

UNITED STATES

GDP growth:	1.2%
GDP:	$14.40trn (PPP: $14.40trn)
Inflation:	2.1%
Population:	304.8m
GDP per head:	$47,330 (PPP: $47,330)

Democrat Hillary Clinton is likely to become America's first woman president as a war-weary country turns its back on incompetent Republicans and the painful Bush years. Until November, the year will be dominated by non-stop electioneering, with some state primaries starting in early January. The party nominees could be chosen earlier than ever, setting the stage for months of bitter campaigning. Deadlock between the president and Congress will bring legislation to a halt. The economy will slow appreciably and just might dip into recession as the housing slump drags on. Some troops will leave Iraq, or at least withdraw to less exposed positions.

To watch: Island USA. Growing Democratic influence will push the country in a more isolationist direction, reflected in a less assertive foreign policy but also a more protectionist economic one. Global trade talks may languish.

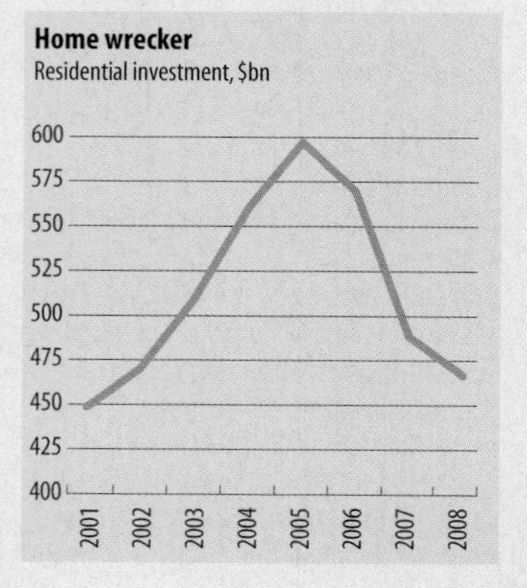

Home wrecker
Residential investment, $bn

SOUTH AMERICA

Main event: Chávez-watching **Latin American growth**: 4.5%

ARGENTINA

GDP growth:	5.7%
GDP:	$270bn (PPP: $772bn)
Inflation:	10.5%
Population:	39.8m
GDP per head:	$6,790 (PPP: $19,420)

Cristina Fernández, wife of the outgoing president, Néstor Kirchner (see In Person), will enjoy a short political honeymoon as she assumes power following end-2007 elections. The economic boom during her husband's tenure was the product of heavy state intervention in markets and prices. Unwinding those distortions will be risky. As economic growth slows, the budget surplus narrows and inflation climbs, discontent will resurface.

BOLIVIA

GDP growth:	4.4%
GDP:	$15bn (PPP: $45bn)
Inflation:	7.3%
Population:	9.7m
GDP per head:	$1,510 (PPP: $4,630)

A disciple of Hugo Chávez, President Evo Morales lacks the Venezuelan leader's oil wealth, and must also deal with a bigger and better-organised opposition. Even so, he remains popular, and may seek a fresh mandate by bringing forward elections. Worker remittances will help to sustain GDP growth.

To watch: Divide and rule. Demands for regional autonomy were to have been resolved in the national assembly, but will probably go to referendum. Opinion is polarised, and violence is possible.

BRAZIL

GDP growth:	4.5%
GDP:	$1.27trn (PPP: $1.97trn)
Inflation:	4.1%
Population:	191.9m
GDP per head:	$6,600 (PPP: $10,290)

Bottom bric
GDP growth, %
Brazil, India, Russia, China
12, 10, 8, 6, 4, 2, 0, -2, -4, -6
1998, 1999, 2000, 2001, 2002, 2003, 2004, 2005, 2006, 2007, 2008

Politics will be dominated by campaigning for the mid-term elections in late 2008, bringing tensions in the ruling coalition to the surface. The anti-corruption credentials of the ruling party have been shattered during its two terms in power, and the trials of leading figures will embolden critics. The market for Brazil's exports remains strong, but uninspiring economic growth will weaken Brazil's bid for superstar status.

CHILE

GDP growth:	5.1%
GDP:	$178bn (PPP: $241bn)
Inflation:	3.8%
Population:	16.8m
GDP per head:	$10,590 (PPP: $14,339)

The political consensus behind the liberal economic model is intact, but Chilean society is becoming more liable to protest, and the president, Michelle Bachelet, will face rising unrest. The post-Pinochet glue binding the centre-left coalition that has run things since the strongman's departure is weakening. Conservative management will insulate the economy from political instability.

COLOMBIA

GDP growth:	5.8%
GDP:	$169bn (PPP: $462bn)
Inflation:	4.5%
Population:	47.6m
GDP per head:	$3,550 (PPP: $9,690)

Álvaro Uribe will continue his second presidential term backed by a congressional majority and solid approval ratings. But longstanding allegations of collusion between the state and illegal paramilitary forces will come to the fore as the Supreme Court presses its investigations. Despite some discomfort, Mr Uribe's position is secure. Economic growth will remain healthy at around 5.8%.

CUBA

GDP growth:	5.4%
GDP:	$49bn (PPP: $134bn)
Inflation:	4.3%
Population:	11.2m
GDP per head:	$4,350 (PPP: $11,970)

The country is changing, but at an evolutionary rather than a revolutionary pace. The coming year will see Fidel Castro (81) move upstairs—either to take on the role of elder statesman or to meet his maker. His brother, Raúl (76), will consolidate his power as acting president, but at the head of a government team rather than as undisputed leader. More open political debate will be tolerated.

To watch: Relations with the United States will rise a degree or two above absolute zero as reforms progress in Cuba and hardline Republicans lose influence in Washington.

ECUADOR

GDP growth:	1.7%
GDP:	$45bn (PPP: $65bn)
Inflation:	3.5%
Population:	13.8m
GDP per head:	$3,260 (PPP: $4,710)

President Rafael Correa, another Chávez protégé, has completed step one of the Bolivarian revolutionary blueprint, winning control of an assembly that could give him sweeping authority via a rewritten charter. Notably less strident than Mr Chávez, Mr Correa has nevertheless hinted that he will intervene heavily in the economy, with the big oil companies among the early victims.

To watch: Debt doubts. Oil exports and worker remittances will give Ecuador the means to pay its debts, but the government's willingness to do so is another matter.

PARAGUAY

GDP growth:	4.0%
GDP:	$13bn (PPP: $29bn)
Inflation:	8.8%
Population:	6.2m
GDP per head:	$2,100 (PPP: $4,620)

The April presidential election will probably pit a former bishop, Fernándo Lugo, against a former general, Lino Oviedo, with the ex-cleric best positioned to win. Mr Lugo admires Venezuela's Hugo Chávez but will emphasise social policy within a sound macroeconomic framework.

PERU

GDP growth:	5.4%
GDP:	$111bn (PPP: $227bn)
Inflation:	2.3%
Population:	29.2m
GDP per head:	$3,820 (PPP: $7,770)

Strong global growth and high prices for Peru's commodities have allowed President Alan García to pursue modestly populist policies. But a weak position in the legislature, resurgent union activism, corruption scandals and rebellious provincial administrations will weaken his authority. Rising wages and strong investment will sustain the economy.

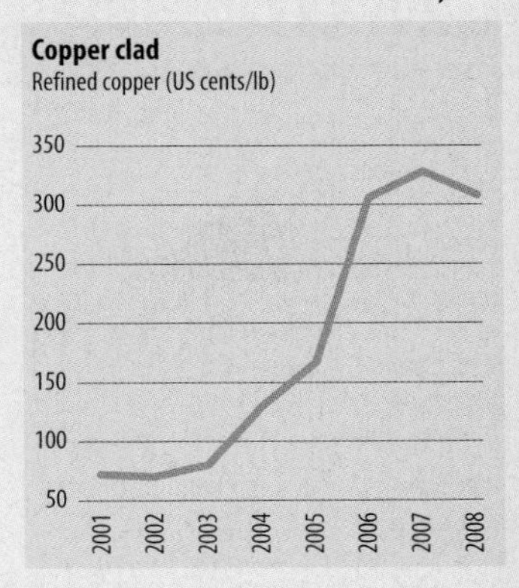

To watch: Swansong. Lima will host one of George Bush's last foreign visits when he attends the Asia-Pacific Economic Co-operation forum in November.

URUGUAY

GDP growth:	4.0%
GDP:	$24bn (PPP: $43bn)
Inflation:	7.2%
Population:	3.3m
GDP per head:	$7,300 (PPP: $12,780)

A stalwart of Latin America's "responsible" left, President Tabaré Vázquez will manage the economy prudently, though any delay in social spending will raise tensions within his Frente Amplio coalition. Another year of economic growth will favour the economy minister, Daniel Astori, in his bid to succeed Mr Vázquez from 2009.

VENEZUELA

GDP growth:	4.0%
GDP:	$268bn (PPP: $239bn)
Inflation:	19.6%
Population:	27.8m
GDP per head:	$9,650 (PPP: $8,620)

President for life? Hugo Chávez, well into his third term, will seek to eliminate presidential term limits through a referendum. The president faces no serious political challenge from a divided opposition, but the economy will be less robust as oil revenue contracts and inflation soars towards 20%. Weaker economic performance may spell trouble, though not in 2008.

2008 IN PERSON

As the successor to her husband, Argentine President Néstor Kirchner, **Cristina Fernández** will make easy copy for foreign editors because of two eye-catching similarities. First, there is Eva Peron, spiritual leader of the nation glorified on stage and screen as "Evita". Perhaps unsurprisingly, Ms Fernández prefers the similarity with another president's wife, America's Hillary Clinton, a lawyer and senator who is competing for the top job. Beyond the headlines, Ms Fernández could end up outshining both, at least in terms of her contribution to her nation's fortunes. If she can continue the economic revival begun by her husband and place it on a more sustainable footing, she could lay the foundation for a period of remarkable growth.

Oil's reward
Current-account balance, % of GDP

Non-oil exporters
Oil exporters (excl Iraq)
Brent crude, $/barrel (right scale)

1998 1999 2000 2001 2002 2003 2004 2005 2006 2007 2008

MIDDLE EAST AND AFRICA

Main event: Iran's nuclear ambitions and the world's response

Middle East & North Africa growth: 5.6%

Sub-Saharan Africa growth: 6.3%

ALGERIA

GDP growth:	5.3%
GDP:	$132bn (PPP: $287bn)
Inflation:	4.0%
Population:	34.4m
GDP per head:	$3,850 (PPP: $8,340)

Stability, political and economic, will be the order of the year. The president, Abdelaziz Bouteflika, will win public approval for a constitutional amendment allowing him to seek a third term in 2009, and will consolidate civilian control. The economy will continue to benefit from strong hydrocarbons prices and big-ticket investments in infrastructure and manufacturing, and more market-friendly reforms will trickle through.

To watch: Jihadi franchise. Algeria's main Islamist radical group has officially joined the al-Qaeda network, and may strike big foreign-linked targets.

ANGOLA

GDP growth:	21.1%
GDP:	$66bn (PPP: $88bn)
Inflation:	13.4%
Population:	17.3m
GDP per head:	$3,820 (PPP: $5,120)

Assuming voter registration can be completed, the country will hold its first legislative election for 16 years, with a presidential contest to follow in 2009 (to coincide with the 30th anniversary in power of the president, José Eduardo dos Santos). The elections will confirm the grip on power of both the ruling party, Movimento Popular de Libertação de Angola, and Mr dos Santos, against an opposition still struggling to complete the transition from rebel army to political movement. Improved economic management and rising oil production—Angola still enjoys an OPEC quota waiver—will push economic growth to 21.1%, the highest of any country in 2008.

CAMEROON

GDP growth:	4.3%
GDP:	$21bn (PPP: $56bn)
Inflation:	2.5%
Population:	19.0m
GDP per head:	$1,100 (PPP: $3,000)

President Paul Biya is popular, healthy (though 74) and backed by a parliamentary majority, so political stability will not be an issue. But there is growing public disenchantment with the government, exceeded only by disgust about the bickering opposition. The government will use the country's natural resources to attract foreign firms, diversifying investment away from France. Foreign-debt relief has raised expectations of better public services.

EGYPT

GDP growth:	7.3%
GDP:	$145bn (PPP: $440bn)
Inflation:	5.7%
Population:	77.5m
GDP per head:	$1,870 (PPP: $5,680)

The five-term president, Hosni Mubarak, will push ahead with economic reforms, which have included sharp cuts in income taxes and customs duties, to improve growth rates and raise living standards. This is a political strategy, designed to cut the popularity of Islamists such as the outlawed Muslim Brotherhood. In the meantime, police repression and strict curbs on civil liberties will remain the weapons of choice against the Islamists.

ETHIOPIA

GDP growth:	8.0%
GDP:	$20bn (PPP: $84bn)
Inflation:	12.0%
Population:	85.1m
GDP per head:	$229 (PPP: $990)

Not 2008 at all, but 2000 according to the Ethiopian calendar. This millennium year offers the chance of greater political co-operation. The release is expected of 40 opposition figures accused of conspiring to overthrow the state, and for whom the chief prosecutor had requested the death sentence. The amnesty will clear the air and should allow more effective lawmaking. Bumper harvests and the government's agriculture-led industrialisation strategy are driving the economy.

To watch: Borderline case. The territorial stand-off with neighbouring Eritrea will fester, but a return to war is unlikely.

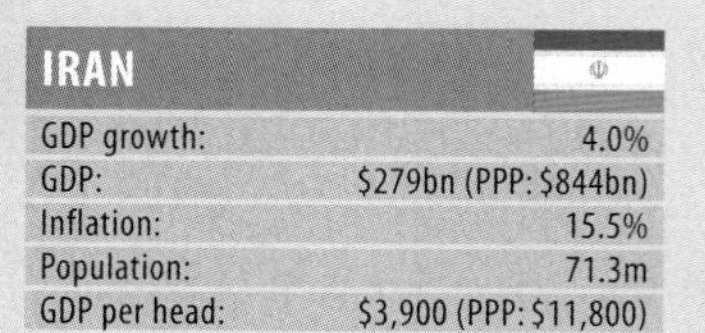

IRAN

GDP growth:	4.0%
GDP:	$279bn (PPP: $844bn)
Inflation:	15.5%
Population:	71.3m
GDP per head:	$3,900 (PPP: $11,800)

The firebrand president, Mahmoud Ahmadinejad, may find his position increasingly threatened as the reformers he once subdued engineer a comeback. Parliamentary elections in March will provide the test, and a strong showing for reformers would undermine the president's authority and provide the platform for an assault on his job in the 2009 presidential election. This would probably come in alliance between reformers and conservatives of a more pragmatic bent than the hardline leader, under their powerful figurehead Akbar Hashemi Rafsanjani.

To watch: Toxic talk. Far from bringing a moderation in nuclear policy, a stronger reformist camp is likely to intensify the chest-thumping as it competes with hardliners for popular support on this issue of national pride.

IRAQ

GDP growth:	3.0%
GDP:	$63bn (PPP: $91bn)
Inflation:	39.0%
Population:	29.4m
GDP per head:	$2,150 (PPP: $3,100)

The drawdown of American troops will remove one of the last constraints on Iraq's religious and tribal factions, freeing them to intensify their turf wars. This will distract from the political process at the centre, making life even more difficult for Nuri al-Maliki's government. The only thing in its favour is the lack of an obvious replacement.

This may be the year Iraq tips towards de facto break-up, with relative stability in some fiefs contrasting with the continuing battlegrounds in and around Baghdad.

To watch: Invasion. Turkey's government has so far restrained army commanders who want to sweep up Kurdish rebels attacking from over the border in Iraqi Kurdistan, but pressure for military action will rise if attacks continue.

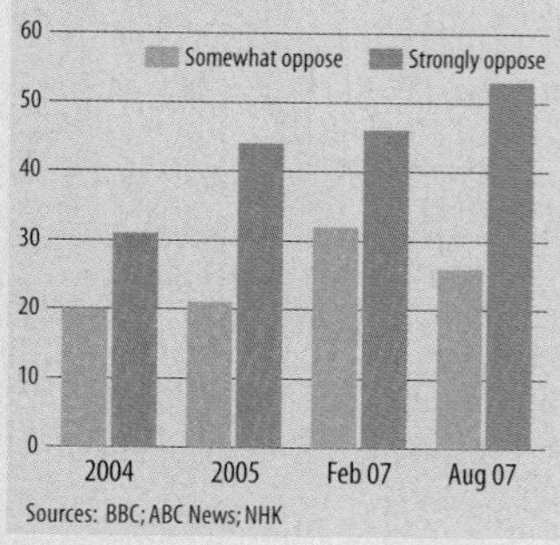

Troops out!
How do Iraqis feel about coalition forces in Iraq?
Sources: BBC; ABC News; NHK

ISRAEL

GDP growth:	4.5%
GDP:	$172bn (PPP: $226bn)
Inflation:	2.3%
Population:	7.3m
GDP per head:	$23,520 (PPP: $31,000)

Fear of facing voters in a fresh election is the main force holding the five-party coalition government together. The prime minister, Ehud Olmert of the Kadima party, has been wounded by his perceived mishandling of the Lebanon war in 2006 and by subsequent corruption allegations. But Labour and its new leader, political veteran Ehud Barak, are gaining in the opinion polls. If the rebound continues, Labour may feel it can give the opposition Likud party a run for its money, and try to bring early elections.

Strong export growth and business investment will keep the economy growing nicely, with low inflation and a current-account surplus.

To watch: Missing peace. Political uncertainty, combined with disarray in Palestinian politics, means the peace process with the Palestinians will remain bogged down.

JORDAN

GDP growth:	5.6%
GDP:	$18bn (PPP: $38bn)
Inflation:	5.3%
Population:	6.2m
GDP per head:	$2,900 (PPP: $6,310)

The ruler, King Abdullah II, retains a firm grip on power, and needs it to balance conflicting forces: his strategic alliance with the United States is resented by many subjects; war and conflict among neighbours threaten to suck Jordan in; parliament stifles economic reforms; and the country remains as reliant as ever on foreign grants.

Even so, strong investment in tourism and property (much of it from oil-rich neighbours) will keep the economy growing smartly.

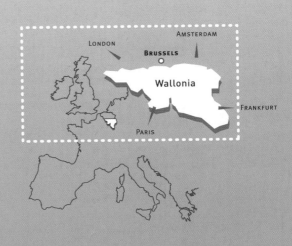

2008 IN PERSON

Marwan Barghouti, an imprisoned leader of the Palestinian Fatah faction, may just be the man to bring about a reunification between the Palestinians' warring factions. In a cautionary tale in these days of asymmetric warfare, Mr Barghouti's popularity was boosted when an Israeli court sentenced him to five life terms in 2004 over his role in the second Intifada. This was the latest in a career of incarcerations, but the one that really made his name among Palestinians looking for a figurehead. If he seemed a thorn in the side to the Israelis then, they may be coming to a different view now as Palestinian in-fighting dims peace prospects. Mr Barghouti may be no Mandela, but his acceptance of a two-state solution and appeals for Palestinian ceasefires to be honoured mark him out as a moderate in comparison with Hamas.

KENYA

GDP growth:	5.6%
GDP:	$25bn (PPP: $63bn)
Inflation:	7.4%
Population:	38.5m
GDP per head:	$640 (PPP: $1,640)

It looks like a new year and a new term for the president, Mwai Kibaki, who led the pack ahead of the end-2007 presidential election. Pre-election spending will inflate the budget deficit, leaving the government reliant on privatisation proceeds and domestic borrowing to make ends meet. The IMF is back on board after suspending funding in 2006 over governance issues, and adherence to IMF-style economic policies should keep GDP growth above 5%.

LEBANON

GDP growth:	1.5%
GDP:	$23bn (PPP: $33bn)
Inflation:	3.5%
Population:	4.2m
GDP per head:	$5,620 (PPP: $7,890)

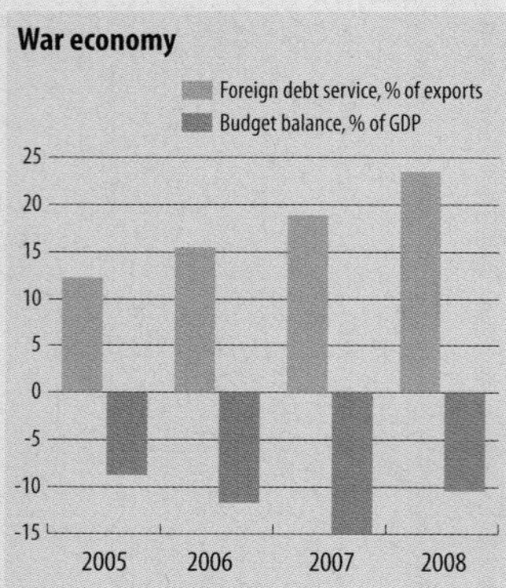

A chessboard for neighbouring powers, Lebanon's domestic politics are as fraught as the region's, and the spectre of civil war will hover overhead. The tussle over plans for an international tribunal to investigate the murder of a former prime minister, Rafiq al-Hariri, will be the centre of tension. Economic reforms will be a neglected sideshow, and the economy will limp along with the help of rising foreign borrowing and a wide budget gap.

MOROCCO

GDP growth:	5.1%
GDP:	$71bn (PPP: $185bn)
Inflation:	2.5%
Population:	31.8m
GDP per head:	$2,250 (PPP: $5,820)

The shift towards the conservative Istiqlal party in the late-2007 parliamentary elections strengthens the hand of the monarch, King Mohammed VI, and checks the advance of the Party for Justice and Development, moderately Islamist and sharply critical of the government. A high abstention rate, though, was the real news, with only 37% of voters turning up. The government is aiming to boost employment and living standards, but will struggle to make progress. After drought damaged the economy badly in 2007, a rally is on the cards.

To watch: Saharan samba. Morocco will host leaders from 34 countries in the second Arab-South American summit as both sides seek to diversify trade links.

NIGERIA

GDP growth:	7.8%
GDP:	$152bn (PPP: $212bn)
Inflation:	7.6%
Population:	149.5m
GDP per head:	$1,020 (PPP: $1,420)

Nigeria is Africa's most populous semi-democracy, but voters have little say on the appointment of national leaders. President Umaru Yar'Adua exemplifies the system, having come to power in a prodigiously rigged election in April 2007. The new president's first full year in office will reveal whether he is to be the instrument of reform that his background and platform promise. Even a modest push for electoral transparency, official accountability and economic even-handedness would help the country to realise its considerable potential. High oil prices will underpin continued GDP growth, but the rest of the economy—dominated by agriculture—is backward.

SAUDI ARABIA

GDP growth:	5.6%
GDP:	$401bn (PPP: $397bn)
Inflation:	3.2%
Population:	24.9m
GDP per head:	$16,100 (PPP: $15,950)

Political reform will lag behind even the modest aspirations of the king, Abdullah bin Abdel-Aziz al-Saud, as he balances the ambitions of his extended family and tries to keep the loyalty of the influential clerical establishment. Islamist radicals will be an immediate threat, and manoeuvring by Iran to become the regional heavyweight will demand attention in the longer term (though the response will fall short of support for military action against Iran). High oil prices will boost government revenue and attract energy investment.

SOUTH AFRICA

GDP growth:	5.1%
GDP:	$261bn (PPP: $695bn)
Inflation:	5.7%
Population:	47.8m
GDP per head:	$5,460 (PPP: $14,530)

The political focus will be on the battle to succeed the president, Thabo Mbeki, in 2009. The ruling African National Congress, with the support of two-thirds of the electorate, is in the driving seat, and the appointment of a party chairman at the close of 2007 will set the scene for the internal contest. Mr Mbeki is likely to step down from the party leadership and endorse a similarly pro-market and centrist successor, probably the deputy president, Phumzile Mlambo-Ngcuka. Rivals on the party's left will rally behind a former deputy president, Jacob Zuma, though lingering corruption allegations may force an early change of horses. Economic policy will remain pragmatic and fiscally conservative. The construction and investment boom shows no signs of slowing.

TANZANIA

GDP growth:	7.2%
GDP:	$14bn (PPP: $57bn)
Inflation:	4.9%
Population:	40.4m
GDP per head:	$353 (PPP: $1,420)

The president, Jakaya Kikwete, has proved less efficient in office than during his successful election campaign, and Tanzanians will increasingly clamour for delivery of his ambitious platform. Political divisions on the semi-autonomous islands of Zanzibar will fester, despite early promises from Mr Kikwete to resolve the problem. The administration's performance will remain steady rather than stellar, but there is little danger it will not complete its term. The farm-based economy will surge, if the weather is good.

UGANDA

GDP growth:	6.4%
GDP:	$13bn (PPP: $54bn)
Inflation:	5.5%
Population:	32.0m
GDP per head:	$415 (PPP: $1,680)

President Yoweri Museveni's government will be kept busy by a host of troubles, any one of which would flummox the most capable administration. Ending the 20-year insurgency of the Lord's Resistance Army, which has impoverished the north, is a particular challenge, but would yield a handsome political dividend. The top prize, a tilt at a fourth term in 2011, would require progress on another front, the growing fissures between Mr Museveni and his National Resistance Movement party. Meanwhile, energy shortfalls will continue to hold back the economy; growth of 6.4% sounds fast, but is below potential.

To watch: Terror trial. Tensions will persist over the trial of individuals accused of belonging to the People's Redemption Army (which the opposition says is a figment of the government's imagination).

ZIMBABWE

GDP growth:	-2.0%
GDP:	$2bn (PPP: $22bn)
Inflation:	4,200%
Population:	13.2m
GDP per head:	$133 (PPP: $1,640)

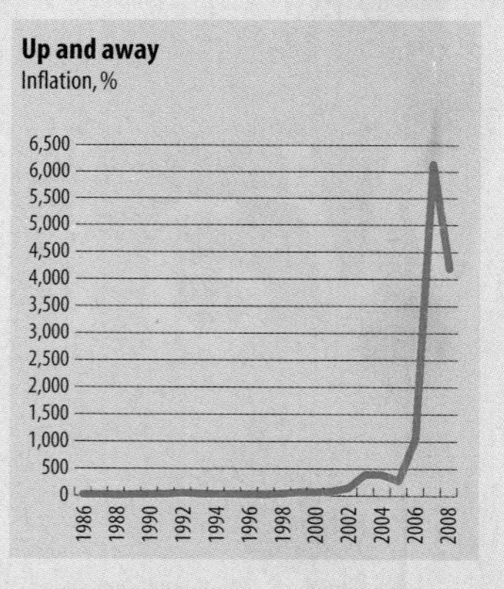

For most of its citizens, Zimbabwe has ceased to function as a state. The government issues policies and statistics, but they mean nothing and no one pays much attention. A third of the population has already left the country, and more than half of the remainder will spend 2008 relying on food aid to stay alive. President Robert Mugabe, a spry 83, will award himself a new term in the March 2008 election and continue suppressing competition from outside and within his Zanu-PF party.

The economy can be summed up in one very big number and one very small one: 4,000%-plus inflation, -2% growth.

The world in figures: Industries

Agriculture 123
Automotive 123
Consumer goods 123
Defence 124
E-commerce 124
Energy 124
Entertainment 124
Financial services 125
Food and drink 125
Health care 125
Information technology 125
Media 126
Raw materials 126
Telecoms 127
Travel and tourism 127

BUSINESS ENVIRONMENT

The Economist Intelligence Unit forecasts global GDP growth of 4.6% in 2008 (on a purchasing-power-parity basis), down from 5.1% in 2007. Beyond that top-line figure, most of the action will be in developing countries, which as a group will grow by more than 7%. China, India and Russia will lead the charge. The rich industrial countries, led by the United States, the euro-zone economies and Japan, will expand by only 1.8%.

The risk of recession in America will be great as the collapse in the housing market undermines consumer confidence. Credit will be more difficult to obtain in many countries as commercial banks tighten lending standards. But central banks worldwide will keep markets flush with cash, cushioning the global economy from too sharp a slowdown. Inflation will remain mostly under control. A weak dollar will help American exporters but weigh on those in most other countries. The price of a barrel of oil will hover around $69, lower than in 2007. Commodity prices will rise by only around 1%, down from 16% in 2007, as supply catches up with demand.

World trade will grow at a healthy 7.1%, despite the WTO's beleaguered Doha talks. China will work to regain international confidence in the safety of its exports. Trade between emerging markets will be a growing feature of global commerce.

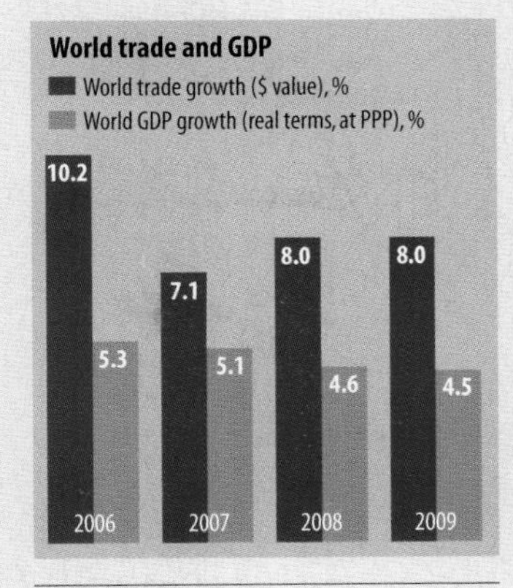

2008 forecasts unless otherwise indicated. World totals based on 51 countries accounting for over 95% of world GDP.

Source:

Economist Intelligence Unit

london@eiu.com

AGRICULTURE

CLOUDY FAIR SUNNY

America's agricultural exports will be worth a record $83.5bn in 2008, up $4.5bn from a year earlier, according to the US Department of Agriculture. Much of the increase will come from rising international commodity prices, rather than larger volumes, but Asian countries will boost demand for crops such as soybeans and cotton. American beef exports will climb by an impressive 18% in 2008, helped along by healthy appetites in Asia.

The world's livestock biodiversity will continue to decline, with at least one breed becoming extinct each month, continuing a seven-year trend. The UN Food and Agriculture Organisation says 20% of the world's species of cattle, goats, pigs, horses and poultry are at risk unless countries improve their management of genetic resources.

Demand for ethanol will spur sugar production. The International Sugar Organisation expects record output of 170m tonnes in the year ending September 2008. India will overtake Brazil as the world's biggest producer of the sweet stuff. But as increasing amounts of farmland are switched over to biofuel crops, other produce, such as oranges, will suffer.

Wheat prices will remain at record highs as global stocks dwindle. The International Grains Council forecasts output of 607m tonnes for the year to June 2008, down from earlier projections because of weak production in Ukraine and drought in Argentina and Australia. Another season of poor harvests will mean higher bread prices at best and a global food crisis at worst.

The global trade in rice—a famously protected commodity—will increase by around 2.3% a year between 2008 and 2017, by which time 8% of the forecast production of 36m tonnes will be traded. This will be the highest share since before the second world war. Rising import demand from Indonesia, the Philippines, Bangladesh, the Middle East and Africa will spur the increase in the global rice trade.

To watch: Death of the "poverty" insect. Africa's first large-scale fly factory in Ethiopia will release millions of male flies, sterilised with gamma-ray technology. Wild tsetse fly females will mate with the altered males, but create no offspring. Eradicating the flies could boost Africa's agricultural output by $4.5bn a year.

AUTOMOTIVE

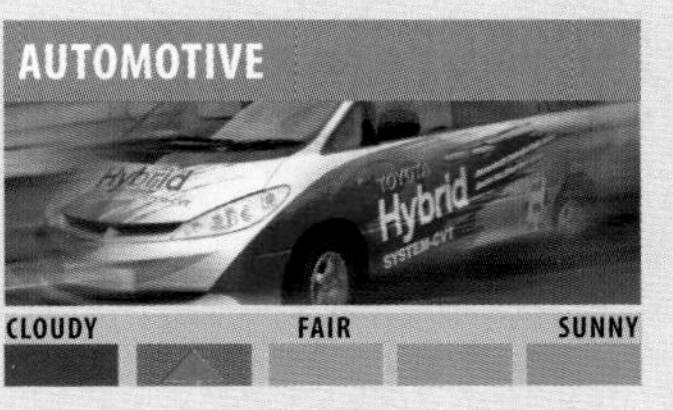

CLOUDY FAIR SUNNY

Global car sales will rise by 3% in 2008 as the American market remains stagnant and sales in India and China roar, increasing by 14% and 16% respectively. Truck sales globally will motor ahead by nearly 6%, reflecting rising investment in emerging economies. In the developed world, truck demand will be driven by tighter environmental regulations.

High oil prices will stoke demand for cars with greater fuel efficiency. Following the pioneering lead of Toyota and Honda, most manufacturers will have an electric or hybrid vehicle on the drawing board or in production in 2008. Hybrids will face increasing competition from diesel-powered vehicles, which are 20-30% more efficient than the petrol variety, and benefit from scrubbed-up diesel and higher-performance engines.

Honda is also investing heavily in hydrogen fuel-cell technology—with zero emissions—and will begin producing a vehicle, the FCX, in 2008. General Motors says it will have its own hydrogen-powered vehicle in showrooms in 2011.

Japanese and South Korean companies are capturing ever more market share in America and Europe, and Chinese and Indian carmakers will take sales at the lower end of the market before the decade is over. With no let-up in price competition, radical restructuring to trim overcapacity and boost margins—particularly in Europe and North America—will be the order of the day. Ford, which aims to sell its British-based Jaguar and Land Rover brands to improve its shaky finances, will not be alone in focusing on core brands and streamlining production.

To watch: Income-generating cars. Using a modified plug-in version of Toyota's popular hybrid, the Prius, Google and Pacific Gas & Electric are working on a system which generates electricity from the parked car and feeds it into a nearby power grid.

CONSUMER GOODS

CLOUDY FAIR SUNNY

Consumer spending will have its fifth straight year of solid growth in 2008, with global retail sales jumping 3.3%. Whereas strong American demand propelled growth earlier in the decade, it is now being fed by eager shoppers in China, India, Russia and eastern Europe.

In the developed world, mid-market retailers will be caught between consumers willing to pay a premium for high-quality brands but eager for low-priced everyday products, particularly when these are considered commodities. This will boost the fortunes of discount stores in mature markets and increase their appeal in emerging economies.

Wal-Mart, the world's largest retailer, aims to generate a third of its sales from non-American sources by 2010, up from 22% in 2007. A tie-up with Bharti Enterprises will help, with hundreds of stores set to open in India between 2008 and the end of the decade. Tesco, from Britain, will invade Wal-Mart's home turf, starting with convenience stores on America's west coast.

Consumers in China and Russia will increase retail spending by a blistering

12% in 2008. In Russia, big-city residents with incomes well above the national average will lead the way. In China, a rising minimum wage and the abolition of the agricultural tax will give consumers in rural areas and second-tier provinces more to spend.

To watch: Your fridge online. New standards developed by the Swiss-based International Electrotechnical Commission will usher in the long-awaited networked home, creating links between household appliances and audio-visual equipment such as PCs and televisions.

DEFENCE

CLOUDY FAIR SUNNY

With or without troop withdrawals, the wars in Iraq and Afghanistan will strain defence budgets. America, as ever, will lead the way, spending as much on defence as the rest of the world combined.

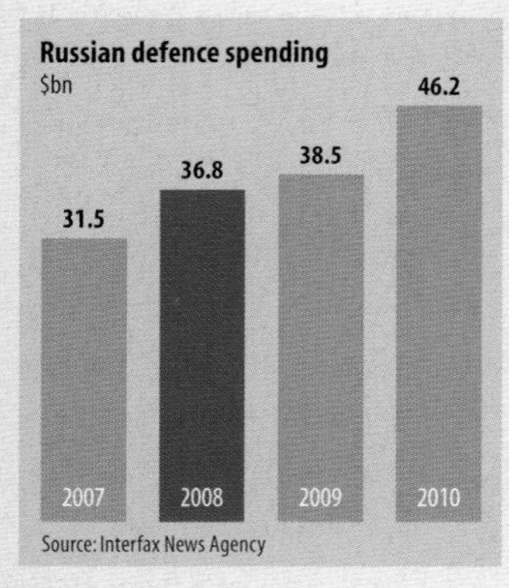

President George Bush is requesting $481bn in regular Pentagon spending in 2008, a 10% increase. To that must be added $142bn to cover the two wars. Pile on $17bn for nuclear weapons and $5bn for other odds and ends, and the total is more like $645bn—and that still doesn't include a further $36bn in homeland-security costs. Britain's defence budget, by contrast, will receive a spending increase of only 1.5% annually between 2008 and 2011, though the navy can look forward to two new 65,000-tonne aircraft carriers as part of that plan.

Most analysts put China's annual defence budget at just over $100bn, which is more than enough to keep Taiwan on tenterhooks. With the Olympics looming, though, Beijing will want to be on its best behaviour.

India's booming economy has given it the means to spend vigorously on arms: it will devote 960bn rupees ($24bn) to its defence in 2008, a rise of 7.8%. Natural-resources-rich countries such as Algeria, Azerbaijan, Saudi Arabia, Chile and Peru will also spend more on defence, thanks to rising revenue from oil, gas and minerals. Israeli spending will rise to $11.8bn from $10.7bn; this includes $3bn of defence aid from America, a 25% rise.

Determined to show it is not a spent force, Russia will boost defence spending by 16.3% to 956bn roubles ($36.8bn), with even bigger investments to come in the following two years. Under its plan to restore Russia's cold-war might, the Kremlin is planning to double production of combat aircraft by 2025 while adding more nuclear missiles, aircraft carriers and tanks.

To watch: Better protection. A Pentagon task force is evaluating a new generation of protective body suits to safeguard soldiers from the improvised explosive devices that have taken so many lives in Iraq and Afghanistan.

E-COMMERCE

CLOUDY FAIR SUNNY

Nearly 1.5bn of the world's citizens will be online in 2008, and a third of those will have access to a high-speed connection. For the first time China will have more broadband subscribers than the United States, says a British research firm, Ovum. By 2010, 21% of China's households will have broadband.

More Americans will use the internet to research products before travelling to shops to make the actual purchase. Forrester Research says this kind of shopping will grow at an annual rate of 17% over the next five years, resulting in shop sales of $1trn by 2012. That's not to say that online business-to-consumer transactions will suffer: eMarketer, a consultancy, predicts such sales in America will reach $139bn in 2008, up from $114bn in 2006. Although the distinction between online and offline retail is rapidly eroding, Europeans have embraced internet shopping as well: online retail sales there will be worth €263bn by 2011, with British shoppers accounting for more than a third of all revenue.

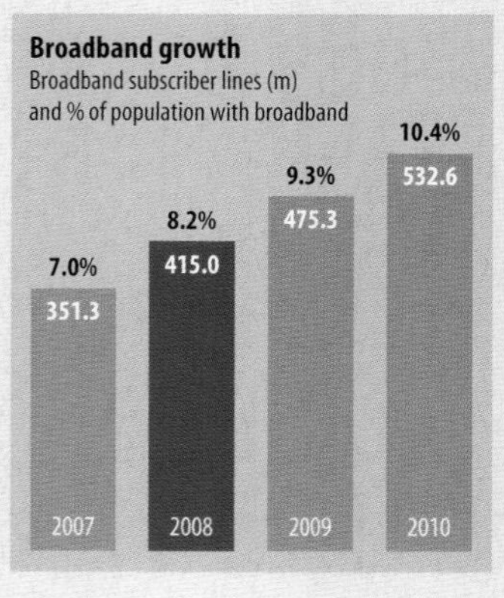

Business-to-business e-commerce sales will reach $650bn in America in 2008 and $1trn worldwide, according to IDC, a consultancy. Improvements in site search and navigation will help to promote new sales.

Governments in the emerging world will follow the example set by ChileCompra, an e-procurement system for public tenders that will conduct about $4bn-worth of business in 2008, most of it with Chile's smaller companies.

To watch: Asia learns to relax. Online travel planning is poised to take off in Asia. By 2010 India alone will account for more than $2bn in internet bookings, according to Euromonitor. The boom will not be limited to the subcontinent: travellers in Vietnam, Indonesia and China will also log on in search of the best deals.

ENERGY

CLOUDY FAIR SUNNY

Worldwide demand for energy will continue to rise in 2008 despite high prices and environmental concerns. Global energy consumption will climb by 3.5%, mainly because of buoyant economic growth in China and India.

With supplies still tight, oil prices will remain high in 2008, at around $69 a barrel for Brent crude, the European benchmark. OPEC has grown accustomed to the fruits of expensive oil, and has little interest in seeing prices fall by very much. Prices will, though, begin to ease in 2009 as new crude capacity comes on-stream in the former Soviet Union and several OPEC countries. Saudi Arabia says that by 2009 it will have the capacity to produce more than 12m barrels of oil a day, up from 10.7m in 2006.

Global consumption of natural gas will grow by 3.4% in 2008, helped by its relatively clean image and advances in transporting the fuel. The International Energy Agency expects natural gas to overtake coal as the world's second-largest primary energy source by 2015. Interest in nuclear power will also increase in 2008, led by the larger EU states, Japan, America and some developing countries. China alone is planning to build 30 nuclear plants during the next decade.

Although the risks of global climate change are becoming better understood, there will be little progress in cutting carbon emissions in 2008. According to the IEA, world CO_2 emissions from power plants will increase by about two-thirds over the next 25 years, with China and India accounting for nearly 60% of the rise.

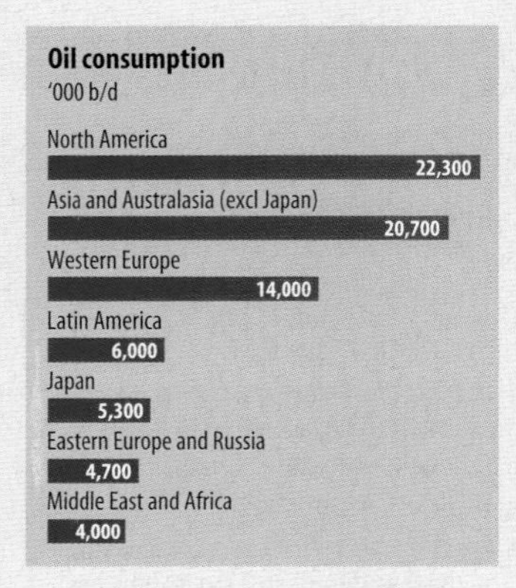

To watch: Dirty-water power. Scientists at Oregon State University have designed a biological fuel cell that uses bacteria to convert biodegradable materials into electricity. The technology should be commercially viable at large wastewater treatment plants.

ENTERTAINMENT

CLOUDY FAIR SUNNY

The war between Blu-ray and high definition (HD) DVD—two technologies battling to replace the DVD as the main entertainment-industry format—will gather pace in 2008. Walt Disney will bring a "virtual castle and multi-player activities" to the Blu-ray launch of the film, "Sleeping Beauty". Toshiba, leading the opposing camp, will begin shipping HD DVD drives as standard equipment in all its laptops. A winner will emerge by the end of the decade. HD DVD is still in the lead because of its lower production costs.

India's Bollywood will churn out more than 800 films in 2008, compared with about 600 from Hollywood. PricewaterhouseCoopers estimates that revenue from Indian films—about $1.8bn in 2006—will reach $3.4bn in the next three years as working practices become more professional. Percept Holdings, a media and entertainment company, will spend $100m on the 2008 launch of the first movie theme park in Mumbai, complete with film sets, cafés and gaming booths.

Digital cinema and 3D screens will

invigorate the American film market, but PwC says Asia will be the fastest-growing region for film-going and video rentals, with annual growth of 4.5% over the next few years. In Europe, online subscription rentals will cannibalise shop sales.

Asia will also be the fastest-growing region for recorded music, including physical formats and downloads, climbing 5.4% a year and overtaking America in market size in 2008. The region will also maintain its lead in the games market, expanding 10% annually to 2011. As the YouTube generation grows up, internet video streaming and downloads will surge, accounting for 30% of all internet traffic by 2011.

To watch: Daniel Craig's biceps. The 22nd James Bond film will be in cinemas in November, starring this soulful English actor. Other 2008 releases: a fourth Indiana Jones film, a Star Trek sequel and further Chronicles of Narnia.

FINANCIAL SERVICES

After more than five years of buoyant lending and extraordinary global liquidity, the credit cycle is turning and the effects will be felt deeply in 2008. The crisis in the American subprime mortgage market laid the foundation for this shift in mid-2007 as lenders and investors, left holding worthless mortgage-related assets, began to reprice all kinds of risk.

Many of these questionable mortgage loans (provided to people with poor credit) will reset at higher interest rates in 2008, leading to a steady rise in delinquencies and defaults. As the loans turn bad, securities based on these mortgages and sold to investors—including banks—from Germany to China will fall in value.

With financial institutions unsure of where the troubles lie, lending and borrowing will be subdued, keeping credit relatively tight. This will undercut mergers and acquisitions generally and private equity in particular, both of which have enjoyed a sustained boom for the past few years. Less dealmaking will remove what had been a strong source of profit for financial-services companies.

Although some property lenders may fail, the world's leading financial institutions should be strong enough to absorb the more stressful conditions that lie ahead. Most large financial firms are well positioned to withstand a slump in borrowing, a modest rise in problem loans or lower returns on assets. Balance sheets are strong, risk

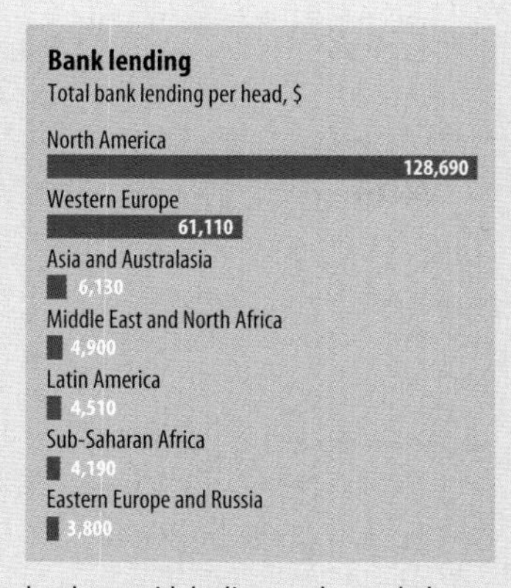

has been widely dispersed—on balance a good thing—and costs are mostly under control. Central bankers will play a key role in providing financing when conditions demand, while tightening regulation of off-balance-sheet vehicles where questionable assets were held.

Isolated from American and European markets, financial services in emerging economies will make rapid strides. In China, for example, only 12m people held credit cards in 2006 in a population of 1.3bn. In India, another booming economy, bank credit will grow by more than 20% in 2008.

To watch: Texting for cash. Mobile banking is taking off in places such as Kenya and the Philippines. This allows low-income workers to use their mobile phones to make and receive small payments at neighbourhood kiosks, eliminating the need to visit a bank.

FOOD AND DRINK

After two straight years of 15-20% annual growth, the Economist Intelligence Unit's price index of food, feedstuffs and beverages will rise by only around 5% in 2008. A slump in the price of drinks, especially tea, coffee and cocoa, will help push the index down. But the prices of many other foodstuffs,

including grains, oilseeds and sugar, will outperform the wider index. Big investments in biofuel crops and strong demand for feed and food, especially in emerging markets, have left the oilseeds and grain markets thinly stretched. This, plus continued resistance by retailers and consumers to higher prices, means life in the food-and-drinks industry will remain difficult.

Spending on food, drinks and tobacco as a share of all household spending peaked at 17.1% in 2007 and will edge down to 17% in 2008 and 16.9% a year later. Spending on food will not actually fall; rather, wealthier consumers in developing economies will spend more of their cash on electronics and home appliances, cutting food's share of the pie.

Consumers in rich countries, meanwhile, will move up the value chain as concerns over health, welfare and the environment spur demand for higher-quality food, including organic and locally grown produce. Food manufacturers and retailers will be pressured by consumers and governments to reduce packaging and curb the use of fats and additives in their products.

With indoor public smoking bans certain to gain ground in 2008, multinational tobacco firms will hungrily eye China, which accounts for 30% of world tobacco demand but is still closed to foreigners. But the wait could be a long one. The authorities are considering tighter restrictions on tobacco ahead of the 2008 Olympic games, which will be a smoke-free event.

To watch: Safe peanuts. A researcher at North Carolina Agricultural and Technical State University has developed a simple process to make allergen-free peanuts. The technique could provide relief to millions of peanut-allergy sufferers.

HEALTH CARE

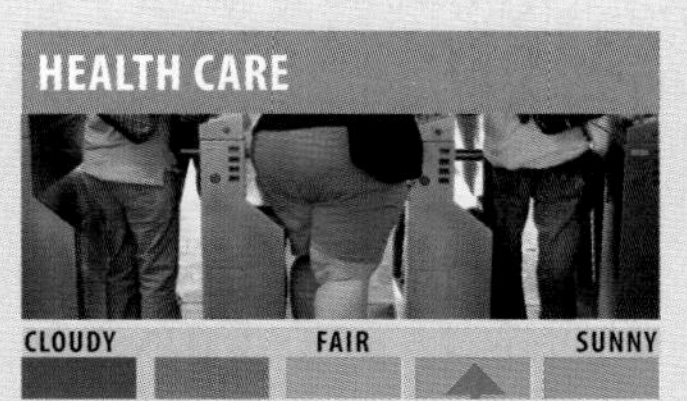

Cancer, respiratory ailments, diabetes and cardiovascular disease are becoming increasingly common in the world's developed economies as populations age. Indeed, while infant mortality and deaths from infectious disease will continue to fall worldwide in 2008, deaths from chronic ailments will rise at a double-digit pace. Efforts to combat these chronic conditions will be the driving force behind health-care spending, which will reach a record 10.6% of global GDP in 2008.

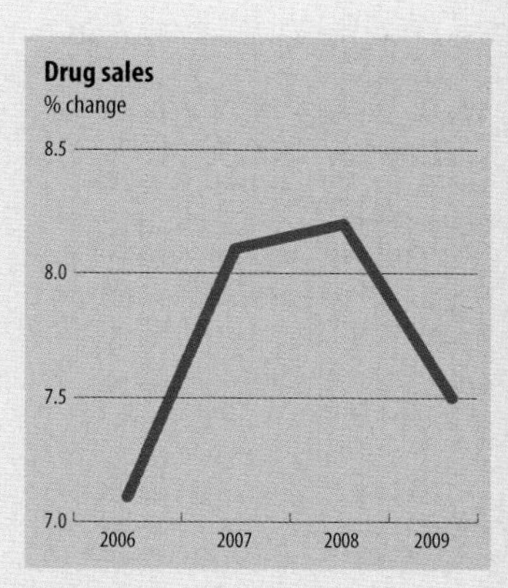

As governments clamp down on drug prices, pharmaceutical sales growth will slow—to 8.2% in 2008, and down to 7.5% the following year. According to IMS Health, a research firm, sales of cheaper generic drugs will grow by 14-17% a year to the end of the decade. Sales of generics will also be helped by a steady stream of expiring patents through to 2011. Patent expirations will include some of the world's major biotechnology drugs, paving the way for the development of a new market—biogenerics.

The prevalence of non-communicable "lifestyle" diseases such as obesity will become a major health issue in 2008, with international agencies such as the World Health Organisation co-ordinating a global response focused on prevention.

To watch: Molecular diagnostics. Researchers at Stanford University have developed a molecular probe that illuminates tumour cells. The probe identifies protein-destroying enzymes in cancerous cells, attaching a fluorescent tag that can be seen with a special camera. This eliminates the need for mammography or other x-rays.

INFORMATION TECHNOLOGY

Sales of personal computers (PCs) and semiconductors once were the benchmark for the health of the global IT sector. Today, it is sales of internet protocol (IP) networking equipment, broadband subscriber lines and the latest net-enabled gadgets. In 2008 demand for all of these will be driven by the continuing success of on-demand, online services—from downloadable video clips to collaborative software. Growth in IT spending in 2008 will, as a result, rise by a robust 5.6%.

PC shipments will grow at a slower rate—just 4.3% annually—during the next three years. There are signs that the digital divide is starting to narrow. PC ownership in the Middle East and Africa will leap to 17% of the population in 2008 from 7.2%, its biggest jump on record, due to lower taxes, falling prices and concerted government efforts to get PCs into schools. In Asia, excluding Japan, PC penetration will be a more modest 11%.

To watch: Smart attire. University of South Australia researchers are developing smart garments that can download monitored data into a computer. Uses range from tracking the vital signs of the disabled to shirts that can download news and music.

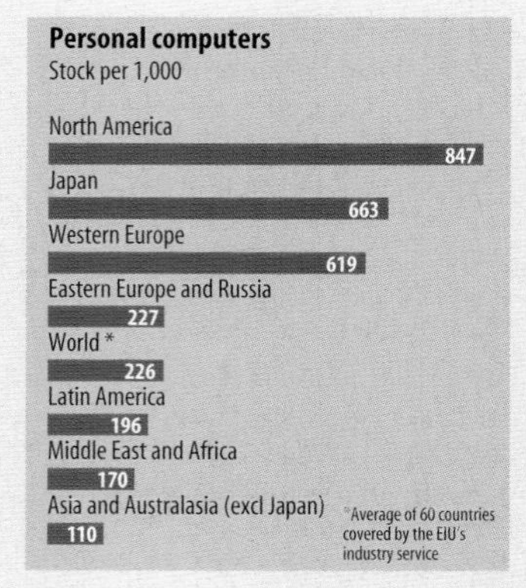

MEDIA

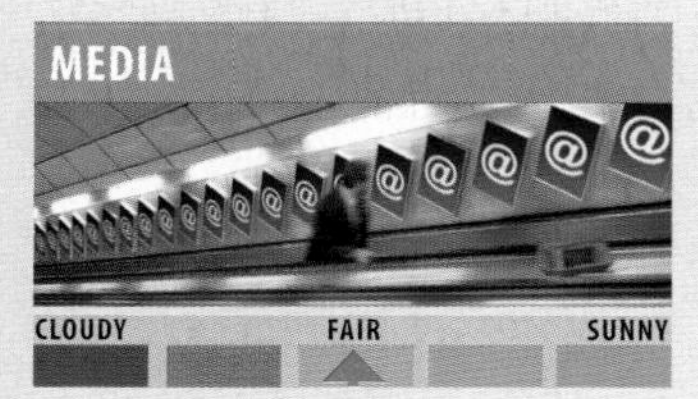

The Beijing Olympics will be a media bonanza, and not just for the eager host, China. The broadcast rights to the event will earn the International Olympic Committee an estimated $1.7bn, up from $1.5bn in Athens four years ago. In America, with presidential campaign war chests at record levels, the candidates will spend more than ever on advertising, mostly on broadcast and cable television. Wall Street analysts predict television stations could reap as much as $3bn from the 2008 election cycle, up from $1.6bn two years earlier and $900m in 2004.

The internet will account for 8% of global advertising spending in 2008, says London-based ZenithOptimedia. For the first time, the web will outperform radio, which will account for 7.9% of global advertising outlays. The internet is growing six times faster than traditional media, and by 2009 will account for more than 10% of ad spending in 11 countries, including Norway, Sweden and Britain. Forrester Research predicts European firms will spend 18% of their media budgets on online marketing by 2012.

Despite declining newspaper and magazine circulation in most Western countries, the news for print is not entirely grim. PricewaterhouseCoopers says Asia-Pacific newspaper revenue, including advertising and subscription sales, will grow to $53.5bn in 2011 from $45.2bn in 2006, an annual growth rate of 3.4%. Latin American magazine publishers are also in a good mood; their market will expand by 6% a year, to $4.2bn in 2011 from $3.1bn five years earlier.

To watch: Bragging blogs. More than 90% of marketing departments will launch a "social media" campaign, such as a blog, in 2008, according to Lewis PR, a United States-based global agency. By 2009 two-thirds of marketers will set aside up to 25% of their budgets for online social media.

RAW MATERIALS

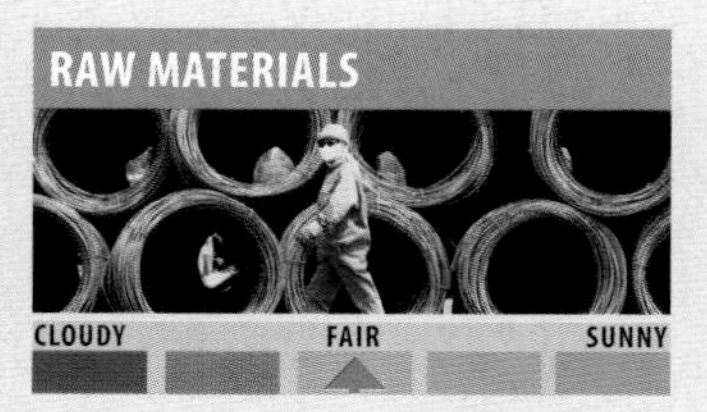

The Economist Intelligence Unit's industrial raw materials (IRM) index will fall by around 3% in 2008 as increased investment in metals production kicks in. This is a fairly gentle drop, however, given the IRM's meteoric 150% rise over the past six years.

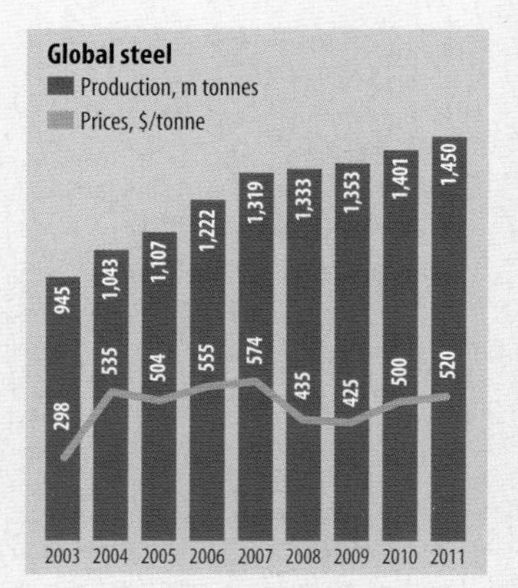

A growing desire for national self-sufficiency in steelmaking will push producers to invest in new factories and equipment. By 2010, China's annual steel output will be well above 500m tonnes, according to Britain-based MEPS International. Global steel production will rise by about 6% annually through to 2010, with both India and Russia becoming increasingly important players. By the end of the decade, global finished steel consumption will top 1bn tonnes.

A combination of weaker American

demand and high inventories will send world copper prices plummeting by 12% in 2008, to an average of $5,900 a tonne. However, consumption will rise by 5%, mostly because of China.

By contrast, global demand for nickel will grow by 7.4% in 2008, but the market will remain tight as output increases by only 7.3%. If Chinese demand for stainless steel is greater than expected, rationing may be necessary.

Renewed interest in nuclear power is boosting confidence in uranium production. Uranium One of Canada will increase output in 2008 to 7.5m pounds, from only 2m in 2007, as four projects get under way. The company wants to compete with its Canadian rival and the world's leading producer, Cameco. Both companies are forecast to produce about 28m pounds of uranium by 2013.

To watch: Carbon fibre. Ten times stronger than steel, rust-proof and ultra-light, carbon fibre should be traded as a commodity on global markets, say its supporters. The material is already being used in Boeing's new 787 Dreamliner aeroplane and in the Airbus A380. Demand for carbon fibre is soaring from manufacturers of everything from bullet-proof vests and golf clubs to wind farms.

With half the world's population now owning a mobile phone, growth rates will at last drop out of double digits in 2008, edging down to 5% in 2010. Phones are no longer just for talking. Revenue growth from data downloads (video, music, e-mail) will be triple that of mobile voice during the next three years.

Third-generation (3G) phones, which have high-speed internet connections, already outnumber conventional handsets in Japan and will post double-digit growth in developed economies in 2008. Hoping to rescue their fixed-line businesses, most telecoms firms are investing heavily in their networks and turning to broadband.

Not to watch: IPTV. The success of internet protocol television—watching your favourite shows over broadband connections—is not likely to take off for some years, mainly because of competition from cable and satellite operators.

New open-skies agreements between the European Union and America, as well as more trips to emerging markets, will propel growth in the travel industry in 2008. International arrivals will increase by 4.4% to 750m, and the amount tourists spend will jump by 5.5%.

With the Superjumbo Airbus 380 already in the air, the Boeing-Airbus rivalry will intensify as the American planemaker's Dreamliner takes to the skies in 2008.

The smaller Dreamliner will be 20% more fuel-efficient and have a range of nearly 10,000 miles, creating the option of new long-haul routes such as Seattle-Shanghai or Madrid-Tokyo.

Under the new EU-US open-skies agreement, which takes effect in March, any European airline will be able to fly to the United States from any European capital. Although this will bring welcome choice and price competition to transatlantic travellers, it will hurt the traditional European flag fleets and may well bring a wave of consolidation. Airlines, having been forced to undergo substantial restructuring in recent years, are now healthier. The industry may well return to profitability in 2008.

Also in this section:
Europe's business stars 130
Gadgets galore 132
Mobile phone as wallet 134
Cash calls in the poor world 135
A talent shortage in China 136
The world's cheapest car 139
OPEC on top again 140
Indra Nooyi: The responsible company 143
Jargon 2.0 144
Money makes the world better 145
Green accounting 146

Business

Freeconomics

Chris Anderson

Online, there really is such a thing as a free lunch

In 1954, at the dawn of nuclear power, Lewis Strauss, the head of the Atomic Energy Commission, promised that we were entering an age when electricity would be "too cheap to meter". That did not happen, mostly because the risks of nuclear energy hugely increased its costs. But what if electricity had in fact become virtually free?

The answer is that everything that electricity touched—which is to say nearly everything—would have been transformed. We would be using electricity for as many things as we could—we would waste it, because it was so cheap that it wasn't worth worrying about efficiency.

All buildings would be electrically heated. We would all be driving electric cars. Desalination plants would turn sea water into all the fresh water anyone could want, irrigating vast inland swathes and turning deserts into fertile acres, many of them making biofuels. Compared with free electrons, fossil fuels would be seen as ludicrously expensive and dirty, and so carbon emissions would plummet. The phrase "global warming" would never enter the language.

Unlikely? Just such a transformation is already under way, but not in electricity. What is getting too cheap to meter is processing power, storage, bandwidth and all the other enabling technologies of the digital revolution. Thanks to the exponential doublings of Moore's Law and its equivalents for hard drives and communications, the cost of a given unit of computation, storage or transmission is inexorably dropping towards zero.

One of the first to notice this and consider its implications was a Caltech professor named Carver Mead. In the late 1970s he was reflecting on the amazing learning curve that the combination of quantum mechanics and information science had started on the surface of silicon wafers. Like Moore before him, he could see that the 18-month doublings in performance would continue to stretch out as far as anyone could see. But he went one step further to consider what that implied about computers. He realised that we should start "wasting" them.

Waste is a dirty word, and no more so than in the 1970s and 1980s. An entire generation of computer professionals had come to power doing just the opposite. In the glass-walled computer facilities of the mainframe era, they exercised their power in deciding whose programs should be allowed to run on the expensive computing machines.

> Be the first to give away what others charge for

The Beijing Olympics deliver a television audience of 4 billion, but Eastman Kodak and General Motors say Beijing marks their last time as **Olympic sponsors**.

2008 IN BRIEF

Chris Anderson: editor-in-chief, *Wired* magazine; author of "The Long Tail" (Hyperion and Random House)

Among Mead's disciples was Alan Kay, working at Xerox's Palo Alto Research Centre. Rather than conserve transistors for core processing functions, he developed a computer that would frivolously throw them at such silly things as drawing icons, windows, pointers and even animations on the screen. The point of this profligate eye candy? It was ease of use for regular folks, a previously neglected market. Kay's work became the inspiration for the Apple Macintosh, which changed the world by opening computing to the rest of us.

Today the same is happening in everything from bandwidth to storage. The learning curves of technology cut prices at a rate never before seen. The cost of storing or transmitting a kilobyte of data really is now too cheap to meter. Soon the same will be true for a megabyte, and then soon after that a terabyte. And the internet touches nearly as much of our economy as electricity did when Lewis Strauss issued his prediction.

Creative disruption

Bandwidth too cheap to meter brought us YouTube, which is revolutionising (and possibly destroying) the traditional television industry, and Skype, which is hollowing out the phone industry. Storage too cheap to meter brought us Gmail, which in 2004 upended the webmail market by increasing—free—the capacity available to all by a factor of 1,000, to say nothing of the huge free photo capacity of Flickr or MySpace's invitation to put anything on your personal page for no cost.

Before the iPod, people weren't asking to carry their entire music collection in their pockets. But Steve Jobs and a few others at Apple understood the economics of storage abundance. They could see that disk drives were gaining capacity for the same price even faster than computer processors were. Demand for massive music collections wasn't driving this—physics and engineering were. Anyone could extrapolate the curves and see what was around the corner, but only the Apple engineers "listened to the technology", to use Mead's phrase, and saw that putting 10,000 songs on a drive smaller than a deck of playing cards was going to be possible by 2001.

The dominant business model on the internet today is making money by giving things away. Much of that is merely the traditional media model of using free content to build audiences and selling access to them to advertisers. But an increasing amount of it falls into the free-sample model: because it is so cheap to offer digital services online, it doesn't matter if 99% of your customers are using the free version of your services so long as 1% are paying for the "premium version". After all, 1% of a big number can also be a big number.

In 2008, the year of free, Yahoo! will go one better than Google and expand its free webmail to infinity. More music labels will give away music as a promotion for concerts, following Prince's free distribution of his album in Britain's *Daily Mail* in 2007 and Radiohead's offer to let fans choose their price—free, if they want—when they download the latest album. And more newspapers will publish their content free on the internet.

All this marks a pattern. When the cost of serving a single customer is trending to zero, smart companies will charge nothing. Today, the disrupter's motto is "Be the first to give away what others charge for". If you listen to the technology, it makes sense. ■

Movers and shakers

Iain Carson

European businessmen (and one woman) who will make the headlines

It is no accident that the thick of the action for Europe's leading business people in 2008 will be utilities and technology companies. Liberalisation in energy and changing technology in the IT and telecoms sector will continue to reshape many companies, creating opportunities for some and huge problems for others. There will be disproportionate activity in France, driven by a new president keen to remodel the French economy.

A new style at Fiat...

...a star at Areva...

...and a whizz kid at Deutsche Telekom

This was already in evidence in 2007, but 2008 will see Gérard Mestrallet and Jean-François Cirelli trying to make a success of the GDF-Suez energy merger, shaped in President Nicolas Sarkozy's Elysée palace. Another object of political interference will be Airbus Industrie, where France's Fabrice Brégier, the planemaker's chief operating officer, must quickly get the company back on course if he is to fulfil his ambition of succeeding to the top Airbus job.

Airbus will also prove a challenge for François Bertrand, boss of Latécoère, a Toulouse maker of aircraft fuselage parts that wants to take over one of the Airbus factories being hived off. A friend of Mr Sarkozy, François Bouygues, who runs the construction firm of that name, will pop into the news by taking a stake in Airbus's corporate parent, EADS.

Deregulation of electricity could be the making of Charles Beigbeder, a French dotcom millionaire who sold his online broking firm in time just as the bubble burst. Now he has an electricity firm, POWEO, signing up retail customers who do not like buying direct from the mighty EDF. This will be the year for him to break through into the big time as an independent, selling power bought from the EDF giant.

Yet another Frenchman making waves will be Jean-Bernard Lafonta, of the Wendel investment company. After floating about 70% of BureauVeritas in 2007, he will be seeking to build strategic ▶

Lightening up

Nicholas Valéry

Leave the laptop behind

As smart phones take over chores that trusty old laptops used to perform, road warriors are stuffing their overnight bags with other tools of the trade instead—and the trend will increase in 2008 as gadget prices fall. But beware: what you lose in weight you may make up in quantity. Thanks to miniaturisation, some of the new accessories are far lighter than their predecessors. But where before they were luxuries to take along, their newfound lightness is making them "must haves" for the road. Here are a few of the gadgets the well-armed business traveller will need in 2008.

The **Visioneer RoadWarrior** (street price around $170) and the **Plustek OpticSlim M12 Corporate** (around $130) are portable document scanners that will make mobile professionals wonder how they ever managed without one. The answer is that until recently portable versions were heavier than even a bulky old luggable laptop. Now they weigh in at less than ten ounces (283 grams).

The handy thing about a portable scanner is that it can double as a personal photocopier and fax machine, or provide digital copies of printed documents for e-mailing as attachments. Best of all, it allows you to fax or e-mail signed documents—great for clinching a deal with a signed contract. You can then scan in all the business cards and expense receipts before heading home.

Another former luxury that will become a near-essential is a portable GPS (global positioning system) navigation device. **Netropa's** clever little **Intellinav 3** can be had for less than $330. **Garmin's nuvi 260** is priced typically around $420. And the **Navigon 7100** (with built-in Zagat ratings of hotels, restaurants, golf courses and nightlife) can be bought for $530 or less. These and other "sat-nav" devices have moved from the dashboard into the pocket, as both their bulk and price have shrunk. Rent a car at the airport, key your destination into your personal navigator—and you'll never get lost again.

Just one would do

The latest models show not only rolling route maps, with verbal directions and announcements of the names of upcoming streets, but also relay the latest traffic and weather reports, and give warning of school zones and speed restrictions. Some let you play music you've downloaded to the device, or watch your favourite movies when unable to sleep at night.

One more gadget finding its way into the mobile professional's luggage is the ultra-small multimedia projector. The size of a chunky paperback, the **Toshiba TDP-PX10U** is the best of the current breed, able to throw a bright, high-resolution image on to a boardroom screen in less than total darkness all for less than $1,000. Most of these digital gems can now be used without a laptop. They get their PowerPoint files or charts direct from a portable hard-drive plugged into the projector's side. Laptop, rest in peace. ■

Nicholas Valéry: writer on technology for Economist.com

2008 IN BRIEF

Clean Gum, a non-stick, degradable **chewing gum**, is launched, and starts to cut street-cleaning costs around the world.

shareholdings, such as his stake in St Gobain. Businesswomen are in short supply in France (as everywhere), but Anne Lauvergeon is making her mark both at home and in America, where Areva, the nuclear company she runs, will capture much of the market as America warms again to nuclear power.

Germany in 2007 lost one of its few top entrepreneurial managers when Klaus Kleinfeld was unfairly hounded out of Siemens for his Americanised style as he rebuilt the company. He was quickly snapped up by Alcoa, the world's second-largest aluminium firm, where he recently took over as chief operating officer. Sticking with the fatherland is René Obermann. The mobile-phone whizz (he started his own company while still a trainee at BMW) is in his second year rebuilding troubled Deutsche Telekom after the meltdown that consumed two previous bosses in five years. Meanwhile the veteran Hartmut Mehdorn's task in his penultimate year on the footplate of Deutsche Bahn will be to privatise it successfully. He might also rescue the ailing freight business of French state railways, through a joint venture.

In the Netherlands Ad Scheepbouwer, boss of the KPN telecoms operator, will bid for the mobile-phone business of French Bouygues later in the year, having shied away in 2007. This will also be the year when another Dutchman, Hans Wijer, discovers whether he paid too much for ICI in adding it to Akzo Nobel.

In Italy Alessandro Benetton, son of Luciano (who founded the clothing group in the 1960s), is taking the reins at the traditional heart of the now diversified Benetton Group. Another scion of a business family, John Elkann, has everything to prove running the Agnelli business empire—including Fiat—founded by his grandfather. He will build on the expansion of 2007, when he moved into the international property services business, buying America's Cushman and Wakefield.

In Spain the band of bold construction bosses will be subdued as the property market weakens and credit becomes tight. Under most stress will be Rafael del Pino, boss of Ferrovial, a firm controlled by his family: its purchase in 2006 of BAA is proving a terrible headache thanks to endless problems at Heathrow airport.

In Britain the biggest business battles will be on the high street. Sir Philip Green will have to rebuild the fortunes of his Top Shop group just as signs of a retail slowdown appear. His arch-rival, Stuart Rose, chief executive of Marks & Spencer (for which Sir Philip once plotted a hostile takeover bid), will outshine him as a revitalised M&S powers on. Both men, however, may be overshadowed by Sir Terry Leahy, chief executive of Tesco and a man who has brought impressive profits to the supermarket chain. Sir Terry's big challenge for 2008 will be to make Tesco, and its subsidiary Fresh & Easy, a success in America. ■

Iain Carson: Europe business editor, *The Economist*; co-author of "Zoom: The Global Race to Fuel the Car of the Future" (Twelve)

Buying and celling

Tom Standage

Pay with a wave of your mobile phone

2008 IN BRIEF

Richard Branson's **Virgin Galactic** makes test flights of its six-passenger plane for space-tourists.

There are three things that people generally take everywhere with them: keys, wallet and mobile phone. One of these hopes to do away with the other two. During 2008 the mobile phone will take a big step towards replacing your wallet. And the same technology could eventually enable it to replace your keys, too.

Paying for things by using a mobile phone has been possible for a while, though it is generally a bit of a fiddle. That is because it is most commonly done using text messages, which were not designed for the purpose. Various schemes let you pay for parking by using your phone, for example, provided you register your credit-card details in advance. Similar schemes make it possible to buy train tickets and items from vending machines. Some mobile-payment systems also allow cash deposits, withdrawals and person-to-person funds transfers, all of which have particular potential in the developing world (see box on next page). But the lack of a single common standard, bickering between mobile operators and banks over business models, and the simple fact that using cash or a card is usually much more convenient than fiddling with a mobile phone, mean that wallets have so far not had much to worry about.

> The phone can be your wallet, your ticket or your key

That will change in 2008 as a new technology, called "Near-Field Communication" (NFC), starts to gain traction. NFC encompasses several short-range wireless standards that are already used in building-access passes, in a new breed of contactless (no touch needed with the terminal) travel passes such as London's Oyster and Hong Kong's Octopus cards and in contactless credit cards. With an embedded NFC chip and suitable software, a mobile phone can mimic any or all of these cards, in effect carrying several of them like a wallet. Rather than waving one card at the station, another to get into the office and a third to pay for lunch, people in many parts of the world are starting to use NFC-enabled wallet-phones for these things instead.

Making all this happen depends on rolling out the appropriate scanning equipment. But that is now happening. In Japan, which has led the way with this technology, 20m people use contactless Suica cards, issued by the East Japan Railway Company, to pay for train fares and make purchases from shops and vending machines. Suica is just one of a bewildering array of contactless payment and ticketing schemes in Japan, many of which also work with wallet-phones, around 40m of which are now in circulation in the country. In the case of Suica, some 350,000 people have adopted Mobile Suica, which allows their phones to act as Suica cards. It is then possible to see the Suica balance on the phone's screen and to top it up while on the move, via a mobile-internet connection.

In America several banks are issuing contactless credit cards and providing shops with the appropriate equipment to read them. Around 160,000 terminals had been installed in 50,000 shops by September 2007, according to industry figures. For small transactions, below $25 or so, customers can "wave and pay" at the till, which is much quicker than processing a conventional credit-card transaction. This makes contactless cards particularly attractive in time-sensitive environments such as shops in railway stations. For larger purchases, the customer waves the card at the reader and ▶

Tom Standage: business editor, *The Economist*

Cash on call

Tom Standage

Mobile payments in the developing world

For people in the poorest countries, where bank branches are few and far between and most people do not have bank accounts at all, using a mobile phone for financial transactions may make a lot of sense. A lack of access to financial services increases the cost of borrowing and hampers entrepreneurship. Carrying large amounts of cash around, or storing it under the bed, is insecure. And sending remittances, which dwarf official aid flows for many developing countries, is subject to high transaction costs. Mobile banking and payment schemes can address all of these problems. And, unlike banks, mobile phones are proliferating fast.

A good example of the potential can be seen in Kenya, where a mobile-payment system called M-PESA was launched on a pilot basis in 2005, and went fully commercial in March 2007. It is operated by Safaricom, Kenya's biggest mobile operator, which is an affiliate of Vodafone. Having signed up for M-PESA, customers can deposit and withdraw money at Safaricom's airtime distribution agents. They can also send funds to other people: the recipient receives a text message that can be "cashed in" at a Safaricom agent.

It sounds simple, but the ability to send money by phone makes all sorts of things possible. Casual workers can be paid by phone; taxi drivers can accept payment by phone rather than carrying cash around; money can be sent to friends and family in emergencies. One popular practice is to deposit money before making a long journey and then withdraw it at the other end, which is safer than carrying lots of cash, says Diane Coyle, an expert on mobile phones and development at Enlightenment Economics, a consultancy. Vodafone is considering launching the service in India.

Similar schemes include Wizzit in South Africa and G-Cash in the Philippines. Wizzit is more like a virtual bank. It has no branches, but allows payments and transfers via mobile phone, and issues customers with a debit card—an intriguing low-cost model for banks in the developing world. The big question, says Ms Coyle, is will m-banking merely make life easier for the relatively well-off, or will it bring financial services within reach of poorer people for the first time? So far the signs are very promising, though there are regulatory barriers in some countries that could hold back deployment. But if m-banking takes off, she says, it could be "transformational". ■

2008 IN BRIEF

In a world of 7 billion people, the number of **personal computers** surpasses 1 billion—and the number of **mobile-phone subscribers** exceeds 3.7 billion.

then enters a personal-identification number (PIN) to confirm his identity.

Credit-card companies are keen on contactless technology because they see it as a way to extend their reach into low-value transactions where cash is currently more convenient. Mobile operators like the idea of incorporating NFC chips into phones because they could get a cut of each transaction. And handset-makers are always keen on any new technology that means that everyone suddenly needs a new phone.

Conquering the world

So far NFC is mainly being used for payments in America, for tickets in Europe and for both in Asia, says Gerhard Romen, an NFC guru at Nokia, the world's biggest handset-maker. But that will change during 2008 as the technology spreads. Barclays, a British bank, has launched a contactless card that combines an Oyster travel pass with a credit card and a cashless payment system for small purchases under £10 ($20). It is merely the first of six banks deploying contactless cards in Britain. In Vienna, NFC-enabled phones can be used as tickets on public transport, to buy things from vending machines and to pay for parking. A similar scheme was launched in Frankfurt in October 2007. Contactless-ticketing trials are under way on the public-transport systems in New York, Boston and San Francisco.

The convergence of contactless cards and the mobile phone, made possible by NFC technology, means you will soon be able to leave your wallet at home, some of the time at least. What about your keys? NFC could replace them too, says Mr Romen. Nokia is working with the world's big lockmakers, which are adding NFC support to their products. "The phone can be your wallet, your ticket or your key," he says. "It's like your own magic wand." Open sesame? ■

2008 IN BRIEF

Boeing delivers its **787 Dreamliner**, the first airliner with an all-composite plastic fuselage, to Japan's All Nippon Airways—assuming the target date does not slip still more.

Not enough people in China

Graeme Maxton *HONG KONG*

A shortage of staff means employers will take more risks in 2008

Ask senior executives about their main concerns for the year ahead, and the "shortage of talent" will come at or near the top of the list. Surely help is at hand, with the world's most populous country now open for business? Alas, no: even China has a talent shortage.

It is an odd discovery to those without much experience of the country. In almost every business and every industrial sector, the biggest problem facing employers is a lack of qualified people. It will get noticeably worse in 2008, for several reasons.

First, investment. Flush with cash from Hong Kong IPOs, a new wave of investment will create lots of new jobs in 2008 as Chinese firms expand. Many will seek to grow internationally too, bringing added troubles. What these companies lack are the skills needed to achieve their goals. Nor do they have the time it takes to develop them. So they will poach the staff they need from rivals.

Second, demographics. Thanks to the one-child policy introduced in 1979, the number of workers in their late 20s will shrink further in 2008. Businesses, which typically select the best of this age-group for supervisory jobs or the fast-track to management, will increasingly find a much smaller talent pool to fish from.

Third, migrant workers. The flood will slow to a trickle in 2008. Until now, migrant workers coming from the western provinces have fed the bottom end of the labour market in the richest parts of China. But following government efforts to set up factories away from the coastal regions, and with the drop in the number of people entering the workforce, fewer inland workers will bother to make the trip.

The search for more senior managers, those who can lead businesses in China, will get tougher in 2008 too. The shortage of bosses has been acute for several years, but with more demand and little new supply it will become even more of a headache.

China's universities and many schools were closed for ten years during the Cultural Revolution. This means that most people in their late 50s and early 60s have had little or no formal education. The majority lack any experience of working outside the state sector. Although the government has been hurriedly trying to train the best of them, the demand for top managers will exceed the supply in 2008.

> It is now cheaper to employ factory workers in Malaysia than in parts of China and senior managers often cost more than in Europe

Nor can China's existing skills problems be fixed easily. Much of the shortage of qualified staff is the result of the education system, which has not been able to keep up with China's fast-evolving labour market. The schools system still teaches by rote, producing people who foreign employers often ▶

Graeme Maxton: freelance contributor, *The Economist*

Cheap but not so cheerful

Graeme Maxton *HONG KONG*

The launch of the world's lowest-priced car

Indians will have the first chance to buy the world's cheapest car in 2008. Delayed by design changes and protests over the site of its new factory, the car is due to appear on the market around mid-year. With a two-cylinder, 30-horsepower, rear-mounted engine and four doors it is aimed at those trading up from scooters and three-wheelers. In launching it, Tata Motors, part of India's largest private firm, will start a controversial trend.

When it was first conceived, the 1 lakh (100,000 rupees) car was to have cost the equivalent of $2,000 before tax. With the drop in value of the dollar and the hike in raw-material costs it is now likely to be more like $3,000. Yet this is still less than half the price of today's best-known low-cost car, the Renault Logan.

Tata achieves its staggeringly low price by approaching the development and assembly process anew. The car uses more plastics than usual and adhesives are used to stick some of the bits together. This is faster and cheaper than using conventional robots and welding. Many of the suppliers will also work on-site, cutting inventory and delivery costs.

To increase volumes and achieve economies of scale quickly the company is establishing a series of small satellite factories, working with the mother plant in Bengal. These will build the cars from kits and then sell and service them as well, doing away with the costs and margins taken by more traditional dealers.

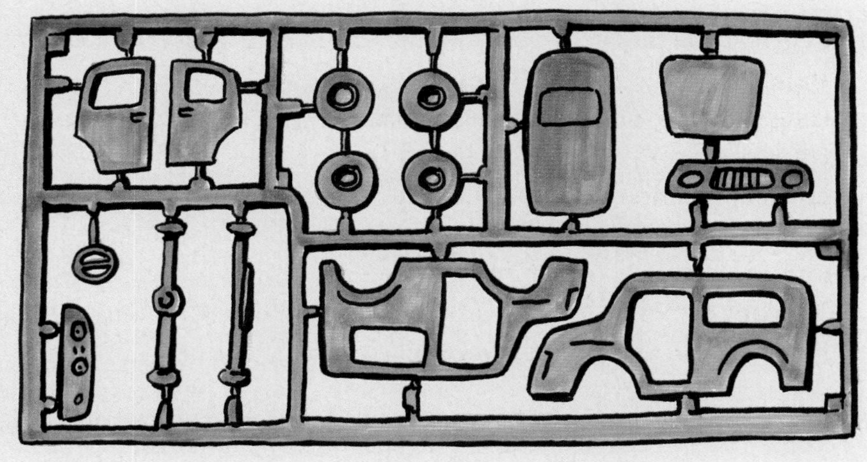

With an initial target of 1m units a year, the new vehicle will double Indian car output. The company says it plans to replicate the approach in other developing countries too, so volumes can grow bigger still. Moreover, after scoffing at Tata's plans, other big carmakers such as VW, Renault, Toyota and GM are hurriedly designing ultra-low-cost cars of their own.

> Adhesives are used to stick some of the bits together

This is good news for the world's (comparatively) poor, and for those seeking the status, mobility and independence that comes from a car. It should be good for the manufacturers too, although margins will be extremely thin. But with concerns about oil security, fuel prices and the environment reaching new highs in 2008, hardly anyone else will welcome this flood of more cars on the world's roads. ■

say are inflexible, lacking in creativity and initiative. Staff turnover is very high, too. It is not uncommon for fast-expanding factories to find that 40% of their staff are new each year. Wages have also been rising quickly. It is now cheaper to employ factory workers in Malaysia than in parts of China and senior managers often cost more in China than in Europe.

With the outlook less rosy still, what will employers do? According to Michael Bekins of Korn/Ferry in Hong Kong, there will be a shift in the mindset of head-hunters and HR bosses in 2008. "Developing retention plans will become a bigger issue than recruiting," he says. He thinks managers will start being measured explicitly on how well they keep their team.

Jürgen Kracht, the head of Fiducia, a China-specialist consultancy, says there will also be "many more Chinese returnees and more Asians moving from countries like Singapore and Malaysia" to make up the shortfall. This, he says, means that the shortage will be exported to the rest of the region.

Employers are also likely to take more risks in 2008 to entice the best, or even the very-nearly-good-enough. Foreign and domestic companies will bring more expatriates from Europe and America. As well as raising costs further, the newcomers will bring new headaches. Without any experience of working in such a difficult place more mistakes will be made, resulting in more product recalls and safety scares. There will also be a trend towards promoting people before they are ready, of "placing people in big shoes", says Vanessa Moriel of Human Capital in Shanghai. Tax-saving pay deals, where part of someone's salary or a sign-on bonus is paid in vouchers or overseas, will become more common in 2008, as employers try to find cunning ways of paying people more, more cheaply.

"Foreign companies risk doing deals in China that they would never do in Europe or the United States," says Mr Kracht. Yet for many companies bending the rules and making compromises will be the only way they can attract the skills they need in China in 2008. ■

2008 IN BRIEF

An **amphibious three-seater car**, the Aquada, is launched into the market, with a road speed of 175kph (110mph) and a river speed of 50kph.

OPEC rules again

Edward McBride

The oil cartel is riding high, at least for now

For much of the past few years, energy analysts have been consumed by the fear that the amount of oil pumped each year is reaching a pinnacle, and will soon be in precipitous decline. Fears of "peak oil" have helped to push oil prices to record levels, in nominal terms at least. But in 2008 it will gradually become apparent that it is not oil output that has reached its apogee so much as the power of the cartel that controls its price: OPEC, the Organisation of the Petroleum Exporting Countries.

In the 1970s OPEC held the globe to ransom, pushing oil prices past $100 per barrel in today's money, and tipping the world economy into recession. But the oil shocks it induced ultimately proved self-defeating. Rich nations began making much more efficient use of the oil they bought, and demand for OPEC's crude started growing far more slowly than the cartel had expected. Western oil companies and OPEC's state-owned behemoths alike were left with lots of excess capacity.

To stave off a total collapse in prices, OPEC had to mothball lots of its own rigs. Non-members, meanwhile, pumped as much oil as they liked, and so profited at OPEC's expense. So even as OPEC's share of the world's oil reserves rose, its share of actual production fell. Worse, many of OPEC's own members gave in to the temptation to cheat, producing more than their allocated quotas and so making it difficult for the cartel to maintain a steady price.

This debilitating cycle has broken down only in recent years, thanks chiefly to a seemingly unquenchable thirst for oil from booming regions like China, India and the Middle East, which have mopped up almost all the world's spare oil-pumping capacity. Since these places will continue to want ever more oil, there will not be much of a fall in demand in 2008, even if the economies of America or Europe wobble.

In theory, big Western firms should respond to buoyant demand and giddy prices by finding and developing more oilfields. But since they made hay during OPEC's decades of self-denial, and extracted most of the easily tapped oil in the countries to which they had access, they have run out of easy options for expansion. Instead, they are reduced to tremendously expensive projects to coax crude from beneath the icy oceans of the Arctic, for example, or out of viscous deposits of tar.

The only bright spots are regions such as the former Soviet Union and Africa, where OPEC does not hold sway and where prospecting with modern technology is only just getting under way. But the countries with the most promising terrain for exploration have begun to develop a nationalist streak: Russia and Kazakhstan have made life difficult for foreign oil firms, for example, and Angola has joined OPEC. No wonder, then, that the oil majors are having trouble raising their output: they will continue to flounder in the coming year in the face of limited opportunities, exacerbated by shortages of engineers and equipment.

> The only bright spots are regions such as the former Soviet Union and Africa, where OPEC does not hold sway

Meanwhile, since OPEC was always the first to rein in its production in the past, it still has big reserves of oil that are relatively easy to get at. It alone is capable of raising its output quickly—although it will probably choose to prop up the oil price by developing new fields at a leisurely pace. In 2008 the cartel will aim to sell each barrel for between $60 and $80, roughly three times its typical level in the early part of this decade.

The cartel's members are particularly fearful of increasing quotas just as the world economy is slowing, since the combination of lower demand and expanded supply could cause prices to plunge. So OPEC is more likely to worsen a global slowdown by keeping prices high than it is to ease one by allowing them to fall.

This hardline stance will cause plenty of friction with big oil importers. OPEC's meetings will attract as much attention and opprobrium as they did in the 1970s. American presidential candidates will issue plenty of ringing denunciations of Saudi Arabia, let alone more militant members of OPEC, such as Venezuela and Iran.

For their part, advocates of biofuels will cite high oil prices, and OPEC's hand in them, as justification for more subsidies for ethanol and biodiesel. Sales of fuel-efficient cars and hybrids will roar ahead, while gas-guzzling SUVs will fall further behind. Frightened Western governments will announce efficiency drives, and throw money at scientists working on potential miracle fuels and vehicles. In short, OPEC's latest period of ascendancy, like its brief heyday in the 1970s, contains the seeds of its own destruction—but that will be scant consolation to hard-pressed drivers in 2008. ■

2008 IN BRIEF

Google, the world's most successful search engine (motto: Don't be evil), celebrates its tenth birthday in September. One thing for it to celebrate will be the launch of a **Google "gPhone"**, pre-loaded with its search facility.

Edward McBride: energy and environment correspondent, *The Economist*

Getting rusty?
OPEC, % of world oil production

* Forecast Sources: BP Statistical Review of World Energy 2007; EIA

The responsible company

Performing with purpose is the new challenge, argues **Indra Nooyi**, chairman and CEO of PepsiCo

The big breakthrough of 2008 will be the emergence of a new idea of the corporation. It will be based on two dimensions, performance and purpose, both rich in substance and responsible in execution.

Corporations in 2008 will take a longer-term view of themselves. The tendency to manage for quarterly results will yield to a new mindset where short-term performance metrics are complemented by measures capturing the long-term health, vitality and thus sustainability of the enterprise. Regulators may ask for these long-term metrics to be included in the annual filing of corporations. This will be a monumental move for corporations and many investors will welcome it.

The fundamental dynamic, which will become more apparent in 2008, is that companies must embrace "purpose" in all they do. Large companies will want to be known not just for the financial results they generate, but equally for the imprint they leave on society as a whole. Their focus will and should manifest itself along three lines. First, ensuring that their products contribute positively and responsibly to sustaining human civilisation. Second, operating in a way that approaches a "net-neutral" impact to the natural environment. And, third, cherishing their people.

First, products. In the era of heavy industry companies were criticised for damaging public health. They were forced, usually by law, to take the safety of the public more seriously. Happily, most of the conditions that afflicted our grandparents have either been conquered or substantially alleviated: life expectancy has grown sharply and infant mortality has all but disappeared. Yet, in developed economies, the morbidity associated with obesity will remain a problem. PepsiCo, of course, recognises its responsibility here: our task is to continue to transform the portfolio, making the healthier choice the easy choice. In 2008 this effort will intensify in all food and drinks companies.

So far, most governments have taken a voluntary approach to the problem, challenging companies to respond. In 2008 that approach will begin to show positive results. Moreover, the argument will broaden. Obesity is a net condition: calories in minus calories out. There needs to be a lot of thought about how to increase physical exercise in an age when our lifestyle is more sedentary—less exercise is taken, work is less physically demanding, work in the home likewise. Our "*Vive Saludable Escuela*" programme in Mexico teaches children that a correct diet coupled with physical activity promotes a healthy lifestyle.

Second, the most conspicuous issue of our time is our collective impact on the environment. Responsible companies have taken this seriously for a long time. In 2008 these responsible companies will make surprisingly good progress on their environmental obligations (we have joined with other concerned companies and NGOs in the United States Climate Action Partnership to encourage the federal government to enact climate legislation). There will also be greater prominence for both the North America and World Indexes of the Dow Jones Sustainability Index.

It is often said that the contribution of developed nations to climate change will be dwarfed with the industrialisation of China and India. In fact the better response is to improve our performance in those countries too. In 2008 we will see corporate investment rise in environmental technology, water conservation, waste-heat recovery, electricity co-generation, renewables and so on. The goal of a net-neutral impact on the environment will increasingly be the rallying cry of the corporation.

The goal of a net-neutral impact on the environment will increasingly be the rallying cry of the corporation

The third aspect of the modern company is the way we manage relationships with our workforce. In 2008 this is partly about remuneration in the traditional sense. But only partly: it is also about the kind of company you are, the image you project, and the way in which you "cherish" your people.

Taking care of the employee

A more literate generation has emerged, armed with good qualifications, comfortable in societies with many cultures and able to pick and choose between companies. Such people are both more demanding and more in demand. The deciding factor is the kind of company that they want to work for.

The time has come for a company to treat its employees as real assets. In the broadcasting industry they refer to their people as "the talent". The rest of the corporate world will have to adopt the practice. Tools and methods to spot new talent—and train, retain and re-train—will also take centre-stage.

The new idea of the corporation means companies will want to "do better by doing better". Voiced in harmony by employees, regulators, consumers, customers, communities and many other stakeholders, it will leave no doubt that performance without purpose is not a long-term sustainable formula. ■

The good jargon guide

Andrew Palmer

Has the perfect storm reached a tipping point? Does the black swan have a long tail?

Profits rise and fall, bosses come and go. Management jargon has its own rhythm too. First comes the initial idea. The term "offshoring", for instance, gained ground at the start of the decade to describe the process of sending business processes overseas. As both the practice and the terminology become more common, variations emerge. Offshoring, an ugly parent, fathered even uglier children. Firms can now relocate processes to be farther away ("farshoring") or closer to home ("nearshoring"), or they can do a U-turn and repatriate activities ("onshoring"). The cycle fades when an idea has played itself out or when the language is so mutilated that no further harm is possible ("rightshoring").

The jargon cycle will keep rolling in 2008. Executives need to know which phrases to avoid and which to adopt. Here's a guide.

Old boom

The dotcom boom spawned a host of new phrases, "dotcom boom" among them. Some have staying power ("B2B"); some quickly disappeared ("vortal", a word for an industry web portal, had a mercifully brief lifespan). For others, 2008 will be their extinction year. Any manager who says "clicks and mortar" or "disintermediation" in 2008 should be preserved and kept for posterity.

Too flat

First, globalisation was going to make everything the same ("Coca-colonisation"). Then it was going to make the differences between us all-important ("localisation"). Now it is going to make some things the same and other things different ("glocalisation"). Some of these ideas have geometric echoes: inspired by Thomas Friedman's best-seller, executives pontificate about whether the world is flat or spiky. Business leaders of 2008 will think it insightful to say that the world is round.

BRIC-speak

It's a big world out there but jargon helps to break it down into manageable chunks. The "BRIC countries" (Brazil, Russia, India and China) is a term that emerged in 2003, courtesy of Goldman Sachs, as shorthand for the world's biggest emerging markets. Mutations include BRICET, bringing eastern Europe and Turkey into the mix, and BRICS, which adds South Africa. Time-pressed executives have found other creative ways to save microseconds when talking about the world: why faff around saying China and India when you can say "Chindia"? Watch for more elision in 2008: with luck, growing links between Spain and Latin America will go Splat.

Heads and tails

No presentation about the internet is complete without a reference to the "long tail", a theory on how the web can make lots of niche products more important than a few blockbusters (the short head). Tails are not just long. As risks of one sort or another jostle for managerial attention, executives of all stripes will worry about fat and heavy tails, a term to describe extreme events that occur more frequently than theory predicts. (Still on the theme of risk, references to black swans, code for something that is wholly unexpected, are to be wholly expected throughout 2008.)

> Business leaders of 2008 will think it insightful to say that the world is round

Crowds

An old idea—that many heads are better than one—is dressed up as dazzling insight today, thanks to a popular book called "The Wisdom of Crowds" and the ability of the internet to tap the expertise of lots of people. Modish phrases such as "crowdsourcing", "wikinomics" and "swarm businesses" all tap into the same concept. Others in the same vein will emerge in 2008. The slang of social networks will also move from the schoolyard to the boardroom: it is only a matter of time before middle-aged managers talk about "poking" when planning marketing campaigns.

Anything 2.0

Web 2.0 is a dull piece of jargon to describe the internet becoming a platform for interaction and collaboration. The term became popular in 2004 and "2.0" has since been slapped on to all sorts of things to give it a shine. The web and the telly are converging? Television 2.0. Citizens are becoming more involved in public policy? Government 2.0. Free food in Silicon Valley canteens? Lunch 2.0. And so on. With grim inevitability, people have been talking about Web 3.0 for a while now and the term will gather momentum in 2008 (the latest version of Mr Friedman's book is "The World is Flat 3.0"). Like most software upgrades, the new version won't do anything notably different from the last one.

One area that has yet to spawn much in the way of management-speak is the environment. There is a small but growing glossary. "Greenwash" is the environmental version of whitewash. Executives fret about carbon footprints and embodied costs. Sustainability will spread everywhere. The green shoots of jargon will flourish in 2008. ■

Andrew Palmer: jargon-fighter, *The Economist*

For the love of mankind

Matthew Bishop *NEW YORK*

A big year for big giving

On June 30th 2008, after what will seem an endless stream of valedictory articles, interviews and speeches about how Microsoft has changed the world, Bill Gates will leave his day job at the software giant he co-founded in 1975. The following morning he will begin to work full-time at his charitable organisation, the Bill & Melinda Gates Foundation. True, he will remain somewhat involved with Microsoft as its non-executive chairman, and he has hardly been uninvolved in his foundation these past few years. Nonetheless, this is a significant and symbolic career change for one of the world's most talented businessmen, who is still—aged only 52—at the peak of his powers.

The business mantra for 2008 will be "doing well by doing good"

There will be plenty for him to do. Thanks to Warren Buffett's decision in 2006 to add the bulk of his $44 billion fortune to the $30 billion with which Mr Gates has endowed his foundation (not to mention the further $50 billion that may one day follow), Mr Gates needs to scale up its operations fast. As the foundation fights against disease, ignorance and poverty, his plan is to be giving away $3 billion a year by 2009. That will be far more than any other charitable foundation in the world, and will represent quite a surge from the $1.36 billion given away in 2005. Mr Gates will have his work cut out managing a workforce likely to swell from around 240 in 2006 to something over 1,000 and, more fundamentally, figuring out how to ensure all those dollars are used effectively.

Already the astonishing sums given away by Mr Gates and Mr Buffett (respectively the first and second richest men in the world according to the 2007 *Forbes* "rich list") have inspired other billionaires to follow suit. Carlos Slim Helú, a Mexican telecoms billionaire (reckoned now to be richer than Messrs Gates and Buffett), has promised to give some $13 billion to his foundations. Dubai's Sheikh Mohammed al-Maktoum pledged a similar sum to a new foundation to promote education across the Middle East.

In 2008 still more tycoons will embrace philanthropy, especially those who have been criticised in the press for stinginess—as were Messrs Buffett, Gates and Slim before they began to give away serious amounts of money. One (slim) possibility is Mr Gates's old rival, Larry Ellison, the boss of Oracle, who has often been accused of tightfistedness. In 2006 Mr Ellison actually cancelled a planned gift to Harvard, apparently in protest at the ousting of the university's president, Larry Summers. Another is Lakshmi Mittal, the eponymous boss of the steel company, but as yet not a star of philanthropy. Or maybe Steve Schwarzman, a private-equity boss who was portrayed as a modern Scrooge in the press after he made several billion dollars in 2007 from the initial public offering of his firm, Blackstone. He has so far given away little of his new fortune, it seems, and could do wonders for his public image by handing over a billion or two to good causes.

But just how deep in 2008 will be the commitment of today's rich to giving if the troubles in the financial markets that began in the summer of 2007 cause significant damage to the economy? All eyes will be on three annual gala dinners-cum-auctions held in the spring—for the Robin Hood Foundation in New York, and the Private Equity Foundation and Absolute Return for Kids in London. Will the financial masters of the universe at these lavish events once again break fund-raising records, or will they start to close their wallets at the first sign of trouble? If the economy has taken a serious turn for the worse, it will not be easy to strike the right balance—seeming, on the one hand, insufficiently generous at a time when giving is needed more than ever, and, on the other, so free with money that the public resents the super-rich givers for being unscathed by the downturn.

But it's good to give

The world's attention will turn to philanthropy again in September, when Bill Clinton will hold the fourth annual meeting in New York of his Clinton Global Initiative (CGI). This will be as much about companies promising to do good as wealthy individuals giving away their fortunes. With the presidential election looming—and Mr Clinton perhaps close to returning to the White House with his wife—corporate America will be hoping that the government will ease the burden of providing health care to their employees; it will hope, too, to avoid heavier taxes. Against this background, it will pay firms to appear as virtuous as possible. In particular, that will mean many more pledges to fight climate change, following the examples of Sir Richard Branson's Virgin companies and Wal-Mart, both of which won reams of positive publicity following their carbon-reducing commitments at past meetings of the CGI. Each promise made at the CGI will be scrutinised for signs that it might be an attempt ▶

The biggest givers

Amount pledged, $bn

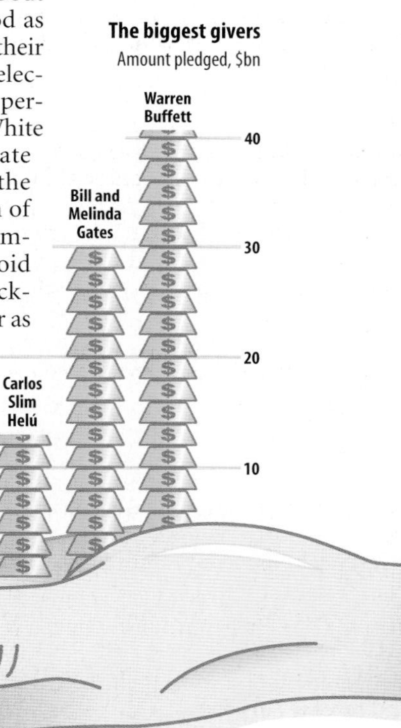

Sources: *BusinessWeek*; *Chronicle of Philanthropy*; *The Economist*

Matthew Bishop: New York bureau chief, *The Economist*. His book on the global boom in philanthropy will appear in 2008.

to buy influence, via Bill, with a putative incoming administration led by Hillary.

The danger is that such headlines in the cynical media will overshadow other debates that need to take place—not least, about what exactly the role of companies should be in terms of philanthropy and corporate social responsibility (CSR). Just as wealthy individuals such as Mr Gates are turning to philanthropy in greater numbers and on a greater scale than ever before, so too leading companies around the world have started to think more seriously about how they can help solve the world's biggest problems, not just by extending their activities with corporate philanthropy and CSR programmes but increasingly by embedding philanthropy in their core business strategy.

A growing number of companies will talk about how they intend to profit by investing in activities that make the world a better place—ranging from developing environmentally clean technologies to designing products that meet the needs of customers "at the bottom of the pyramid". The business mantra for 2008 will be "doing well by doing good". ■

Sustainable maths

Kate Galbraith *SEATTLE*

Environmental reporting for companies needs teeth

Corporate accounting will not get any sexier in 2008. But it will get cleaner and greener—and perhaps even meaner. With global warming continuing to permeate political discussion, companies will be more eager than ever to offer up environmental indicators to show their good citizenship. A handful of governments—those of Spain, Norway and Canada among them—may create incentives for (or demand) better reporting from troublesome industries.

Helpfully, green accounting is already starting to conform to one standard. The Global Reporting Initiative, an organisation based in the Netherlands, has been issuing reporting guidelines on sustainability since 2000. (It includes human-rights and workforce issues as well as environmental ones.) GRI reporting has grown: the organisation expects 1,750 global companies to issue reports based on its guidelines in 2008, triple the number in 2005.

Deeper shades of green

The concept has a long way to go. Though Europe's carbon-trading scheme does require far more detailed emissions data than the GRI, in most countries green accounting has few teeth. America requires companies to report on their toxic waste and several European countries have for some time required reporting on matters like corporate energy usage.

In America, the world's great energy guzzler, "sustainability reports" are voluntary. It is nice to learn how many tonnes of waste are recycled at UPS, and to read that Proctor & Gamble's Pampers are getting slimmer (so using less material). But what about the issues that companies don't want to report? It would be no surprise if one day California—which has already passed a cap on carbon emissions—decides to require, say, corporate water-usage reports, says Janet Ranganathan of the World Resources Institute.

One big problem is that most sustainability reports are not audited by outsiders (verification is especially rare in America). This could change as investing in "sustainable companies" grows. Environmentalists are putting pressure on America's Securities and Exchange Commission to require companies to disclose their carbon emissions, as well as to quantify (for the benefit of shareholders) the possible impact of climate change on companies' bottom lines—though their chances of success seem rather slim.

> In America, the world's great energy guzzler, "sustainability reports" are voluntary

Informal watchdogs are springing up to monitor companies' green claims. In 2007 an American website called Climatecounts.org created an online scorecard that rates large corporations such as Apple, Dell and Nike on their efforts to reduce carbon emissions. In 2008 the green-besotted media will start investigating corporate environmental claims. Are companies really reducing their energy use as much as they say? And is organic cotton from abroad really organic?

Meanwhile green accounting of a sort for consumers is also poised to take off. Green labels that claim to declare the carbon footprint of products from shoes to food will proliferate. And carbon offsets—such as purchases of guarantees to plant trees, which absorb carbon dioxide and therefore make up for gas-guzzling behaviour—will become ubiquitous. In 2007 General Electric began offering a credit card that buys carbon offsets with reward points, and more gimmicks will surely arrive in 2008.

But the real breakthroughs will come in home energy usage. "Smart meters" that show real-time power consumption (and the cost of it) are on their way. Thus, for example, people will be able to see how much their costs spike when they run the dishwasher or the dryer. This will encourage conservation and off-peak energy use.

America's main green-building certification programme, called LEED, is about to broaden its horizons from commercial buildings to homes. And the more aware consumers become of their own green footprint, the more pressure they will put on companies to come clean. ■

Kate Galbraith: environment contributor, *The Economist*

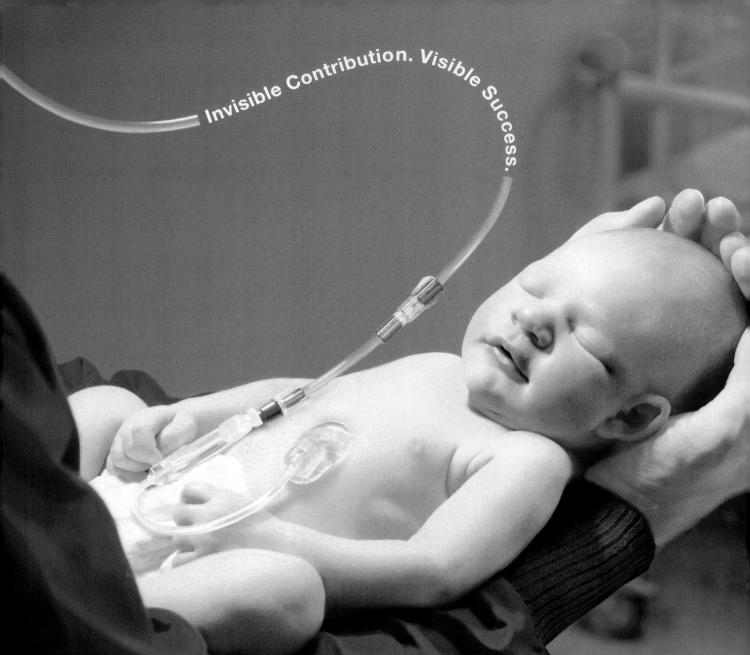

Also in this section:
Sovereign wealth funds, friends or foe? 150
Banks go back to basics 152
Joaquín Almunia: The euro zone—bigger and better? 154
Prospects for trade liberalisation 155
Doha's quartet 155
London's slipping crown 156
Risky business in foreign investment 157
David Rubenstein: The rise and rise of private equity 158

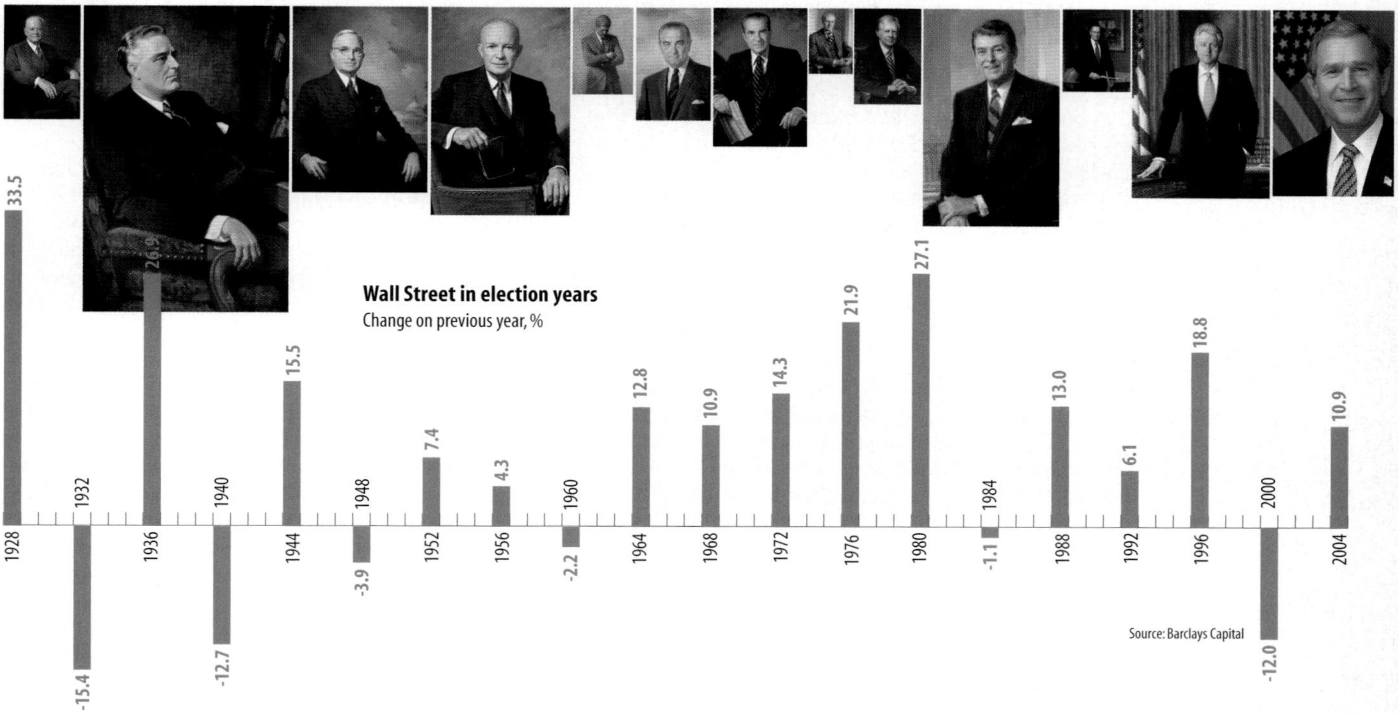

Finance

Wall Street in election years
Change on previous year, %

	%
1928	33.5
1932	-15.4
1936	26.9
1940	-12.7
1944	15.5
1948	-3.9
1952	7.4
1956	4.3
1960	-2.2
1964	12.8
1968	10.9
1972	14.3
1976	21.9
1980	27.1
1984	-1.1
1988	13.0
1992	6.1
1996	18.8
2000	-12.0
2004	10.9

Source: Barclays Capital

History lessons for the markets

Philip Coggan

Investors will be watching politics as well as price-earnings ratios

If history is any guide, 2008 should be a better-than-average year for America's stockmarkets. Figures culled from the Barclays Equity-Gilt Study show that since 1926 Wall Street has risen by an average of 8.8% in presidential-election years, perhaps because politicians pull out all the stops to ensure they get elected.

However, although such statistics may be superficially appealing, this could easily be a random effect. After all, 1932 was an election year and it saw the absolute market nadir after the crash of 1929. The markets also fell in 1940, 1948, 1960, 1984 and 2000. In down years for the stockmarket the incumbent party was just as likely to be re-elected as thrown from office.

If politics has any effect in 2008 it may be to make investors a little nervous. This will be the first presidential election since 1952 in which neither a sitting president nor vice-president is running for office. That will create a climate of uncertainty, which markets traditionally dislike. And, to the extent that either party is the favourite, it will be the Democrats, whereas Wall Street favours the Republicans.

The key question for markets is whether the profitability of the corporate sector can be sustained

The election aside, perhaps the key question for markets is whether the profitability of the corporate sector can be sustained. In America, profits are running at around a 40-year high as a proportion of GDP. Some people, such as Andrew Smithers, an independent strategist, argue that they are doomed to return to the mean. But others argue that profits can be sustained because of the effects of globalisation: the emergence of China and India has shifted the balance of power in favour of capital and against labour.

The question is important because of the measure that investors rely on to assess market valuations: the price-earnings ratio. Optimists argue that, on the basis of forecast profits, shares look cheap by historical standards. But the pessimists say this is because profits are cyclically high; use a smoothed average of profits and valuations are as high as they were before the crash of 1929.

American corporate profits may come under pressure if, as expected, the economy slows under the influence of the turmoil in the housing market. And equities may also lose one source of support if the credit crunch that ▶

2008 IN BRIEF

The Dhaka stock exchange is set to double in value, to more than $15 billion, as **Bangladesh** sells off state-owned enterprises.

Philip Coggan: capital-markets editor, *The Economist*

started in the summer of 2007 lessens the ability of private-equity groups to launch takeovers and also makes it harder for companies to buy back their own shares.

However, as the year rolls on investors may start looking to an economic rebound in 2009, especially if the Federal Reserve continues the cycle of interest-rate cuts that began in September 2007.

In foreign-exchange markets, the big issue will be the durability of the carry trade, which has seen speculators borrow in low-yielding currencies—notably the yen—to invest in higher-yielding currencies and assets. The carry trade has had several wobbles in recent years as investors have taken fright and left some of its more exotic beneficiaries, such as the Icelandic krona or the New Zealand dollar. The main pressure on the carry trade in 2008 will probably come from the combination of falling American interest rates and some modest increases in Japanese rates. The danger is that investors (including those Japanese who have pushed money overseas) will tire of losing money and cut their bets, causing a sharp jump in the yen. However, the good news is that a combination of a weaker dollar and slower American economic growth should reduce the American trade deficit, one of the main imbalances in the global economy.

2008 IN BRIEF: Syria, supposedly socialist, heads towards capitalism by opening the **Damascus stock exchange**.

In bond markets, the credit crunch of summer 2007 will continue to reverberate. Rating agencies are expecting an increase in the default rate on corporate bonds, if only because cash-strapped companies will find it more difficult to find finance. That will inevitably provide a further test for the complex structured products created in recent years, such as collateralised debt obligations (CDOs).

Investors will be looking to see whether the subprime effect is repeated in corporate debt; in other words, whether the repackaging of loans and bonds has led to a lowering of credit standards. That may well be the case, since the dash for yield in 2004-06 made it far easier for companies to raise funds on what, by historical standards, looked rather generous terms. What seems virtually certain is that there will be some scandals; as Warren Buffett has remarked, it's only when the tide goes out that you find out who's been swimming naked.

One sector that might get shipwrecked in 2008 is commercial property. Like residential property, it is vulnerable to higher borrowing costs and slower economic growth. Investors have dashed into property in recent years because of attractive yields; those yields no longer offer quite so much compensation for risk. Office property in London and New York might be adversely affected if credit problems prompt the financial industry to shed jobs.

Finally, investors will also be on the lookout for one of Nassim Taleb's black swans (extreme, unpredictable events), although by definition these cannot be foreseen. A military strike against Iran is not really in the black-swan category, since it has already been widely discussed, but it is hard to believe that the prospect is priced into financial markets. The global economy has coped admirably with oil at $70 and even $80 a barrel; whether it could sustain $100 a barrel for very long (as might happen if supplies from the Gulf are interrupted) is another matter. ■

Superfunds to the rescue

Philip Coggan

Or are sovereign wealth funds a threat?

Threats and opportunities are two standard bits of jargon in the world of management consultancy. But either could apply to sovereign wealth funds, the investment portfolios built up by national governments. Some see them as a threat, leading to the backdoor nationalisation of businesses in Europe and America. But others see the funds as an opportunity, a wall of money that will prop up stockmarkets.

Whether an individual fund is seen as a threat or an opportunity depends on its origin. Nobody is too worried about Norway's government pension fund, built on the back of the country's oil revenues. It is generally seen as a model, building up the kind of diversified portfolio that any big institution might desire and steering clear of controversy. Indeed, Norway has been dispensing advice to up-and-coming wealth funds round the globe.

But Norway is very much the exception. The fastest-growing wealth funds are being built by Russia and China and some of the bigger ones are in the Middle East in countries like Abu Dhabi and Dubai, which might be friendly now but cannot be guaranteed to remain so for ever. What happens if those funds take stakes in defence companies or energy groups: will they be content to remain passive investors or over time might their controlling governments be tempted to wield their influence?

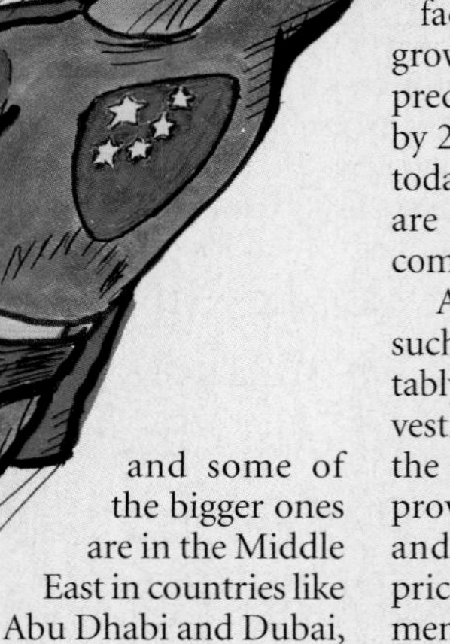

So far the threat has been more theoretical than real. Dubai International Capital, for example, has been able to take a 3% stake in EADS, an aircraft manufacturer, without alarm. But such is the growth of some funds—Morgan Stanley predicts they could be worth $12 trillion by 2015, up from $1.5 trillion-2.5 trillion today—that it will not be long before they are building up sizeable stakes in some companies, banks or markets.

As for the wall-of-money argument, such theories have been heard before, notably in the late 1980s when Japan was investing heavily in American property and the odd movie-maker. Those purchases proved both a bad deal for the Japanese and an inadequate support for asset prices. Big investors will need better arguments for buying shares in 2008. ■

Back to basics

Henry Tricks

Time for the banking industry to relearn its craft

It is with a queasy feeling that the world's bankers enter 2008. Within 12 months, they have seen record profits crumble, once-booming debt businesses blighted by writedowns, and the troubles of some former high-flyers in the mortgage industry threaten the soundness of the financial system. Fresh obstacles loom in 2008, including a new regulatory regime, known as Basel 2, whose shortcomings have emerged even before it has been officially born. More worrying still would be a slowdown in the world economy.

Source: BankScope *To mid-2007 only

That is not all. The maelstrom in credit markets in 2007 exposed flaws in a banking model that has transformed the finance industry: the banks' ability to sell loans that they don't want to keep to investors hungry for high-yielding assets. This "U-Haul" model of distributed risk had been widely considered one of the marvels of modern finance, until trouble hit.

The ability of American banks to turn their loans, via Wall Street's alchemists, into packages of high-yielding securities and sell them to investors was supposed to have enabled banks to diversify their exposure to credit risk. Bank failures had for years been minimal, even during the Asian and Russian debt crises of 1997 and 1998 and the dotcom collapse. By keeping fewer loans on their balance sheets, banks reported stronger returns on their assets, helping to generate bumper earnings.

The coming year will test how much of that risk has indeed been spread, and how much of the diversification was illusory. Did banks simply replace the risk of lending on their own doorstep with exposures from outside their sphere of expertise? Some lenders appear to have bamboozled naive borrowers into taking on mortgages they couldn't afford, knowing they could sell the unsound loans into the market with few questions asked. Others made themselves vulnerable by financing long-term loans in the short-term money markets, rather than from depositors or through issuance of bonds. They were strangled when the money markets seized up.

Taking such risks will be far harder in 2008, because everyone has been sharply reminded of the maturity mismatch between assets and liabilities that is at the heart of banking. So banks will have to court depositors, not the capital markets. When they make loans, they will have to keep them, monitor them and ensure repayment, rather than passing them on like hot potatoes. "There will be a mad rush back to traditional banking," predicts Dick Bove, banking analyst at Punk Ziegel.

The process will not be smooth. Politicians, especially in the American Congress, may tie up lenders with red tape. And Basel 2, with its new capital-adequacy framework for banks, will be rolled out across the European Union from January (it will affect some American banks in 2009). At least for less sophisticated banks, it leans heavily on rating agencies as arbiters of credit quality. But their credibility has been damaged by the over-optimistic assessments they made of some of the riskier debt instruments. Basel 2 also focuses on credit risk, and largely skates over the fickleness of liquidity that bedevilled markets in 2007.

It has been a long time since banks have faced such torments, but their business has always been a cyclical one and only the foolish will have forgotten that. (As the saying goes, a banker is someone who lends you an umbrella when it is sunny, and asks for it back when it rains.) To tide them over, all those profits have left banks with plenty of capital in the vaults. Should that run out, central bankers in America and Europe have also shown a remarkable willingness to provide liquidity to the financial system to prevent panic.

Tougher conditions are also reducing competition from non-bank financial players, which had flourished in the easy-money era. Aggressive mortgage banks, such as Countrywide in America and Northern Rock in Britain, have revealed their frailties. The big American banks—such as Citigroup and JPMorgan Chase—have retail-banking franchises that may expand by acquiring stricken competitors. The same holds true for well-capitalised retail banks in Europe. Investment banks that falter may find nationwide American banks offering to buy them; or European banks such as Italy's UniCredit taking audacious advantage of their hour of need.

> There will be a mad rush back to traditional banking

Lurking in the background is another potential source of support: deep-pocketed governments in China and the Middle East, keen to invest part of their wealth in Western banks' assets and expertise. According to Morgan Stanley, sovereign-wealth funds spent $26 billion in the six months to October 2007 on big financial firms such as Barclays, a British bank, Blackstone, a private-equity group, and the London Stock Exchange. Banks, for their part, covet access to big emerging markets, and a strategic stake sold to the Chinese government, say, may ease the way to a strategic stake in a Chinese bank.

But government ownership of banks is always tricky. That should not be forgotten just because an injection of yuan, roubles or petrodollars might provide a quick and easy way to keep a bad bank on life support. ■

2008 IN BRIEF
The EU adopts a **"Single Euro Payments Area"**, requiring banks to level their prices for crossborder settlements.

Henry Tricks: finance editor, *The Economist*

The euro zone: bigger and better?

Joaquín Almunia, European commissioner for economic and monetary affairs, looks at how to transform a successful decade of monetary union into an even better one

In 1998 Europe's leaders took the momentous decision to launch economic and monetary union (EMU), establishing the European Central Bank (ECB) and creating the euro on January 1st 1999. As we approach the tenth anniversary of what is arguably the most significant step towards an integrated Europe, it is important to recall the benefits and achievements of EMU, but also to look to the challenges ahead.

The first decade of EMU has been a major success. The past ten years have given the euro-zone nations unprecedented and sustained levels of low inflation. Interest rates remain favourable by historical standards and have been consistently lower than in Britain or America. The result is very favourable conditions for investment in a currency area no longer plagued by internal currency realignments, and the emergence of a strong and stable euro that quickly became an international currency on a par with the dollar.

This is a remarkable achievement which reflects the confidence placed both in the single currency and in its underlying economic-policy framework. Without the euro, imagine how much harder the surges in energy prices would have hit those European nations with traditionally weak public finances. After a period of low growth, due mainly to the long-term effects of German unification and insufficient reform in Europe, the European Union and the euro area are now growing above potential. Job creation in the almost ten years since EMU has been very strong, outpacing America and illustrating Europe's ability to meet the challenges of EU enlargement and globalisation.

Such benefits have provided a good incentive for others in the EU to seek membership of the single-currency zone. Cyprus and Malta are set to join in January 2008, following Slovenia's entry in 2007. They will bring the euro zone's membership to 15 countries, with a population of 318m.

Within the euro area, Germany and Austria have experienced a steady improvement in competitiveness, while Spain, Ireland, Italy, the Netherlands, Portugal and Greece have suffered a sustained loss in competitiveness

That monetary union has combined price stability with historically low nominal and real interest rates is thanks to the ECB's credible monetary policy and member states' commitment to fiscal discipline under the stability and growth pact, particularly since its reform in 2005. The euro area's average budget deficit in 2007 is likely to have been around 1% of GDP, a result surpassed only in 2000 when exceptional receipts from the sale of mobile-phone licences boosted state revenues. By the end of 2007 only five out of the 27 EU countries were running a deficit in excess of 3%, one of which was in the euro zone. By comparison, in 2005 no fewer than 13 EU countries were under budgetary surveillance.

But the stability and protection afforded by the euro can be maximised only if euro-zone members continue to face up to certain challenges. This includes using the present good economic times to achieve balanced budgets to be able to weather the next downturn and to cope with the budgetary costs arising from an ageing population. Achieving that objective in all euro-zone countries by the end of this decade is a realistic target. Besides budgetary consolidation, member states are also encouraged to push through further reforms of pensions and health-care systems and to increase employment levels to limit the rise in age-related public expenditure for future generations.

What's needed next

Efforts to put the euro area's public finances on a more sustainable footing must go hand in hand with policies to improve the quality of public spending. Directing government spending towards education and R&D would increase productivity and growth potential, boost innovation and help to safeguard Europe's social model.

Although the euro zone is performing satisfactorily overall, adjustment to EMU has proved somewhat lengthy for some member states, leaving them vulnerable to swings in the level of economic activity. This is also associated with persistent differences in inflation and large current-account imbalances. Within the euro area, Germany and Austria have experienced a steady improvement in competitiveness, while Spain, Ireland, Italy, the Netherlands, Portugal and Greece have suffered a sustained loss in competitiveness, which in some cases also affected growth.

The slow pace of adjustment illustrates the need for more structural reforms. We are starting to see the fruit of the reforms carried out in recent years in terms of job creation and productivity gains. But to consolidate the benefits of EMU, member states must continue to favour the conditions for greater trade and investment, as established in the "Lisbon strategy" for growth and jobs. A stronger political commitment to an effective system of euro-area governance and more determined action to translate at national level the agreements made with the other euro-area partners will also be key to making monetary union fit for the 21st century. ■

Fearful or cheerful?

Patrick Lane

The prospects for the world trade talks

A bouquet for Doha?

Optimism about the chances of a speedy conclusion to the Doha round of global trade talks has long demanded a certain fortitude. Launched in 2001 as a "development" round aimed at helping the world's poorest countries, the negotiations have been snared in disagreement ever since. A ministerial summit in Mexico in 2003 ended in acrimony; lack of progress prompted the World Trade Organisation's director-general, Pascal Lamy, to suspend the round in 2006; and an attempt to bridge the gaps between the principal players (see below) in June 2007 failed.

At first blush the prospects for 2008 are little better. The political timetable looks unhelpful, especially in America. Trade-promotion authority, which allows the president to ask Congress for a straight yes or no to trade agreements, has expired. If a Doha deal could be struck, a Democratic Congress may balk at passing it as a parting gift to any Republican president, let alone George Bush. Worse, the effects of America's tottering housing market and the associated credit crunch will be felt well into 2008, in Europe as well as in the United States. That may make protectionist arguments easier to sell on both sides of the Atlantic.

Is there a case for optimism? Remarkably, yes. Trade negotiators have not been idle. In July the chairmen of the two key Doha-round committees—one on agriculture, one on trade in non-farm goods—put forward "draft modalities", documents that should form the basis of further discussion. After a month or so for reflection, trade officials began meeting again in an attempt to close the many remaining gaps.

As is the way with trade, the proposals are complicated. To take one of the less testing examples, the non-farm draft has a formula for reductions in maximum (or "bound", in the jargon) tariffs on non-farm goods. Developing countries, whose tariffs tend to be higher, are expected to make deeper cuts. How much deeper is to be argued over; they may have some leeway. Those that "bind" less than 35% of their tariffs are exempt from the formula but are expected to cap 90% of their tariffs at a rate of 28.5% at most.

> The political timetable looks unhelpful, especially in America

Quite a lot of progress has been made on other matters—such as allowing freer access to rich countries for goods from the WTO's poorest members. But a lot of work is still to be done: the gaps between the protagonists on both farm and non-farm trade are still wide.

Mr Lamy reckons the WTO could still conclude the round in 2008. But, if Doha is not yet dead, the chances that it will be completed next year are surely worse than 50-50. And even then it would face a difficult passage through Congress. It was President Clinton who skilfully steered through the previous agreement, the Uruguay round; maybe a second President Clinton will have to deal with Doha. ■

Patrick Lane: economics editor, *The Economist*

Square dance

Patrick Lane

Four powers hold the key to Doha

Global trade negotiations have always been long, painstaking affairs. But with previous talks, under the WTO's forerunner, the General Agreement on Tariffs and Trade (GATT), life was simpler in one respect. Agreement between a few rich countries was what counted. Poorer ones, by and large, tagged along—even though, in theory, any member could hold up a deal because agreement had to be by consensus. In the Uruguay round, on which the gavel was at last brought down—after almost eight years—in 1994, agreement between the European Community, as it then was, and America was the main requirement for a deal.

Life is more complicated now. Consensus is still the rule, and developing countries have become much more willing to fight their corner. In practice, this has brought Brazil and India into the small group regarded as holding the key to any agreement under the Doha round.

The developing countries want America to offer deeper cuts in farm subsidies and the European Union to open its agricultural markets further; and the two rich regions have sometimes sniped at each other too. Meanwhile, the Americans and the Europeans would like India and Brazil to cut their tariffs on industrial goods.

Confusingly, the WTO tariff negotiations are about "bindings"—maximum rates. Actual average tariffs for both Brazil and India are less than half their bound levels. Similarly, America's best offer on farm subsidies is above what it spent in 2006. The gap does create room for compromise. But it takes time to get there. ■

London loses its cool

Lionel Barber *LONDON*

Tougher times ahead for the City

Host of the 2012 Olympic games, financial rival to New York, magnet for football-mad billionaires: London's reputation as cool, classy and cosmopolitan has never been higher. The capital's dynamic growth has been driven by the City of London, the location of choice for hedge funds, private-equity firms and Wall Street exiles. Thanks to a favourable tax regime, light regulation and an open-armed welcome to foreigners, the City is the bejewelled crown of Britain's economy.

But that crown is in danger of slipping in 2008. Even before the great credit squeeze of 2007, there were clear signs that mergers and acquisitions as well as private-equity buy-outs had peaked. The return of conservative risk management in the banks and hedge funds will be a prominent theme in the coming year. Inevitably, this will lead to staff culls, lower Christmas bonuses and the disappearance of the more exotic off-balance-sheet financing which proliferated in the era of cheap money.

Watch those smug faces in New York

In 2008 investment banks will still be digesting the more leveraged deals struck at the height of the debt-driven boom. Some of these deals may fall by the wayside; others will have to be renegotiated. As one prominent banker says: "We will still see M&A activity in London, but it will be more of the mid-size and small-cap end rather than the really big deals."

Private equity, which has enjoyed mouth-watering returns, will have a far tougher time in 2008. Not only has competition increased; the industry's image has taken a beating amid accusations of asset-stripping and unduly favourable tax treatment. Gordon Brown's government may tinker further with the tax code, but not enough to drive wealthy partners and non-domiciled London residents to sunnier (or snowier) tax havens such as Monaco or Switzerland.

When money was cheap a plethora of companies, many from the former Soviet Union, raised hundreds of millions of pounds by listing their shares in London. It should be no surprise if one or two high-profile casualties emerge in a less benign environment. Watch those smug faces in New York, where regulators have made rude noises about "casino capitalism" in London.

A slowdown in the financial-services industry will also be keenly felt in the property market, both commercial and residential. Financial firms hold nearly a third of office space in London. With commercial rents rising at a rate of more than 15% a year, estate agents have not blinked at charging up to £140 ($280) a square foot for prime space in, say, London's West End. That will surely change in 2008.

Despite bullish talk among estate agents and property developers, it is hard to see those sky-high rates holding up. True, the vacancy rate in the City (as well as Lower Manhattan) has fallen below 6%. But millions of square feet are under development in the Square Mile, adding to the supply of office space just at the moment when the City's growth is slowing down. Residential prices in London, though unlikely to fall, will certainly witness a slowdown in the rate of growth.

On a brighter note, London's antiquated transport system should receive a face-lift in 2008. Terminal 5 will open at Heathrow airport in March, providing desperately needed relief for frustrated air passengers. In 2008 the government will push ahead with Crossrail—a rail link between Heathrow and Canary Wharf. But overall London's infrastructure is a blight on the City, a shabby remnant of a glorious Victorian heritage.

The music goes on

London still has a few shots left in the locker. The light, one-stop touch of the Financial Services Authority will offer a competitive advantage compared with New York: as a principle, comply-with-the-rules will always trump comply-or-go-to-jail. London's record of innovation—from the invention of the Eurobond market to the launch of *sharia*-compliant bonds—remains second to none.

In 2008 the City's secret weapon may well prove to be money from the Middle East. Peter Weinberg, a former Goldman Sachs banker, estimates that between $50 billion and $100 billion of Middle Eastern capital could come to London. Since September 11th 2001, Arab investors have found London a friendlier place to do business than New York.

In the first years of the 21st century, London never had it so good. Times will be tougher in 2008. But to paraphrase Chuck Prince, boss of Citigroup: the music has not stopped, it has merely slowed down. Would-be dancers should be on notice: more waltz, less samba. ■

No more samba?

2008 IN BRIEF

Accounting begins under the **Kyoto protocol**; by 2012 member countries' emissions should be down by 5% compared with 1990 levels.

Lionel Barber: editor-in-chief, *Financial Times*

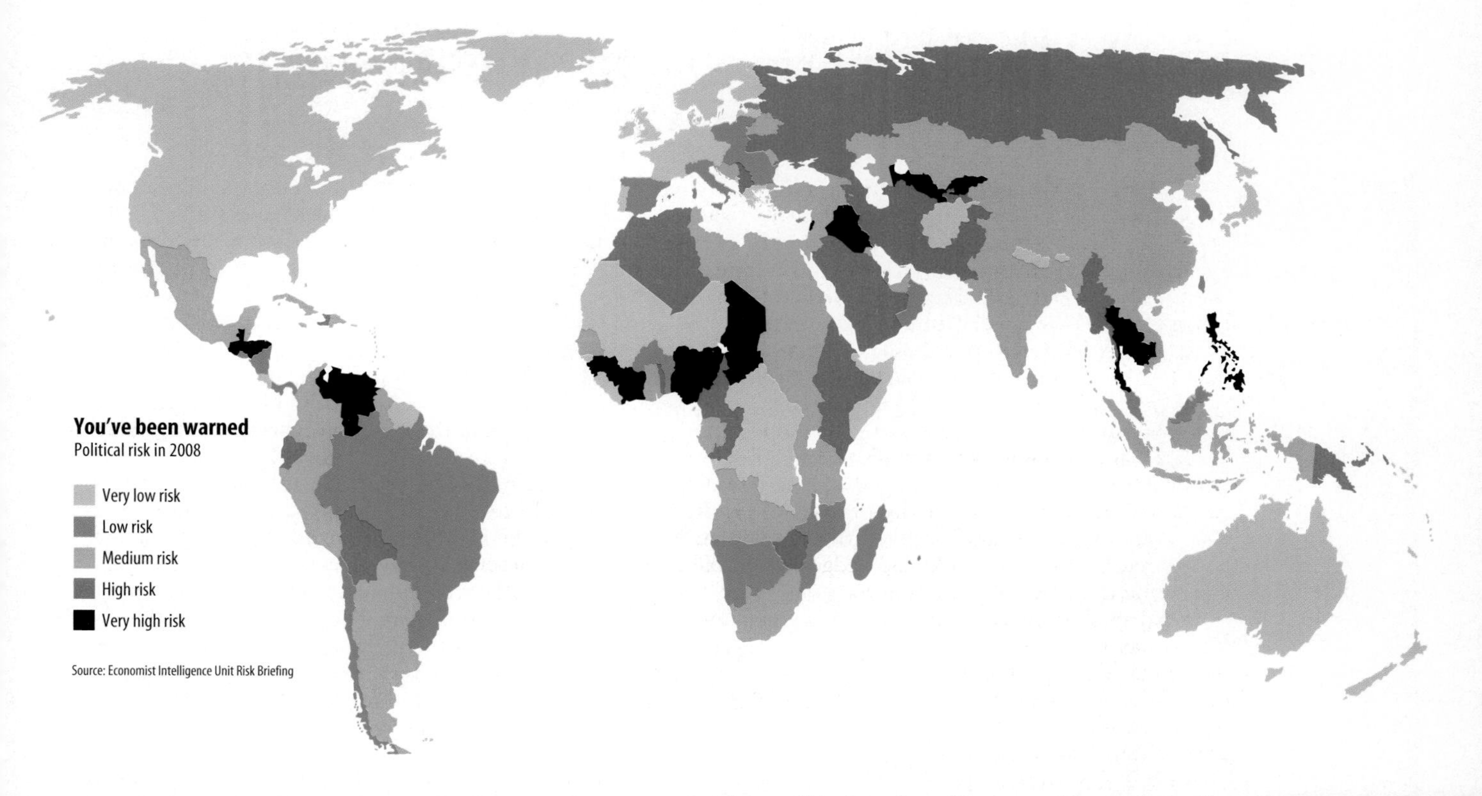

The spread of political risk

Laza Kekic

A growing threat to foreign investment

The terrorist attacks of September 11th 2001 had surprisingly little impact on business decisions. True, the attacks produced a growth industry in doom-laden predictions about the end of globalisation. But those contemplating foreign investments carried on more or less regardless, as before paying scant attention to political risk. They based their business decisions on other things, such as a country's economic prospects, labour costs and overall business environment. Besides, multinational companies have traditionally been a hardy breed, operating in the most inhospitable climates.

But there are signs that things are changing. Political risk has started to flash on the corporate radar. Surveys suggest that businessmen see political risk as a much greater threat than in the recent past. A recent survey of global executives by the Economist Intelligence Unit, a sister company of *The Economist*, found this was especially so for emerging markets, where executives identified political risk as the main constraint on investment. All the main forms of political risk (the danger of political violence, protectionism, geopolitical tensions and government instability) were seen as increasing. In the case of the rich countries, there was widespread concern about rising protectionism, about the threat of terrorism in America and Britain and about the impact of geopolitical tensions (from possible conflict with Iran to frictions between the West and Russia).

Why this heightened sense of political risk? In part it may be psychological—a sluggish reflection of an extreme risk-aversion in Western societies. Worries about the threat that terrorism poses for business are out of proportion with the real risk, which in most parts of the world remains minuscule. Fear of litigation, especially in America, may also be part of it: crippling legal claims are possible if a company's management is shown not to have "prepared" for some nasty mishap abroad.

But to a great extent the increased perception of political risk simply reflects reality. The signs of a protectionist backlash against foreign investment are multiplying: witness, in America, the regulation of foreign acquisitions in the name of national security; or, in Europe, the defence of "national champions" and the outcry against emerging-market sovereign wealth funds; and, in Russia and Latin America, the new barriers to foreign investment and the expropriation of assets in the oil industry and elsewhere. International investment is most likely to flourish in a climate of international political calm. Yet a host of geopolitical risks threatens to disrupt global economic activity.

> The signs of a protectionist backlash against foreign investment are multiplying

Although perceptions of political risk have increased, these do not yet appear to be having a significant impact on decision-making. For now, they are trumped by the perceived good opportunities for investment. But this could change in 2008. Economic and financial risks are rising again. The danger is that these could interact with stronger political-risk perceptions and sharply chill the climate for international investment. ■

2008 IN BRIEF

Hong Kong cuts **income tax** by one percentage point, down to a mere 15% for individuals and 16.5% for corporations.

Laza Kekic: director, country forecasting services, Economist Intelligence Unit

The rise and rise of private equity

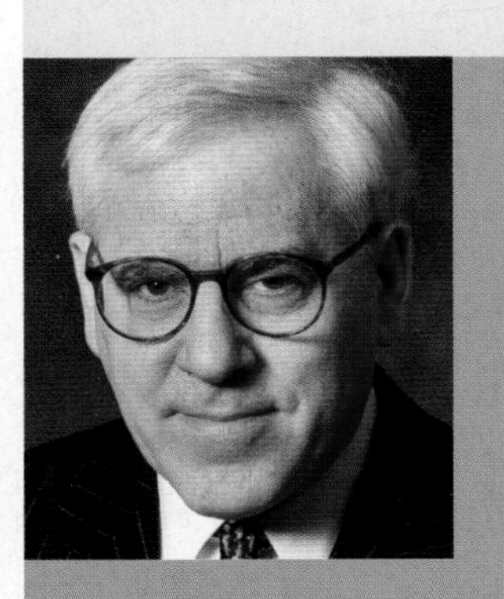

The prospects for the private-equity industry remain bright, and this will be good for the world, argues **David Rubenstein**, co-founder of the Carlyle Group

The private-equity industry is larger, more profitable and more global in scope than at any time in its roughly 40-year history. And despite the recent retrenchment in the credit markets, its expansion will continue in 2008 and beyond, as an increasing number of investors realise that the returns achieved by top-quartile private-equity funds are difficult to achieve elsewhere.

On three key fronts—funds under management, investments completed and returns realised—the industry has achieved a level of success which few would have predicted even five years ago. Today, there are thousands of private-equity firms around the world which could, between them, finance acquisitions worth over $2.5 trillion, an increase of some 50 times in the past 20 years. This is equivalent to 12% of the total equity value of companies traded on the world's principal exchanges.

Two broad trends will shape the continued growth of private equity. First, it will become even more of a mainstream industry. Second, its globalisation will accelerate.

Ironically, private equity's growing public profile has made it something of a misnomer. What started as an unproven, inconsistent investment technique in the 1970s has morphed into one of the world's largest industries. In America alone, the 20 largest pension funds have over $110 billion invested in private equity on behalf of some 10.5m beneficiaries. Private-equity firms own and operate very "public" companies such as Dunkin' Donuts, Hospital Corporation of America and Chrysler.

And many of the largest private-equity firms will be publicly owned in the not too distant future. Already, one of the industry's leaders, the Blackstone Group, has closed an initial public offering. The public's already considerable stake in private equity through public pension funds will get bigger as public investors buy stakes in "private"-equity firms.

Because of the amount of capital that private-equity firms now control and the economic consequence of their decisions, these firms face increasing public criticism and the prospect of more regulation. This enhanced public scrutiny will only intensify—and justifiably so—as private equity's role in the global economy becomes even more prominent.

The expansion of private equity will become an increasingly global phenomenon, and this will happen faster than commonly thought

Private-equity firms should respond by better publicising their efforts to ensure that their business practices are consistent with the welfare of not only their investors but also their portfolio companies' employees, managers, customers, suppliers and local communities. Until recently, they did not always adequately communicate their concerns and plans. They must enhance their new focus on better public communication, so that the benefits of private equity are more widely understood.

These benefits are numerous. Not only do the returns accrue to pension funds and individual investors, the industry is also driving improvements in the local and global economies. Because private-equity firms make money only by increasing the value of their investments, they employ the most effective management practices. The companies they buy tend to become much more efficient and grow more quickly than they would otherwise.

While this enhanced efficiency increases economic output, it also creates jobs and often involves the preservation of companies that would otherwise face uncertain futures. A recent study found that over the past five years businesses backed by private equity in Britain increased employment at an average annual rate of 9% compared with 1-2% for public companies. Businesses in America that might have faced difficult futures without a private-equity buy-out include household names such as Burger King and Toys "R" Us.

Tomorrow, the world

The expansion of private equity will become an increasingly global phenomenon, and this will happen faster than commonly thought. Asia (excluding Japan) saw private-equity deal volume jump from $3.2 billion in 2002 to $51.1 billion in 2006, and growth rates were comparable in eastern Europe and Latin America. Moreover, the enormous amounts of capital generated by emerging economies will give rise to new, local private-equity firms which will compete both locally and internationally with the likes of Blackstone, Carlyle and KKR.

Already, much of the private-equity capital deployed outside developed markets derives from local sources. Soon, funds based in Asia or the Middle East will compete for investment opportunities not only in their home markets but in America and Europe as well. The global private-equity market will become a two-way street. The incipient stages of this transformation are apparent in the Chinese government's pre-IPO $3 billion investment in Blackstone.

Private equity's move into the mainstream, and its global reach, will help the industry to provide new benefits to businesses, economies and investors around the world. It will create a flatter world—in which access to capital and expertise will be far more equal. ■

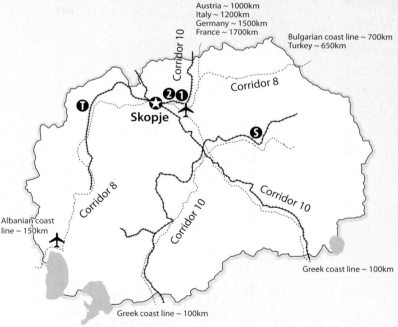

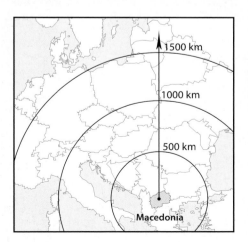

Also in this section:
Printing in 3D 162
Into the deep blue 163
Restoring movement through thought 164
Peter Diamandis: The next space race 165

Science

The great melt

Alun Anderson

For scientists, nowhere will be hotter than the Arctic

It will be a busy year for the Arctic. Thanks to International Polar Year, a programme involving more than 60 nations in over 200 research projects, the region will swarm with more scientists than at any time in history. And the Arctic certainly needs urgent attention.

Everyone has seen those iconic pictures of polar bears sitting on tiny ice floes amid blue open water and knows that global warming is hitting the Arctic. The vast frozen seas are melting away at a staggering rate. In 1987 there were 7.5m square kilometres (2.9m square miles) of sea ice left at the end of the summer melt but by 2007 only 4.1m square kilometres remained. An area of ice equivalent to a third of the land area of America had vanished and the Northwest Passage opened for the first time. Some computer models predict that all summer ice will be gone by 2040. But accurate models are proving hard to make. Frighteningly, the actual pace of ice loss continues to outpace even the gloomiest forecast—and changes in the Arctic might have catastrophic consequences for the rest of the planet.

But there will be scientists in the Arctic in 2008 interested in more than sea and ice. Geologists will be searching for the oil, gas, minerals and diamonds that the melting ice might reveal. Geophysicists will be busy mapping the sea bottom as the circumpolar powers—Russia, Canada, Denmark, Norway and America—try to prove that the Arctic sea floors are natural extensions of their own lands and thus belong to them. Already, in an opening gambit, Russia has planted a titanium flag on the sea bed beneath the North Pole. And there are squabbles over new shortcuts for shipping around the Siberian coast and the Northwest Passage.

It is hard to predict where the great melt will lead because the Arctic is incredibly dynamic. The ice is not just melting away as temperatures rise. Vast currents and winds push the ice around the ocean, some of it remaining trapped in the huge Beaufort Gyre off the coast of Alaska, where it ages and thickens, and some being spat out between Greenland and Siberia in the great Transpolar Drift Stream. As the Earth's climate has changed, once-regular oscillations in these systems have become unpredictable.

The problem is made even more difficult because the frozen ocean is layered. Snow on top of the ice insulates it and slows melting. Under the ice, cold, fresh ▶

2008 IN BRIEF

La Niña, a Pacific current off the coast of Latin America, reaches a peak in January, disrupting normal sea temperatures and causing **extreme weather** around the world.

Alun Anderson: senior consultant, *New Scientist*

▶ water from the huge rivers that ring the Arctic insulates it from warmer waters that leak in from the Pacific and Atlantic. Any changes to these insulating layers can bring melting. The melting will itself generate more warming. Ice is pure white and reflects sunlight back into space. But leads of open sea are black and absorb heat. Once melting begins, more heat pours in and ever faster melting results.

Satellite pictures of the shrinking ice are not enough. Scientists need to get out there to collect data

To understand all this, satellite pictures of the shrinking ice are not enough. Scientists need to get out there to collect data. And some of them have adventurous plans for 2008. A French team working with German scientists will travel by airship from Paris to Svalbard, then on to the North Pole and across to Alaska. Special instruments suspended from the airship will measure ice thickness and create the longest profile of the sea ice ever made. A Russian expedition will go to the pole in 2008 too, but more slowly, drifting for eight months on a station built on an ice floe and studying the sea ice all the way.

Much more data will come from cruises by ship, plane and helicopter and, increasingly, from automated sensors that send data back south by satellite. There are "ice buoys" that drift through the Arctic on floes, and send probes into the water below, measuring temperature, salinity and other critical factors. There are robot vehicles that can travel under the ice, and buoys anchored to the sea floor to measure flows of water into and out of the Pacific and Atlantic. Sensors on land and sea will measure clouds and winds. Many scientists will also be looking at the impact of climate change on the animals and plants of the region as well as on the way of life of its 160,000 Inuit and other indigenous peoples.

Meanwhile other scientists will seek a global-warming silver lining. In 2008 data from the United States Geological Survey will boost estimates that 25% of the world's undiscovered hydrocarbon reserves are in the Arctic. Exploitation has already begun. Norway will start shipments of gas from its "Snow White" field in the Barents Sea in early 2008. Gazprom of Russia and France's Total will start work on a daunting new frontier for the oil industry: the Shtokman gas field, 600km (370 miles) out into the Arctic from Russia's northern coast.

While the race is on to find oil and gas in the melting Arctic, it is the greenhouse gases that came from burning fossil fuels which caused the big melt in the first place. So the treasure-seekers should beware that the Arctic may take its revenge. One threat is of sea levels rising. Another comes from the lakes of floating fresh water amid the sea ice. If Arctic circulation patterns change, this fresh water could travel out into the Atlantic, and turn off the ocean currents that bring warm weather to Europe. Yet another is the release of methane, a potent greenhouse gas. Let's hope that 2008's scientific explorers give us the knowledge to understand the risks. ■

2008 IN BRIEF Construction begins in southern France of the ITER plant, a €10 billion ($14 billion) international project to produce energy from **nuclear fusion**.

A whole new dimension

Alun Anderson

Rich homes can afford 3D printers

If you really want to impress your friends with high-tech wizardry in 2008 then consider shopping for a three-dimensional printer. Already well-established in sophisticated design studios, the price of basic 3D printers is likely to go under $5,000 during 2008, opening them to home use.

Wizardry is the right word, for a 3D printer can really create any three-dimensional object, no matter how complicated, that you can design in a computer. Chain-mail, the coats of interlinking rings that were worn by knights of old, provides a beautiful example. You might think that to make chain-mail you would need a lot of rings, which you then join painstakingly to neighbouring rings, up and down, left and right. That's how medieval armourers made them. A 3D printer can just print chain-mail, already all linked up; it emerges from the printer almost ready to wear.

The underlying process is quite simple. Objects are built up inside the printer (commercial models are about the size of a domestic fridge), thin layer upon thin layer as a printer makes repeated passes, following a sliced-up blueprint provided by the computer. The 3D form grows upwards, at a rate of about 5cm (2 inches) an hour, until it is done.

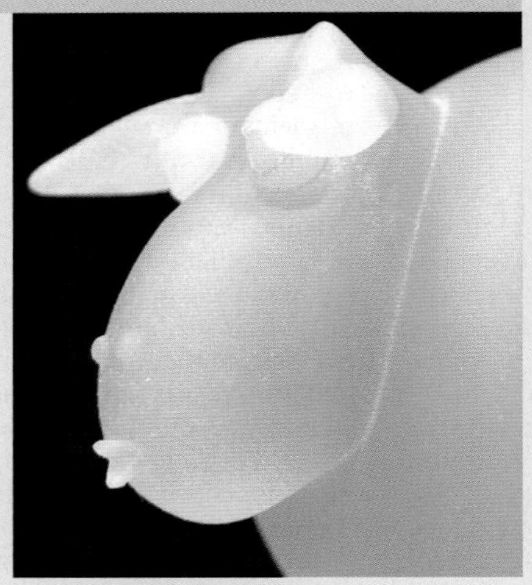

Mary had a 3D printer

Different manufacturers have different approaches. Two leading companies, Z Corp and 3D Systems, offer a choice between powder and polymer as the material from which the object emerges. In either case, an inkjet printer creates the shape of the object, either by adding a glue to the powder, or by pumping out fine drops of polymer that are then cured by an ultraviolet lamp.

Add a 3D scanner and you can reproduce real objects, including your own head. The scan takes a few seconds. Then just wait as a copy of your head gradually grows inside the printer.

More serious uses for high-end machines include making models of buildings for architects, drug molecules for pharmaceutical companies and shoes for fashion companies. Extremely specialised machines can even print in titanium, using powdered titanium and an electron beam, making it possible to create usable one-off parts for aeroplanes and F1 racing cars. There is talk of machines that will print from powdered gold and shake up the jewellery-design business.

But the real fun will come as ordinary folk at home feel free to let their creativity run wild. If you can imagine it, you can make it. ■

Visiting Neptune's kingdom

Geoffrey Carr

Outer space has hogged the limelight for too long. Welcome to inner space

Mankind has permanent bases at the South Pole and even in outer space. Submarines apart, though, the seafloor remains a place for nervous, transient visits. That has led to an astonishing discrepancy between humanity's knowledge of the one-third of the Earth's surface that is above sea level and the two-thirds below it. In 2008, however, that should start to change—not because of a rush to build a network of manned underwater bases but because of a recognition that, like the moon and Mars, the Earth is a hostile planet best explored not by people but by robots.

The Neptune programme, named after the ancient Romans' god of the sea, is the brainchild of John Delaney at the University of Washington, in Seattle, and Chris Barnes at the University of Victoria, in British Columbia. Starting in 2008 they plan to wire up part of the seabed called the Juan de Fuca plate. This is one of the smallest of the tectonic plates into which the Earth's crust is divided. Its northern tip, where the first wires will be laid, is under Canadian waters. The rest is under the auspices of America.

The Juan de Fuca plate is more or less triangular, and it is bounded by the three sorts of edge that such plates can have. Its western side is a volcanic rift where new crustal rock is being created by magma rising from the Earth's interior. Its southern side is a so-called transverse fault along which it slides against its neighbour, the Pacific plate. Its eastern side is a trench, down which it is disappearing into the Earth's interior. There, the rock it is composed of melts, and some then returns to the surface through the vents of the Cascade volcanoes such as Mount Rainier, Mount Hood and Mount St Helens.

> These places support life-forms unknown elsewhere

The Neptune programme plans to string a series of ten base stations along all three of the plate's edges, so that all types of plate boundary can be sampled. The base stations will be connected by seabed cables that will deliver power to them and return the data they collect to Dr Delaney and Dr Barnes, using a fibre-optic link capable of carrying 10 gigabytes per second. Some stations will also include a tethered cable up to 3km (2 miles) long, depending on the depth of the ocean at a particular site. The tether will act as a lift via which equipment can be sent down to the seabed, and then recovered when it needs to be examined. In addition, instruments on the tether will allow the water column to be monitored continuously throughout its depth.

Besides acting as the anchor for this tether a base station will be home to rovers that will crawl over the seabed sampling the rock, the water and the local wildlife. Other robots will swim around in the water nearby. Dr Delaney refers to this arrangement as "telepresence". The rovers will sometimes be under human control, via the data-link, while at other times they will be set to automatic and allowed to do their own thing.

What the rovers will discover remains to be seen—although "hit and run" missions to the ocean depths offer clues. The most exciting plate boundaries are those where new rock is forming to the accompaniment of much volcanic activity. These places are home to life-forms unknown elsewhere, many of which support themselves in very different ways from the living things with which people are familiar. Their genes are thus of great interest to biotechnologists.

Whether Martians exist in any shape or form is a moot point. Neptunians, though, are as weird and wonderful as the imaginings of any science-fiction author. Thanks to Messrs Delaney and Barnes, we should soon get to know them better. ■

2008 IN BRIEF

NASA's Phoenix spacecraft arrives on Mars in May to study ice in the planet's polar region, and in September China launches its third **manned space mission**.

Geoffrey Carr: science editor, *The Economist*

2008 IN BRIEF

A new form of laser treatment for the eye, developed by Professor John Marshall of London's St Thomas' Hospital, could halt the progression of age-related **macular degeneration**, the biggest cause of blindness in the developed world.

The power of thought

Alison Goddard

Restoring movement to the paralysed

A sticking plaster may appear to be a grossly inadequate treatment for a paraplegic. Attach a few electrodes, though, and a device that resembles such a dressing could help translate into actions the thoughts of people who are paralysed. In 2008 a practical version will be shown to work and the first individuals will be recruited to try them for real.

Paralysis is a breakdown in communication. The brain does not forget how to ride a bicycle. Years after paralysis has struck, the same nerve cells fire when someone is thinking about moving; it is just that the rest of the body does not receive the message.

John Donoghue of Brown University in Rhode Island has been working on how to restore that link. He has shown that the technology he has developed works, albeit only for a handful of people who were prepared to endure having a tangle of wires dangling from their heads. In 2008 Mr Donoghue and his colleagues will turn their device into something that looks like a hearing aid and whose use could become almost as routine.

The researchers will implant a silicon chip the size of a small button into the brains of monkeys. The chip will be fitted with an array of 100 thread-like gold wires, each of which will be attached to a nerve cell in the brain. When the nerve cell fires, this electrical activity will be picked up by the wire and conveyed to the silicon chip.

The next step will be to transmit this information from the skull to the outside world. A second device will be attached to the silicon chip to do this. It will transmit data through the skin using pulses of infra-red light, just like a remote control. Power will come via an inductive coil placed under the scalp and next to another on top of the scalp, which will be attached to a battery. This, and a computing unit worn on a belt, will be the only parts visible outside the body. Ultimately the team intends to implant the computer unit in the chest, connected to the brain by a fibre-optic cable.

> The researchers reckon their device will be able to direct a motorised wheelchair or move a robotic hand

The researchers reckon their device will be able to direct a motorised wheelchair or move a robotic hand. But they also want to restore to paraplegics the use of their own bodies. Hence their involvement with Hunter Peckham of Case Western Reserve University. He is developing a system which electrically stimulates muscles to make them move once again. Connecting the two systems together would mimic the way in which the body normally works.

But restoring useful movement to paraplegics involves more than making muscles work once more. It also means restoring a capability that most able-bodied people do not realise they have: the use of sensory feedback to fine-tune actions. Reach out to pick up a cup of hot tea from a vending machine and, as your hand touches the cup, it subtly adjusts its grip so that enough strength is used to lift the cup without crushing it and burning your fingers.

In order to achieve this, in 2008 Mr Donoghue and his colleagues will develop their system to run in reverse. Because the monkeys used in the tests will not be paralysed, the implant will not only broadcast what the brain is doing but also eavesdrop on what happens to the nerve cells when they are receiving information. This could then be mimicked in people. The idea is that paralysed people could operate, say, a robotic hand with sensors that collect information about the pressure and temperature they encounter and convey these data back to the brain. That is, the human brain will be stimulated to feel what the robot senses. Not bad for a device that looks like a sticking plaster. ■

Don't scramble the feedback

Alison Goddard: science correspondent, *The Economist*

The next space race

A new era of private space exploration is in prospect, predicts **Peter Diamandis**, chairman and CEO, X Prize Foundation

NASA. ESA. JAXA. RKA. These are the world's major national space agencies. They are the names that have dominated the past 50 years of space exploration. But over the next 50 years new names will emerge. The names that history will remember from the next five decades will be those of entrepreneurs, members of the private sector who saw in space an opportunity for expansion and vast wealth creation.

Two fundamental realities will drive space exploration forwards. First, wealth is accumulating in the hands of ambitious and visionary individuals, many of whom view space simultaneously as an adventure and as a place to make money. What was once affordable only by nations can now be funded by individuals.

Second, corporations and investors are realising that resources on Earth are limited and are running out. But everything we hold of value on Earth—metals, minerals, energy and real estate—is in near-infinite supply in space. As space operations become more affordable, companies will set their sights on extra-terrestrial resources, and what was once thought of as a vast wasteland will become the next "gold rush".

Alaska serves as an excellent analogy. Once thought of as worthless territory (in 1867 William Seward, America's secretary of state, was criticised for paying $7.2m to the Russians for Alaska, known then as "Seward's folly"), Alaska has since become a trillion-dollar economy. The transport infrastructure has made Alaska's gold, oil, timber and fishing industries super-profitable. The same will hold true for space. A 0.5km (0.3-mile) diameter asteroid is worth more than $20 trillion in nickel, iron and platinum-group metals.

Aside from the economic incentives, technology is reaching a critical point, making space exploration an inevitable component of human progress. Moore's Law has given us exponential growth in computing technology, which in turn has led to exponential growth in nearly every other technological industry. Breakthroughs in rocket propulsion will allow us to go farther, faster and more safely into space. Robotics will help us to explore, map and recover resources from far-off celestial bodies. Improvements in communications and life-support technologies will enable further manned missions, and eventually the colonisation of other places, like Mars. And now all of these technologies are in the hands of entrepreneurs who are willing to take risks and do things that have never been done before.

Wealth is accumulating in the hands of ambitious and visionary individuals, many of whom view space simultaneously as an adventure and a place to make money

Recently, the X Prize Foundation joined with Google to announce a $30m Google Lunar X Prize, to be paid out to the first teams able to land on the lunar surface, rove for 500 metres and send back two video/photographic moon-casts. Amazingly, within the first two weeks following the announcement, we received over 190 requests from 25 countries from prospective teams looking for registration materials. This is the new generation of entrepreneurs who will reinvent space exploration the same way that Apple and Dell reinvented the computer industry.

To boldly go

Crucially, these entrepreneurs are young, in contrast to the grey-beards who are now running the space show. The average age of the engineers who built Apollo was just 26—not 50-plus, the average of today's aerospace industry. Similarly, the dotcom industry was also built by the genius and unconstrained thinking of 20-somethings. Young doers don't know what is impossible, and they have less to risk when proposing bold solutions.

This is not to say that governments will have no role. They will retain the critical work of pure science, and of answering some of the biggest unknowns: for example, is there life on Mars? Governments should play the important role of big customer and get out of the operations business. In the same way that government agencies don't build their own PCs, or fly their own commuter airlines, in the future governments will buy seats on commercial orbital vehicles, and stay aboard commercial space stations. Politicians will also need to determine what laws govern space and its colonies—and how to respond if space colonies strike out on their own and claim independence.

So, in the next 50 years, will we see the stuff of science fiction come to life? Quite probably, though that may be thinking too small. Private tourism to space will become a real-life opportunity. Privately financed human-research outposts will be common sights in the night sky and on the moon. The first one-way missions to Mars will be launched. We will witness the first live births in space. Mining operations will spring up on the moon. Asteroids will be claimed for their natural resources. And, as these things happen, more opportunities that we have yet to comprehend will come out of the frontier. The next 50 years will be when we establish ourselves as a space-faring civilisation. ■

Out with the old, in with the new

Leo Abruzzese *NEW YORK*

Yankee and Shea Stadiums, New York icons, will bite the dust, aged 85 and 44

The house that Ruth built

Baseball, according to American mythology, was first played by barefoot boys in small towns when the country was young. In fact, the first baseball club was organised in New York City in the early 1840s by bank clerks whose work days ended early. New Yorkers have cherished baseball, and the places where it is played, ever since. Which makes 2008 a reflective time for them. The city's two baseball shrines—legendary Yankee Stadium, and the less beloved Shea Stadium—will host their final games, to be replaced by newer, more fashionable places.

Commerce, not tradition, has always driven baseball. New stadiums attract more fans, especially if they are built in the "retro" style that has come to epitomise American baseball. These new baseball parks are designed to look old—brick-and-limestone buildings graced with arched windows and an early-20th-century feel. More important to the teams' owners, new stadiums are stuffed with luxury "sky boxes", which companies eagerly buy to entertain customers.

None of this will make Yankee Stadium's demise easy to accept. Opened in 1923, it was, from the start, baseball's greatest temple. The Yankee owners at the time, Jacob Ruppert and Tillingast l'Hommedieu Huston, built the stadium—it was the first baseball field to bear such a grand name—after the team was evicted from the Polo Grounds, a park it shared with the rival New York Giants. The Yankees had overtaken the Giants in attendance thanks to the exploits of Babe Ruth, whose thunderous hitting turned the Yankees into champions. This was the Roaring Twenties, a time of economic plenty and a growing urban middle class. Many New Yorkers could afford to attend baseball games, and there was no better show than Ruth's Yankees.

The new stadium was a wonder: built of concrete and steel, it had the first-ever triple-deck grandstand, cathedral windows, a roof-line copper frieze and an unheard-of 16 toilets. It seated 58,000 people, more than twice as many as the average baseball park of the time. The stadium cost $2.5m, an extravagance funded by the drawing power of the team's star hitter. The stadium was immediately dubbed "The house that Ruth built".

Yankee Stadium's mystique is bound up in the success of the team, which has won 26 championships. Many of the sport's greatest players—Lou Gehrig, Joe DiMaggio, Mickey Mantle—were Yankees; their ghosts still roam the playing field.

The luckiest man

Baseball's most poignant moment was at Yankee Stadium on July 4th 1939. Gehrig, revered as the "Iron Horse" for his durability, had been stricken by a muscle-wasting disease that would later bear his name. To a crowd gathered to honour him, he tearfully spoke the most famous lines in American sport: "Today I consider myself the luckiest man on the face of this earth... I may have had a tough break, but I have an awful lot to live for." He died less than two years later.

> It had the first-ever triple-deck grandstand, cathedral windows and an unheard-of 16 toilets

Yankee Stadium's history extends beyond baseball. Max Schmeling, Hitler's favourite boxer (though no Nazi), beat Joe Louis, America's great black contender, in Yankee Stadium in 1936. Two years later, on the eve of the second world war, Louis, by then heavyweight champion, avenged the loss by knocking out Schmeling in the first round.

Shea Stadium, home of the New York Mets, lacks the charm of its cross-town neighbour. Opened in 1964 and named for the lawyer who helped bring the team to the city, it was one of a dozen grimly functional stadiums built across the country to accommodate a variety of sports. But fans will remember the place fondly, especially for the 1969 Miracle Mets, who rebounded from a string of last-place finishes to win an improbable championship. The place also had its non-baseball moments, including two iconic Beatles concerts in the 1960s.

New stadiums are being built to replace the old ones. The Mets, like most teams, have sold the naming rights to their stadium, in this case to a big bank. The Yankees, with more tradition to preserve, will call their place, simply, the new Yankee Stadium. Both parks are being built adjacent to the old ones.

The new parks will be good places for baseball, with all the amenities the modern entertainment industry has to offer. What they won't have is the history: Gehrig's voice ringing in the rafters, or the sound of Schmeling hitting the canvas. ■

Leo Abruzzese: editorial director, North America, Economist Intelligence Unit